Byron J. Carter

The Ingenious Inventor
Who Founded the Jackson Automobile and Cartercar Companies

Dean M. Nelson

by

Dean M. Nelson

Cyclorium Press

Second Edition

ISBN 978-0-692-57642-7

Library of Congress Data

Nelson, Dean Michael

      Byron j. carter: the ingenious inventor who founded the jackson automobile and cartercar companies.

      Includes bibliographical references and index.

      1. Automobile industry and trade – Michigan – History. I. Title.

Designed by Jeffrey A. Franke, Art Lab Studios

Printed by The Avery Group at Shapco Printing, Inc., Minneapolis

Printed in the United States of America on acid-free paper

Dedicated to my generous, understanding father, who bought me my first Jackson-made automobile, a 1909 model, when I was 15 years old.

Acknowledgments

During the course of collecting information and completing research for this book, I received generous support from many who offered their historic materials and archives, guidance, and expertise. It is a pleasure to acknowledge this help.

I would first like to thank Byron J. Carter's granddaughters Sallie D. Sparks Kendall and Linda "Buzzy" I. Carter Maurer, and their families, for many years of encouragement and for sharing their extensive family papers, photographs, patent documents, and oral histories with me. They have been exemplary stewards of these important materials, which Byron and Della Carter saved and passed on to their children, Rachel L. Carter Sparks and Kenneth G. Carter. Many of this book's most significant images came from the Carter family collections preserved by Sallie Kendall and Buzzy Maurer.

Dr. Scott R. Matthews and his wife, Joyce Argeropoulos Matthews, have been enthusiastic supporters of my Jackson motorcar research efforts for a long time and have also contributed their own thorough research along with Matthews family recollections, historical materials, and photographs. Scott Matthews is a great-grandson of Jackson Automobile Company founder George A. Matthews. He is also a grandson of Harry E. Matthews, who was a Jackson Automobile Company clerk starting in 1906, and over the next several years served as Jackson's purchasing agent, corporate secretary, and treasurer.

My friends in Jackson, Detroit, and elsewhere in Michigan who are antique-car enthusiasts, collectors, and historians have been instrumental over the years in helping me assemble research materials for this book. Among them are Todd and Faith Holton, Ken and Aggie Soderbeck, Jim Zuleski of the Ella Sharp Museum, Lloyd and Judi Ganton, Leo and Phyllis Warren, Mary Jo Hasselback and her late husband, Dick Hasselback, William Bailey, Paul Osika, the late Ronald G. Bean, and the late Richard P. Scharchburg.

I also would like to thank other friends in the antique-car field or with similar historical interests who have provided expertise, advice, and encouragement and, in some cases, have loaned or sold me materials related to Byron J. Carter, the Jackson Automobile Company, or Cartercar. They include Greg Loftness, William S. Jackson, Lowell Kimble, Ken and Cheri Jones, Tom Rasmussen, Bruce Van Sloun, Kim Dobbins, Gerry Groenewold, Mike Yeakel, David Aschbacher, John C. Meyer III, Gary Hoonsbeen, Bob Johnson, Peter Fausch, Bill Cuthbert, Susan Dunek, Dottie Batho Lasley, Dale Kemmerer, Chris Kidd, Bill Dickenson, Larry Smith, Dale McMurry, Don Boulton, Ron Hellekson, Bob Snyder, Enrique Klein, Bruce Rimmer, John Carter, Charlie Beesley, Alex Blendl, the late Ralph Dunwoodie, and the late Leslie Kulseth. My sincere apologies if I have missed anyone.

The following institutions, and especially the indicated personnel, assisted in providing information:

Ella Sharp Museum, Jackson, Michigan; Jim Zuleski, former director of Collections and Exhibits, and Lynne A. Loftis, former executive director.
Jackson District Library, Jackson, Michigan; Jeannette McDonald, Susanne Weible, and reference department staff.
Jackson County Genealogical Society, Jackson, Michigan.
MLive Media Group, publisher of *The Jackson Citizen Patriot* and MLive.com; Sara L. Scott, Jackson Editor.

Bentley Historical Library, University of Michigan, Ann Arbor.
Burton Historical Collection, Detroit Public Library, Detroit, Michigan; Mark Bowden, Coordinator for Special Collections.
Ford Archives and the Benson Ford Research Center of The Henry Ford Museum, Dearborn, Michigan.
Gilmore Research Library and Archives, Gilmore Car Museum, Hickory Corners, Michigan.
Grand Rapids Public Library, Grand Rapids, Michigan.

National Automotive History Collection, Detroit Public Library, Detroit, Michigan; Mark Bowden, Coordinator for Special Collections, and the late James J. Bradley, former head.

Richard P. Scharchburg Collection of Industrial History (formerly the Kettering/GMI Alumni Foundation Collection), Kettering University, Flint, Michigan; the late Richard P. Scharchburg.

State Archives of Michigan, Michigan Library and Historical Center, Lansing, Michigan.

State of Michigan, Department of Licensing and Regulatory Affairs–Corporations, Securities & Commercial Licensing Bureau, Lansing, Michigan.

Antique Automobile Club of America Library & Research Center, Hershey, Pennsylvania; Chris Ritter, head librarian.

Automotive Research Library of the Horseless Carriage Foundation, La Mesa, California.

Boston Public Library, Boston, Massachusetts.

Free Library of Philadelphia, Philadelphia, Pennsylvania.

Harrah's Automobile Collection Library (now the National Automobile Museum, The Harrah Collection), Reno, Nevada; the late Ralph Dunwoodie, Harrah's automotive historian and purchasing agent.

Indianapolis Motor Speedway Hall of Fame Museum, Indianapolis, Indiana.

James J. Hill Center, Reference Library, Saint Paul, Minnesota.

Library of Congress, Washington, D.C.

Minnesota Historical Society, Gale Family Library, Saint Paul, Minnesota; Jennifer Jones, director, Library & Collections.

Minnesota Historical Society Press/Borealis Books, Saint Paul, Minnesota; Daniel A. Leary, design & production manager, and Josh Leventhal, acquisitions editor.

The Nethercutt Automotive Research Library and Archive, Sylmar, California.

New York Public Library, New York.

Western Reserve Historical Society Research Library, Crawford Auto Aviation Collection Marque Files, Cleveland, Ohio; Derek Moore, Frederick C. and Kathleen S. Crawford Curator of Transportation History.

Wichita State University Libraries, Special Collections & University Archives, Wichita, Kansas.

Other professionals and associates who ably assisted with this effort include:

Jeff Franke of Art Lab Studios, a gifted artist and dedicated ally, who expertly completed photographic work, cover design, and several iterations of artistic book design and layouts, and also coordinated printing of this book.

Laura Silver, whose editing and advice greatly improved the readability of my manuscript.

Deidra Anderson, an Adobe Photoshop whiz who performed miracles in recovering faded or damaged images and in formatting others.

David Heide of David Heide Design Studio, a great friend and accomplished architect, who guided me through many aesthetic decisions.

Dawn Johnson, an especially well-read, longtime close friend, who helped me map out and launch the writing of this book.

Helga Thielen, a printing adviser and proofreader for this project.

Jeff Baker, account manager for The Avery Group of Shapco Printing, Inc., a highly valued consultant in all paper, printing, and book manufacturing details.

Jason Johnson, owner of Midwest Editions, Inc., who contributed the exceptional capabilities of his custom bookbindery.

Lastly, I would like to thank my dear mother and late father and grandparents, who instilled in me an appreciation for the past. I am also grateful to other family members and friends who consistently encouraged me over the duration of this time-consuming project.

Contents

Fig. 1. Byron J. Carter, with his hand on the steering tiller, sits next to his father, Squire, in Carter's improved steam carriage powered by the three-cylinder steam engine Carter designed and later patented. Carter's improved steam carriage was first announced and described in the August 5, 1901 issue of the *Jackson Daily Citizen*. This photograph, which was taken in front of the Carters' 204 West Cortland Street bicycle shop, is a close-up view from fig. 111. The identities of the two men perched on the auxiliary folding front seat are unknown. *Courtesy of Sallie Sparks Kendall*

Preface

Byron J. Carter of Jackson, Michigan, was a clever, innovative inventor, skilled engineer and machinist, and a bold, ambitious entrepreneur at the dawn of the motorcar age in the United States. He was intensely interested in the myriad new mechanical devices that had been developed in the 19th century, particularly steam and gasoline engines, bicycles, phonographs, and, ultimately, horseless carriages. Despite several false starts and persistent difficulties to secure financing, Carter became a tenacious force in America's nascent automobile industry and was at the center of founding two important, prominent auto enterprises of the day: the Jackson Automobile Company in July 1902 and the Motorcar (later "Cartercar") Company in 1904. Byron Carter is perhaps best known today for his patented invention of the friction-drive automobile transmission used in the Cartercar, which some engineers consider to be the precursor of today's continuously variable transmissions used on certain hybrid cars. Carter's considerable contributions were essential in launching the City of Jackson as one of Michigan's major automotive-industry centers.

Unfortunately, comprehensive historical information about the many achievements of B. J. Carter has often only been recorded piecemeal in works that typically have had a broader focus and, in many instances, contain inaccuracies or rely too heavily on conjecture and erroneous secondary sources. There are, however, some notable exceptions. Former professor of history at Eastern Michigan University and an automotive industry authority, the late George S. May, PhD, in his exceptional 1975 book, *A Most Unique Machine: The Michigan Origins of the American Automobile Industry*, wrote that Byron J. Carter "is possibly one of the most important of Michigan's auto pioneers, but he has not fared well at the hands of historians."[1] May's research was thorough, and he accurately chronicled many of Carter's earliest automotive endeavors in the context of the entire pre-1910 Michigan automobile industry. Another book, *Cartercar and Jaxon, 1900–1923: A Story of the 'Jackson' and 'Cartercar' Automobile Companies*, first published as a series of four articles in *The Bulb Horn* magazine, was written by the late Ronald G. Bean in 1970.[2] This work was a concerted effort by Bean to document B. J. Carter's early life and his post-1900 automotive work and activities, which led to Carter's formation of the Jackson Automobile Company and the Motorcar (later "Cartercar") Company. We owe considerable gratitude to Ronald Bean, with whom I spoke on several occasions, for his tenacious efforts to interview then surviving early Jackson and Cartercar automobile men, as well as the descendants of the Jackson Automobile Company founders, B. J. Carter, George A. Matthews, and Charles Lewis. Bean also collected and preserved many historic Jackson and Cartercar photographs and images, which could easily have been lost or discarded over the last 45 years.

This book will attempt to expand on the narratives of Ronald G. Bean, Professor May, and others by referencing many contemporary newspaper accounts and city directories, primarily from Jackson and Detroit, and national automotive journals of the day, which provide greater detail about and pinpoint the specific timing of events in B. J. Carter's life and career. Additionally, it relies on historical accounts, photographs, and other information generously provided by the descendants of Byron J. Carter and George A. Matthews. Lastly, this book includes 250 photographs and images, many of which have never been published before. These will, I hope, better illuminate and illustrate Carter's impressive endeavors.

My interest in the Jackson Automobile Company surfaced early, at the age of 15, when my father, after much cajoling, bought me a 1909 Jackson-made automobile from the estate of a car-collector friend. This particular auto was offered as a 1900 Jackson, which I soon found out was not possible because Jackson motorcar production had not actually commenced until 1902. Shortly after, I also realized my "Jackson" car had been incorrectly branded by earlier owners, as it was in fact a 1909 Fuller Model "B" high-wheeled touring car, originally offered by the Fuller Buggy Company and likely built in the Jackson Automobile Company factory. After more research and discussions with a handful of early motorists who were still around in the mid-1970s, I came to understand this brand confusion: Fuller automobiles were sold by the same sales agents who handled Jackson cars; these agents often called the Fullers either "Jackson Fuller" or "Fuller Jackson" models at the time. This preliminary research set me on the path of pursuing the Jackson Automobile Company's history; the associated thousands of hours in libraries, archives, museums, and antique car shows, and my many trips to Jackson, Detroit, and elsewhere became a true labor of love. The unsung achievements of Byron J. Carter persistently continued to surface, and I developed a fascination with this tireless, ambitious, and ingenious automotive pioneer who had done so much to launch and promote the automobile industry in Jackson and Detroit, and across Michigan and the nation. In addition to my research interests, I am pleased to say that I own five Jackson automobiles, including two of the titans with 50-horsepower overhead-cam-and-valve engines that the Jackson Automobile Company produced between 1908 and 1912. These 50-horsepower machines were built with the same motors that powered Jackson's most successful race cars.

My lifelong curiosity and discoveries about Byron J. Carter, George A. Matthews, Charles Lewis, the Jackson Automobile Company, and the Cartercar have provided me considerable enjoyment, and I hope readers will share this sentiment once they have perused this book.

Byron J. Carter's Early Life

Byron J. Carter, who typically identified himself as "B. J. Carter" in correspondence and business advertising, was born August 17, 1863, to Squire B. Carter (January 16, 1837– February 8, 1914) and Martha J. Carter, née Crum (July 14, 1841–December 1, 1916), near the village of Hanover, Jackson County, Michigan (as noted in B. J. Carter's 1896 marriage certificate). It appears that Byron was Squire and Martha Carter's only child. During the 1870s and 1880s, Squire Carter bought and sold various Jackson County acreage in Sandstone and Spring Arbor townships and within the Jackson city limits, and by 1884, the Carters' address was 119 West Avenue North in Jackson.[3] B. J. Carter's youth was spent on the family's farms and on the nearby Spring Arbor Township farms of his grandfather Peter T. Carter and his uncle Anthony Carter. In the 1884 *Jackson City Directory*, Byron, like his father, was listed as having the occupation of farmer.[4]

The author could find nothing to confirm whether B. J. Carter secured any formal education beyond high school; nonetheless, he obtained extensive training to be a mechanic and engineer through his many mechanical endeavors and his collaborations with more experienced machinists and early mechanical-device builders. As one of Carter's obituaries stated, he "was naturally of a mechanical turn of mind and early appreciated the possibilities of the automobile."[5] He was the sort of young man who learned quickly through observation and close study and by relentlessly asking many questions. Carter pursued his inventive ideas and business propositions in a seemingly tireless manner and ultimately perfected his technical skills to become an expert mechanic, inventor, and engineer. He was, without question, someone who was very driven to acquire knowledge and to succeed in business.

Fig. 2. B. J. Carter as a young man, circa 1883. *Courtesy of Buzzy Carter Maurer*

Fig. 3. Squire B. Carter, circa 1890. *Courtesy of Sallie Sparks Kendall*

Fig. 4. Martha J. Carter, circa 1890. *Courtesy of Sallie Sparks Kendall*

RES. OF P.T. CARTER

SEC. 21 SPRING ARBOR TP. JACKSON CO. MICH.

Fig. 5. An 1874 engraving of the Spring Arbor Township farmstead owned by B. J. Carter's grandfather Peter T. Carter from *Everts & Stewart New Illustrated Atlas of Jackson County, Michigan. Courtesy of Todd and Faith Holton*

First Business Ventures of B. J. Carter and Squire B. Carter

When he was 21 years old (in late 1884), B. J. Carter began his long association with steam-driven machinery—which eventually led him to design and build steam-powered automobiles—when he established his first steam job printing and rubber stamp manufacturing business, initially located at 112 West Main Street (now West Michigan Avenue) in Jackson; the operation prospered, and by 1887 Carter had moved it to 167 West Main Street, which was a three-story building called the Bronson Block.[6] Carter's print shop was located at the back of the building on the second story.[7] The other second-floor tenants were all lawyers and judges, and the first floor was occupied by a grocery store and a boot and shoe maker.[8] (A Jackson reference map showing certain locations mentioned in this book is included as Appendix A.) Small "jobbing" printing presses had been developed in the 19th century and were readily available. These devices, typically run by steam engine or foot treadle, were well suited for quick setup and rapid printing of small-format items such as letterheads, billheads, business cards, and envelopes. One operator running a steam-powered jobbing press could normally attain speeds of at least 1,500 impressions per hour on simple print work.[9] Steam job printing, with its relatively modest start-up cost, was a logical choice for Carter's first business, particularly given his mechanical interests and abilities.

In late 1884, B.J.'s parents, Squire and Martha Carter, took another residence in Jackson, at 338 West Washington Street (now Avenue), where B.J. was listed as a "boarder."[10] In 1885 or 1886, Squire opened a grocery store at 217 Francis Street in Jackson, where he offered groceries, provisions, flour, and feed.[11] Both father and son were now Jackson businessmen. By 1888 Squire had once again shifted his entrepreneurial efforts and became a furniture dealer with partner, William S. Barnard, at 134 North Mechanic Street.[12]

One of B. J. Carter's early print shop clients was Louis P. Ganger, publisher of the *Jackson Weekly Tribune* newspaper, which called itself "the labor organ of the city."[13] Carter printed this newspaper for Ganger starting in late 1886, and the two operations shared leased premises on the second floor of the Bronson Block.[14] Shortly after they had formed this client arrangement, fire broke out in the Bronson Block building, and many of the tenants sustained severe fire and water damage.[15] Fortunately, Ganger's "Jackson Tribune escaped with little or no damage, their office being out of the range of water. B. J. Carter's printing house suffered a loss of $1,000. He has $2,500 insurance."[16]

Carter was not so lucky four months later, in August 1887, when a protracted bill-collection and personal-property legal dispute came to a head between Carter and Louis P. Ganger.[17] Carter claimed that under his October 23, 1886 contract with Ganger for the *Jackson Weekly Tribune* printing work, ownership of the newspaper (and its mailing lists and "forms") would transfer to Carter if Ganger missed any monthly payments.[18] In a *Jackson Daily Citizen* newspaper interview entitled "The Tribune Trouble," the 23-year-old Carter said, "Mr. Ganger failed to comply with the conditions of the contract almost from the first, but I have been very lenient with him, taking from time to time such small sums as he was able to pay me. Finally I went to him and asked for a payment of some sort, and to my surprise, he declared that he owed me nothing whatever. I then brought suit for recovery of the property, before Circuit Court Commissioner Blakely, claiming non-fulfillment of contract."[19]

During the course of this exchange between Carter and Ganger, Ganger brazenly shifted his printing work from Carter to the *Jackson Patriot* newspaper's print shop and moved the *Jackson Weekly Tribune's* mailing list and "forms" to the *Patriot* as well. (These were the materials that Carter claimed became his property, along with the *Jackson Weekly Tribune*, when Ganger stopped paying his newspaper printing bills.) Carter, in turn, requested that a search warrant be issued for Ganger's home and barn to find the mailing list and "forms." When they could not be located, a warrant was issued for Ganger's arrest. Said Carter, "I went to the press room of the Patriot to make one more search for the 'forms.' It occurred to me to look in the coal bin, which is in the darkest part of the dark basement. After removing a lot of bags, old papers and rubbish, I found the 'forms' and had them removed to my office."[20] Five days later, Ganger's attorney issued a writ that charged Carter "with falsely, wrongfully, and maliciously, and without any reasonable or probable cause, procuring a search warrant and causing plaintiff's [Ganger's] house to be searched for

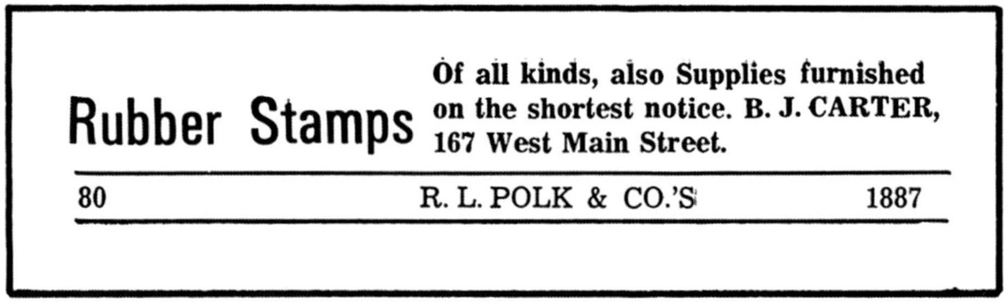

Fig. 6. An advertisement in *R. L. Polk & Co.'s 1887 Jackson City Directory* for B. J. Carter's first rubber stamp manufacturing and steam job printing business at its second address, 167 West Main Street, in the Bronson Block; this business was first located at 112 West Main Street in Jackson when it was established in late 1884. *Courtesy of the Jackson District Library*

stolen goods."[21] Ganger's attorney continued to bother B. J. Carter in November 1887, when he filed a further declaration in a libel action against Carter stating that Carter had "maliciously made a complaint against [Louis Ganger in] charging him with concealing the forms and mailing lists of the Jackson Tribune, and claiming damages to the amount of $5,000."[22] On March 6, 1888, a hearing was held for arguments to be presented in a case Louis P. Ganger had brought against B. J. Carter to recover Ganger's "costs."[23] The matter was dismissed on July 9, 1888, with no recovery of costs for either party.[24] It remains unclear whether Ganger ever paid Carter his initial debt. This unpleasant situation was likely the young Carter's first exposure to the inherent complexities and conflicts, legal and otherwise, that can arise in business transactions.

During the Ganger debacle, B. J. and his first wife, Evaline C. Carter, née Petrie, lived in an apartment at 169 West Main Street, which was next door to Carter's printing operation in the Bronson Block building.[25] The couple announced the February 29, 1888 birth of a son, George Rayland "Ray" Carter, in the *Jackson Daily Citizen*; tragically, Ray Carter died of accidental electrocution on February 22, 1913.[26]

Shortly after his contentious dispute with Louis P. Ganger, B. J. Carter renamed his steam job printing and rubber stamp business Carter & Co., and moved his operations to 132 North Mechanic Street, next to his father's furniture store.[27] Apparently Carter's printing business was growing, as Carter

hired Frank A. Palmer to serve as print shop foreman for Carter & Co.[28] Palmer came to Carter's enterprise with valuable experience, as he had previously run Frank A. Palmer & Co., a job printing company at 220 West Main Street.[29]

Squire Carter's businesses evolved as well, and by March 1889 he had set up operations in the northwest corner of Cortland Street's intersection with Jackson Street, where Byron and he would continue in various successful endeavors until late 1905. The elder Carter started the expansion at the new site by first taking over the two-story wood-frame building (using an address of 202 West Cortland Street, which was essentially a side entrance to the structure) and then advertising that he would store stoves over the summer and return them serviced and "blacked."[30] The building had formerly been a combination boardinghouse and hotel known as Carter House, which, according to the 1887 *Jackson City Directory*, was operated by Charlotte M. De Wolf, as proprietor.[31]

In May 1889, B. J. Carter reinforced his reputation as a steam-engine mechanic when he served as engineer and builder for a 20-passenger steam engine–powered yacht, christened *Mrs. Falsom*; the ship was launched in nearby Michigan Center and was touted by the *Jackson Daily Citizen* as "monarch of the sea."[32]

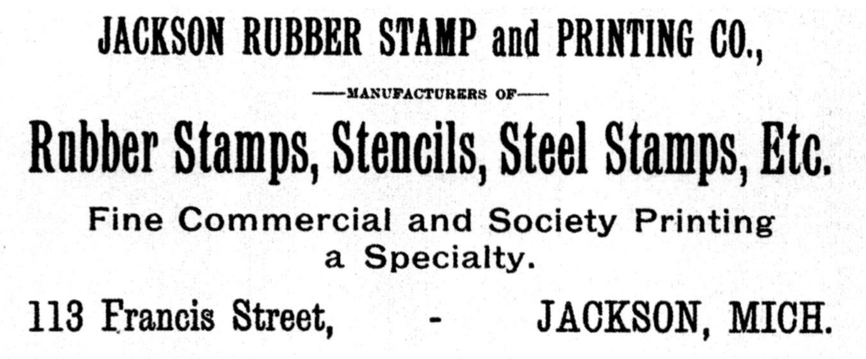

Fig. 7. An 1890 *Jackson City Directory* advertisement for B. J. Carter's last rubber stamp and steam job printing business, Jackson Rubber Stamp and Printing Co., established by 1890 and located at 113 Francis Street; Carter sold out of this business within a year. *Courtesy of the Jackson District Library*

B. J. Carter continued in the steam job printing and rubber stamp manufacturing business, and by 1890 he had reorganized Carter & Co. and formed a new company called the Jackson Rubber Stamp and Printing Co., located at 113 Francis Street. Frank A. Palmer, the shop foreman from Carter & Co., was now B. J. Carter's partner in the business.[33] Jackson Rubber Stamp and Printing Co. was a short-lived venture, and within a year of its formation Carter sold his interest in the business to a cigar manufacturer and the mayor of Jackson, Martin G. Loennecker, who then established and published the *Industrial News*.[34] Carter's former partner in the job printing business, Frank A. Palmer, stayed on with Loennecker's Industrial News Co. as a printer.[35]

It seems safe to say that during the late 1880s and early 1890s, B. J. Carter was becoming quite familiar with the mechanical principles of steam engines, their applications in manufacturing operations and as a motive power. This engineering knowledge would serve him well in his later experiments with boat building and automobile construction and engine design and building. Carter's curiosity about horseless carriage development was likely piqued in the early 1890s, as information about the first European automotive innovations was starting to make its way to American engineers and mechanics.

Fig. 8. Squire B. Carter in the entrance of his grocery store at 217 Francis Street, where he offered groceries, provisions, flour, and feed, circa 1885.
Courtesy of the Jackson District Library

Earliest Bicycle Pursuits

B. J. Carter also developed a strong interest in another fledgling technology of the age, the bicycle (frequently called a "wheel" in the 1880s and 1890s). Carter was an active "wheelman" and a pioneer cyclist in Jackson, who, by the age of 21 (in mid-1885), already owned a bicycle.[36] In a January 26, 1964 letter to Carter's granddaughter Marcia Gene Carter, B. J. Carter's then 87-year-old cousin, Vie D. Moore, née Patch, recounted, "One of my early memories of him was his wheeling into [our] driveway on one of those high wheel bicycles." Carter was also a charter member of the Jackson Bicycle Club founded in the mid-1880s.[37] B. J. Carter's first bicycle jaunt recorded in the *Jackson Daily Citizen* occurred in August 1885, when he and four other members of the newly formed Jackson Bicycle Club cycled to a "Knights' camp" outside of Jackson.[38] During this trip the group had frightened a horse and buggy; the newspaper article stated: "It's understood they will quietly chip in and settle for the buggy that the frightened horse wrecked."[39]

A July 1886 bicycle ride from Jackson to Leslie and back (34 miles round-trip), with B. J. Carter "mounted on a new Star bicycle," was also reported.[40] Similar to the standard high-wheel bicycle, which was the predominant style in the 1880s, the Star bicycle was also built with a huge drive wheel (42–60 inches in diameter, depending on the different Star model specifications).[41] Despite this gigantic wheel, the Star was considered to be a "safety" bicycle because its much smaller stabilizing wheel was placed at the cycle's front and was used for steering.[42] Conversely, on the standard high-wheel bicycle, often called an "Ordinary," the smaller wheel was located at the back and the large drive wheel was in front and used for steering.[43] The innovative Star cycle design was considerably safer because it essentially eliminated the risk of dangerous "headers," which occurred when a rider of an Ordinary high wheeler hit an obstacle and was pitched forward (head first) over the large front wheel. The Star was not free of design flaws, however, as it did not distribute the rider's weight over the small front wheel, which caused the front wheel to be skittish on sand and gravel surfaces, and the wheelman was sometimes thrown off sideways instead.[44] The Star cycle's general wheel configuration and ratcheting-pedal arrangement were invented by George W. Pressey

of Hammonton, New Jersey, who was granted a U.S. patent (no. 233,640) for this "velocipede" on October 26, 1880.[45] With at least two additional federal patents (nos. 293,284 and 331,199), the Star bicycle was manufactured by the H. B. Smith Machine Co. in Smithville, New Jersey.[46] It is not surprising that the young B. J. Carter would have been drawn to the Star bicycle's cutting-edge design and technical improvements, even though its cost was substantial in 1886 and 1887, ranging from $75 to $127 depending on the model, wheel size, and finish level (e.g., a Star could be purchased entirely nickel plated).[47]

Racing and competitions were exciting activities for the enthusiastic wheelmen of the 1880s. One of the earliest bicycle races in Jackson, perhaps the first, occurred on June 1, 1886.[48] The next year, B. J. Carter was part of a committee that planned "a series of bicycle races during the state fair . . . entirely under the direction of the Jackson Bicycle Club, and some valuable prizes will be offered; not cash prizes, as they are forbidden by American league rules, but handsome cups, medals, etc., will be offered to winners."[49] Carter was also a member of the committee for the September 3, 1889 Jackson Bicycle Club races, which they would conduct at the "Michigan fair."[50] According to one of his obituaries, Carter "became identified with the bicycle industry in his early youth. During the eighties he was one of the fastest riders of the old-style ordinary in Michigan."[51] This obituary suggested that Carter's bicycle-racing success triggered his interest in establishing a bicycle business, which he (and his father) would do in 1893.[52]

Fig. 9. Photograph of an Ordinary high-wheel bicycle with a fashionable wheelman from the mid-1880s, likely wearing a cycling club uniform; with its precipitous mount, high center of gravity, and small wheel at the back, the Ordinary put riders at significant risk for "dreaded headers." This style of bike was labeled a "penny farthing" in England because its side view appeared a bit like two British coins of different diameters. *Author's collection*

Fig. 10. Two wheelman in cycling clothing typical of the mid-1880s pose with their bicycles. The young man on the left steadies an expensive Star Special "safety" bicycle, similar to the Star bicycle B. J. Carter purchased new in 1886. The cycle on the right is a standard high-wheel Ordinary. The Star was considered a safety bicycle because its smaller steering wheel was placed ahead of the large drive wheel to prevent headers. *Author's collection*

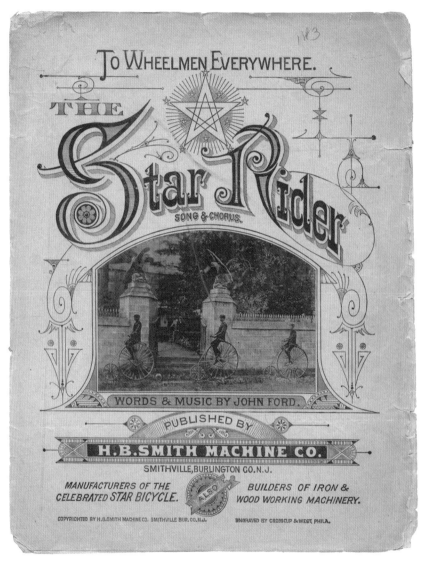

Figs. 11 & 12. The Star safety bicycle became so popular in the 1880s (purportedly over 4,000 were sold) that at least two promotional songs were commissioned by the cycle's manufacturer, the H. B. Smith Machine Co. of Smithville, New Jersey: "Star Bicycle Galop," in 1882, and "The Star Rider Song & Chorus," in 1883. *Courtesy of Dottie Batho Lasley, custodian of the Norman Batho Collection*

B. J. Carter Temporarily Relocates to Sheffield, Alabama

The young B. J. Carter encountered a setback in his personal life that was considered controversial at the time: the April 26, 1890 *Jackson Daily Citizen*, in a harshly worded article, reported that Carter and his first wife, Evaline C. Carter, had applied for a divorce.[53] This newspaper piece publicly chastised 21 Jackson couples including the Carters, as "matrimonial failures" and "hopeless malcontents" for filing divorce applications in the Jackson County Circuit Court.[54] Shortly after (in 1891 or 1892), B. J. Carter relocated to Sheffield, Alabama, about 637 miles from Jackson. Sheffield is a small industrial city and railroad center in northern Alabama. There, he executed at least one employment contract (this one was dated July 11, 1892), with the Standard Machine Works, which, according to the firm's letterhead, were "dealers in engines, boilers, and machinery of every description."[55] This company also manufactured the "Gray's Patent Revolving Head Screw Machine." Even though it is not specifically stated in the contract, this employment agreement may have been part of an apprenticeship for the 29-year-old Carter, who it appears had no formal engineering education. Apprenticeships were a career rite of passage for most engineers and machinists in the 19th century. Under the highly detailed employment contract, Carter was to construct a 34-foot-long steam launch (yacht) of white oak and yellow pine. Carter's experience with engineering the steam launch *Mrs. Falsom* in Jackson three years earlier was undoubtedly invaluable in the Sheffield shipbuilding project. For this extensive steam-powered launch project with the Standard Machine Works, Carter was to be paid a total of $300, drawn in installments, as funds were needed by him for building the boat. It is unknown whether Carter executed any additional work contracts with the Standard Machine Works, and the full term of his employment in Sheffield is ambiguous. The *Jackson City Directory* indicated that, by the end of 1892, B. J. Carter had moved back to Jackson, was working in his father's business, and once again boarded in his parents' 338 West Washington Street home.[56]

Fig. 13. The 34-foot steam-powered launch B. J. Carter built in the summer of 1892 for the Standard Machine Works of Sheffield, Alabama; the railroad bridge in this photograph still spans the Tennessee River connecting Sheffield and Florence, Alabama. *Courtesy of Buzzy Carter Maurer*

Fig. 14. The Carters' furniture and bicycle buildings in the northwest corner of Cortland and Jackson streets (looking south on South Jackson Street). The policeman in this May 19, 1898 photograph holds two-year-old Verne Alva Trask, son of Jackson machinist Charles A. Trask. Verne is perched on the tiny bicycle Trask had built in early 1898 to promote his bicycle-manufacturing business. The wheels were only 13 1/2 inches in diameter and it was labeled "the smallest bike made for use." The tower and smokestack of the Jackson Corset Co. are visible over the roofs of the Carters' buildings. *Courtesy of Alex Blendl (from a Lockwood negative)*

Business Operations in the Northwest Corner of Cortland and Jackson Streets

Squire Carter had, by 1889, taken over the wood-frame building in the northwest corner of Cortland and Jackson streets, which had several entrances, making tracking his various addresses today a little confusing (S. B. Carter first used 202 West Cortland Street as his business address, and shortly thereafter used 120 South Jackson Street); there he offered "new and second-hand furniture and pawnbroker" services.[57] Soon after (by October 1891), Squire Carter revised the address of his stove-storage and sales facility and furniture and pawnbroker business yet again (within the same wood-frame building) as 122 South Jackson Street and added a "loan office."[58] To accommodate his ever-growing businesses, the senior Carter attempted to expand the wood-frame building in March 1892 by adding another story, but the Jackson City Council rejected Carter's petition for a building permit variance.[59] This large wooden structure would soon be the first facility for Squire and Byron's bicycle and sundries sales and repair business, which commenced in late 1893.[60]

Fig. 16. This 1894 advertisement promotes S. B. Carter's various businesses at the corner of West Cortland and South Jackson streets. *Courtesy of the Jackson District Library*

Fig. 15. Verne Alva Trask and his miniature bicycle with a police officer, circa 1898, on the front lawn of the Jackson sheriff's office and Jackson County Jail; the Carters' brick bicycle repair shop is visible in the background. *Author's Lockwood negative collection*

Fig. 17. Carters' bicycle repair shop and the Jackson sheriff's office and Jackson County Jail, circa 1898; the tower of the Jackson Corset Co. factory, on West Cortland Street, is visible over the top of the Carters' brick building. *Author's collection*

Fig. 18. The Jackson Corset Co. factory at 225 West Cortland Street, circa 1915, which was located opposite (and west of) the Carters' 204 West Cortland Street bicycle sales and repair building. *Author's collection*

Fig. 19. A busy day on South Jackson Street north of West Cortland Street during the late 1890s (photograph taken from a second-floor window of the Carter bicycle repair shop); the corner of the Jackson County Jail is visible on the left. *Author's Lockwood negative collection*

Fig. 20. A military parade on South Jackson Street just north of West Cortland Street (photograph taken from the roof of the small store in front of the Carter bicycle repair shop); based on the uniforms, the first row of marchers appears to be a combination of Union veterans from the Civil War in the Grand Army of the Republic and veterans' sons from the Sons of Union Veterans of the Civil War; the row behind may consist of members of a Zouave honor guard regiment or drill team. *Author's Lockwood negative collection*

BICYCLES.

VICTOR MODEL D.

VICTORS!

RAMBLERS!

IMPERIALS!

The best line of Wheels in the world for cash or on payments.

A complete line of Extras for repair work kept in stock—Pneumatic Tires, Rims, Etc.

All kinds of Repairing done on short notice.

Old Wheels taken in exchange or fitted with Pneumatic Tires.

Bargains in the way of Good Second-Hand Wheels.

A few Good Wheels for Rent.

S. B. CARTER,

Cor. Cortland and Jackson St.

Fig. 21. An advertisement from the March 29, 1894 issue of the *Jackson Daily Citizen*, which is believed to be the first S. B. Carter bicycle-shop advertisement in the newspaper. *Courtesy of the Jackson District Library*

The Carter Bicycle Enterprise and Other Business Expansions during the 1890s

Father and son embarked, by late 1893, on what would become a robust bicycle sales and repair operation, as the 1890s bicycle craze was in full swing.[61] The more conventional safety bicycle, with two similar-sized wheels and close in design to today's bikes, had by then completely replaced the high wheelers, and everyone, including ladies, had to have one. Jackson's bicycle business grew rapidly throughout the 1890s; by 1898, the *Jackson City Directory* indicated that 16 bicycle dealers, manufacturers, and repairers were operating in the city.[62]

The Carters' bicycle enterprise had achieved a certain level of success by March 1894, when Squire Carter started placing prominent, frequent bicycle advertisements in the *Jackson Daily Citizen*, first offering Imperial, Rambler, and Victor cycles (fig. 21).[63] These advertisements, with multiple variations and additional bicycle brands, continued in the Jackson newspaper under the name of S. B. Carter (except for a brief period in early 1895, when B. J. Carter's name inexplicably appeared in ads) until early 1899, when B. J. Carter took over bicycle business management (and advertising) from his father.[64]

It was not long after the Carter bicycle business had commenced that thieves made off with a couple of cycles. On July 31, 1894, the *Jackson Daily Citizen* reported that a Rambler bicycle, "which one John White rented of S. B. Carter Friday afternoon, for a two hours' ride" had been sold to "a Leslie man for $16"; the bike was recovered but "the whereabouts of 'John White' are unknown."[65] A month later, a buyer, who purchased a bicycle from Squire Carter on an installment plan, sold his cycle before paying Carter the full amount owed.[66] The man was arrested, pleaded guilty to embezzlement, and was sentenced to a two-year prison term.[67]

United States Tag Co.,

MANUFACTURERS OF THE

Hercules 3-Hole Wired

Shipping Tags.

The Strongest Tag in the World.

And all styles of Shipping Tags,

Plain, Printed, Wired or Strung

S. B. CARTER,

Corner Cortland and Jackson Sts.

Get your Tags at the factory.

Fig. 22. An April 9, 1895 *Jackson Daily Citizen* advertisement for S. B. Carter's newly formed business, the United States Tag Co., which manufactured shipping tags of all styles in the Carter "factory" at the corner of South Jackson and West Cortland streets. *Courtesy of the Jackson District Library*

Squire and B. J. Carter expanded their business by establishing the United States Tag Co., with B. J. Carter as manager, which was advertised at the 122 South Jackson Street wood-frame building for the first time in April 1895.[68] There they manufactured the Hercules three-hole wired and other styles of shipping tags.[69] The 1897 *Jackson City Directory* indicated that the factory for United States Tag was located at 202 West Cortland Street.[70] One can presume that the printing presses and paper-cutting devices for manufacturing tags were driven by steam engines or perhaps large electric motors, which were a relatively new technology. Squire, in 1896, added foundry and machining work to his expanding business, and also continued to offer furniture for sale and stove storage and worked as a pawnbroker in this same building.[71] By 1897, he found it necessary to hire a full-time bookkeeper, Emma M. Smith, to keep track of his various diverse endeavors.[72]

Bicycle Operations Grow in an Impressive New Facility

Squire B. Carter acquired the land adjacent to his wood building and later built a handsome two-story brick structure at 204 West Cortland Street. The January 30, 1896 *Jackson Daily Citizen* wrote that "Mr. Carter has just recently completed a building at 204 West Cortland Street, which he will occupy exclusively as a bicycle store. He has in the rear of the store the best and most complete repair shop in the state. He carries repair [parts] in stock for all wheels handled by himself. Mr. Carter has been in the bicycle business from the first, handling the best lines of wheels and selling his share."[73] The many bicycle brands offered by Squire and B. J. Carter in 1896 were Cleveland, Clipper, Crescent, Fowler, Lu-Mi-Num, Model, Overland, Rambler, Record, and Remington.[74] Over the next six years, the Carters would drop some of these cycle lines and add or reacquire agencies for several others including American, Columbia, Daycycle, Dayton, Eagle, Featherstone, Fox Flyer, Hartford, Ideal, Imperial, Monarch, Pennant, Racycle, Stormer, United States, Victor, and World. The 1897 *Jackson City Directory* still listed S. B. Carter's bicycle operations at 122 South Jackson Street and had added the 204 West Cortland Street address as well.[75] Within three years the new brick Carter bicycle facility would become the first hub of automotive activity in the City of Jackson.

The above cut represents the front of our Bicycle Store, built exclusively for Bicycle business, 204 W. Cortland street, near Jackson street, where can be found a carefully selected variety of the best makes of bicycles, all made by old experienced and reliable manufacturers.

In the rear is our repair shop which was also built and arranged especially for Bicycle Repairing, where by the aid of the best and most modern and special tools and skilled mechanics

Bicycles are Repaired

As They Should be.

and at reasonable prices.

Ramblers, Cleveland Swell Specials and Cleveland Line Remingtons by Remington Arms Co , Fowlers, Lu-Mi-Nums, Clippers, Crescents, Records, etc., will be our lines, and a complete stock of Bicycle Sundries.

Call and see them, it costs nothing.

S. B. CARTER,

204 W. Cortland St.

Fig. 23. This February 3, 1896 *Jackson Daily Citizen* advertisement illustrates Squire B. Carter's new brick sales and repair shop, "built exclusively for Bicycle business," located at 204 West Cortland Street. *Courtesy of the Jackson District Library*

Figs. 24 & 25. Photographs of the Carter bicycle shop at 204 West Cortland Street, which opened in early 1896; B. J. Carter is seated on the bicycle shop's front step in the first picture, which also shows a large bicycle shipping crate on the boardwalk. These two storefront photographs were taken no earlier than March 1896 (as the canvas awning had not yet been installed in the March 17 or 18, 1896 Fowler Sextet photograph, fig. 39) and not much later than April 1897 or so, when the Carters dropped Cleveland bicycles from their newspaper advertisements (the folding sign on the boardwalk lists Rambler, Remington, and *Cleveland* cycles). *Author's Lockwood negative collection*

Fig. 26. The Carters' bicycle repair shop at 204 West Cortland Street; Carter machinist Arthur L. Butcher is shown in the right foreground using a metal file, and Frank N. Bradley, a printer for the United States Tag Co. and clerk for Squire B. Carter, is sitting on the wooden stool. The identities of the two men on the left are unknown. *Author's Lockwood negative collection*

Fig. 27. Another view of the Carters' bicycle repair shop at 204 West Cortland Street; Carter employee Lewis "Lou" N. Tussing (left) is shown fixing a bicycle tire on the workbench, and Carter "bicycle repairer" Fred T. Lockwood (right) assembles a bike. A large S. B. Carter bicycle store advertising sign is visible through the back window and may be the backside of a repainted exterior sign (or was perhaps used to cover a broken or missing window). *Author's Lockwood negative collection*

Fig. 28. Bicycle lapel studs and stickpins, made of celluloid, metal, and other materials, were popular souvenirs and advertising items given away by cycle dealers during the 1890s and early 20th century. Original pins and lapel studs representing most of the many bicycle brands offered by the Carters from 1893 to 1902 are shown here. *Author's collection*

Fig. 29. Fred T. Lockwood and his first wife, Florence E. Lockwood, in a photographic self-portrait, around the time of their 1898 marriage. *Author's Lockwood negative collection*

Fred T. Lockwood: Photographer, Carter Employee, and a Boat-Motor Pioneer

Frederick "Fred" Thaddeus Lockwood (April 22, 1873–June 25, 1940) was one of the Carters' first employees in 1895, as a 22-year-old machinist and bicycle repairer.[76] Lockwood was instrumental in the Carters' bicycle business and was part of the group of Carter employees and associates who rebuilt B. J. Carter's first horseless carriage in June 1899 and made it operational.[77] It was Fred T. Lockwood's camera that captured many of the extant images of B. J. Carter's bicycle and automotive activities and other early scenes of life in the City of Jackson around the turn of the 20th century; the author is privileged today to own and preserve 128 of the Lockwood glass-plate negatives. It appears that Fred Lockwood's first wife, Florence E. Lockwood, née Daniels, may have been the most proficient photographer in the Lockwood family, as she won several awards in the Jackson Camera Club's first annual amateur and professional photography exhibition held on November 29, 1898.[78] Prints from some of the more interesting surviving Lockwood negatives were likely featured in this photography exhibition.

In March 1901, six years after first joining the Carter bicycle business, Fred T. Lockwood resigned from his Carter machining and bicycle repairing position to open Lockwood Brothers, along with his younger brother, Arthur L. Lockwood, an electrician.[79] Lockwood Brothers was an electrical, machine-work, and bicycle-repair business, located in space leased at 131 East Cortland Street.[80] Lockwood Brothers' location was about two blocks east of B. J. Carter's bicycle shop, and, given Lockwood Brothers' proximity, Carter may have relied on the firm for electrical and some machining work on a contract basis.

Shortly after setting up shop, Lockwood Brothers entered the motorized-vehicle business in April 1901 by offering for sale the E. R. Thomas Motor Company's Auto-Bi and Auto-Tri motorcycles (two wheels and three wheels, respectively), which several sources claim were the first brand of motorcycles widely available in the United States.[81] The firm also built at least one double-steam-engine-powered yacht that Lockwood Brothers intended to rent "to pleasure parties during the summer": the June 9, 1902 *Jackson Daily Citizen* announced that Lockwood Brothers had constructed a 20-foot launch christened *Puritan*, which had a trial run on Wolf Lake, east of Jackson.[82] Lockwood Brothers would, in 1902, add an Oldsmobile sales agency and they were reported to have hitched a plow to a one-cylinder Oldsmobile in January 1903, as an experiment, to clear snow from "about 10 miles of walk."[83] From late September 1902 through mid-1904, Lockwood Brothers occupied 204 West Cortland Street, which B. J. Carter vacated when he moved his car-manufacturing operations to the Jackson Automobile Company's more expansive plant.[84] After Carter resigned from the Jackson Automobile Company in May 1904 and reclaimed occupancy of his 204 West Cortland Street facility to manufacture friction-drive autos for his new venture, The Motorcar Co., Lockwood Brothers relocated a couple of doors away to 210–212 West Cortland Street.[85]

Fred T. and Arthur L. Lockwood, along with W. L. Ash of Lansing, Michigan, would go on to incorporate the Lockwood-Ash Motor Company, in September 1906, a prominent Jackson enterprise in the field of boat motors, spark plugs, and other marine and automotive products for many years.[86] The first Lockwood-Ash factory was located on East Main Street at its intersection with Horton Street, across from the Jackson Automobile Company's second factory (see figs. 247 and 248). (The Jackson Automobile Company purchased its second factory site on November 30, 1907, about a year after Lockwood-Ash set up operations across the street).[87] The Lockwood-Ash Motor Company is said to have built its first gasoline outboard boat motor in 1914 and, in addition to marketing motors directly, Lockwood-Ash soon developed a robust "private brand" business supplying Sears, Roebuck & Company with its Motorgo boat engines.[88] On February 23, 1929, Lockwood-Ash merged with the original Evinrude Motors and the ELTO Outboard Motor Co. of Milwaukee to create a $4 million enterprise called Outboard Motors Corporation; Arthur Lockwood was named treasurer of the new company.[89] ELTO stood for "Evinrude's Light Twin Outboard" and was a spin-off firm that had been formed by Ole Evinrude, an early inventor of patented outboard boat motors, in the fall of 1920, long after Evinrude had sold his original Evinrude Motors in 1914.[90]

From a 1939 automotive journal reference, it appears that Fred T. Lockwood might have concluded his motor and engineering career as a representative for the Borg-Warner Corp., the worldwide manufacturer and supplier of automotive components and parts.[91] At this time, Borg-Warner would have had its headquarters in Chicago, with major subsidiaries in many locations, including Detroit and Eastern Michigan.[92]

Fred T. Lockwood also served as a Jackson city commissioner starting in 1917, as vice mayor in 1919, and later as a bank department manager, school board member, and teacher.[93] He died in 1940, at the age of 67.

Fig. 30. Lockwood Brothers bicycle repairing, machining, electrical, motorcycle, and later, automobile business, established in March 1901, at 131 East Cortland Street; pictured are Fred T. Lockwood (left), formerly a bicycle repairer and machinist for B. J. Carter, and his brother, Arthur L. Lockwood, an electrician. Lockwood Brothers sold E. R. Thomas Motor Company motorcycles, of which two are displayed: the Auto-Bi at $200 in 1901 and the three-wheeled Auto-Tri at $350. The E. R. Thomas Motor Company would later build the high-powered luxury Thomas "Flyer" automobiles. *Courtesy of the Ella Sharp Museum*

The 1890s Bicycle Craze in Jackson

B. J. Carter continued to be an active cyclist through the mid-1890s, when he was in his early 30s. Despite being arguably past their prime for competing in bicycle races, Carter and several of his employees and associates were still attending bicycle races (and perhaps participating). Even if they did not compete, the round-trips on cycles to these various events would have been grueling. An August 2, 1895 *Jackson Daily Citizen* article reported that "a party of seven bicycle riders left this afternoon for Detroit on their wheels, to attend the Hilsendegen 25-mile road race, which will be run at Belle Isle park tomorrow."[94] The Hilsendegen road races were said to be "among the important cycling events of the country. The value of the prizes to be awarded contestants is $6,000."[95] In the party were Byron J. Carter, machinist Charles A. Trask, H. W. Bowering, Will Jones, and Carter employee John H. Carpenter.[96] This group's enthusiasm for bicycles was certainly demonstrated by their willingness to pedal about 160 miles round-trip to attend a race that was considerably shorter. Carter, Trask, Bowering, and eight other cyclists returned to Detroit only one month later for another vigorous ride.[97] (Charles A. Trask would figure prominently in B. J. Carter's life and career.)

In "Local Bicycle Items," the September 14, 1895 *Jackson Daily Citizen* reported that B. J. Carter and Odie Hunter had departed on bicycles for Michigan City, Indiana, a formidable 300-hundred-mile round-trip from Jackson.[98] Once there, the two cyclists' plan was to take a "steamer" across Lake Michigan from Michigan City to Chicago.[99] Future Carter employee Frank N. Bradley joined Carter and Hunter in cycling back to Jackson from Michigan City a week later.[100]

It was reported that "Frank Bradley and Walter Beach left this morning on their bicycles to attend the Ypsilanti bicycle races" on June 13, 1896, and that "they will return tonight."[101] The distance from Jackson to Ypsilanti, Michigan is about 46 miles. Carter met up with these gentlemen at this Ypsilanti race, although there is no indication whether he pedaled his way there.[102] Carter also attended other bicycle events with his employees and associates; for example, in January 1896, he and Bradley, Trask, and Carpenter all visited the Chicago cycle show.[103]

Carter, Bradley, Trask, and associates Floyd Mitchell and Arthur L. Butcher were all active members of the Jackson Wheelmen, a bicycle club that was formed January 10, 1896.[104] Shortly after, they planned an "informal" Wheelmen's Ball on January 30, 1896, for 220 couples.[105] All Jackson Wheelmen appeared "in dress suits, with black satin knee pants [knickerbockers], black silk hose and low shoes, decidedly swell costume."[106] The Jackson Wheelmen soon built club quarters in Jackson with a "bath room" to promote the cycling sport.[107] And the Jackson Wheelmen, which donated $100, and B. J. and Squire Carter, who together donated $10 to the project, were instrumental in the construction of a smooth new seven-mile cinder bicycle path from Jackson to nearby Clark's Lake (now Clark Lake); in reporting about the new cinder path, the *Jackson Daily Citizen* wrote, "To the rider of a wheel, the country affords the boon of an exhilaration and physical enjoyment of which the city with its noise and smoke, is barren."[108]

Fig. 31. The Central City Music Co. of Jackson, got caught up in the 1890s craze and paid homage to the many bicycle clubs when it published "The Cycling Club March and Two-Step" in 1896. The cover of this sheet music proclaims, "Dedicated to all the Cycling Clubs and Their Cycling friends." The composition was arranged by Louis F. Boos, a music teacher, who by 1910 would lead his own band and orchestra in Jackson. The cover includes a photograph of one of Jackson's several cycling clubs (one was called "The More the Merrier Bicycle Club") assembled along Stonewall Road. *Courtesy of Dottie Batho Lasley, custodian of the Norman Batho Collection*

Fig. 32. A wheel gathering at the corner of West Cortland and South Jackson streets next to S. B. Carter's bicycle, furniture, and stove sales building (note the wall sign), circa 1897; Frank N. Bradley is the front cyclist on the white tandem safety bicycle. *Author's Lockwood negative collection*

Fig. 33. Carter employees Frank N. Bradley (left) and Fred T. Lockwood (right) resting during a tandem-bicycle ride, circa 1897; Bradley is wearing a cycling jersey that displays the Jackson Wheelmen cycling club insignia. *Author's Lockwood negative collection*

Fig. 34. Pictured is Florence E. Lockwood, Fred T. Lockwood's first wife, in typical Victorian cycling attire, circa 1898. Cycling was one of the few sports considered respectable for women in the mid-1890s. Enthusiastic new lady riders are estimated to have made up at least a third of total bike sales during the 1890s craze. Cycling is credited as a dominant force in society's acceptance of the more comfortable, less restrictive women's clothing introduced in the 20th century. Florence Lockwood's wheel is a standard ladies' safety bicycle of the time. The woven cord lacing over the bicycle's rear wheel and the bentwood chain guard with lacing were intended to prevent long skirts from becoming tangled in the spokes and chain. *Author's Lockwood negative collection*

Fig. 35. More adventurous 1890s women cyclists wore controversial "Turkish pants" or riding bloomers and knee-high leggings, as shown in this photograph. The constables in one major city, Victoria, British Columbia, decreed, in 1895, that "bloomers are not suitable for ladies' street wear, even when worn as a bicycling costume." For reasons lost to history, this rider may actually be a man in a women's costume (note the men's safety bicycle). The bike is decorated with ribbons and streamers, which may indicate the getup was intended for a parade or some other town festival in Jackson. *Author's Lockwood negative collection*

Fig. 36. Arthur L. Lockwood posing on a racing bicycle, circa 1896, when he was 20 years old; Lockwood successfully placed second out of 63 racers in the July 21, 1896 Diamond Race Meet's main 10-mile road race, which was run along "the Lansing Avenue course" starting at Ganson Street in Jackson. The elaborate Diamond Race Meet with six different competitions (the main road race and shorter track runs at the Jackson Fair Grounds [now the Jackson County Fairgrounds]) was organized and conducted by the Jackson Wheelmen cycling club. *Author's Lockwood negative collection*

Fig. 37. A racing cyclist astride a Dayton bicycle, with an associate who is preparing him for a competition at the Jackson Fair Grounds; this may have been one of the track events for the July 21, 1896 Diamond Race Meet. *Author's Lockwood negative collection*

Fig. 38. A racing action shot from the same Jackson bicycle event shown in fig. 37. *Author's Lockwood negative collection*

Fig. 39. The Fowler Sextet bicycle was exhibited at the Carter bicycle shop on March 17 and 18, 1896. B. J. Carter sits at the front, behind him is United States Tag Co. employee Frank N. Bradley, third is possibly Carter machinist Arthur L. Butcher, fourth is Fred T. Lockwood, fifth is Lewis N. Tussing, and the last person's identity is unknown. It might be John H. Carpenter, who, at this time, worked for the Carters as a machinist or possibly a 29-year-old Fred P. Hinckley, who joined the Carters' business shortly after this photograph was taken. B. J. Carter's bride-to-be, Dorothy Adell "Della" Gillette, and his father, Squire B. Carter, are visible inside the bicycle shop. *Courtesy of Buzzy Carter Maurer*

The Fowler Sextet

In conjunction with an extensive bicycle show conducted by the Carters at Jackson's Guard Hall, the Carters exhibited a novel bicycle at their new 204 West Cortland Street brick bicycle shop on March 17 and 18, 1896, to promote business: the Fowler Sextet.[109] This contraption, which was built with a truss frame "on the cantilever bridge principle" with six seats for cyclists, was labeled "Largest Wheel in the World."[110] The Fowler Sextet was 156 inches long, weighed 137 1/2 pounds, and had 30-inch wheels. The Fowler Cycle Manufacturing Co. in Chicago claimed that the Sextet's engineered, varied pedal-sprocket sizes for the six cyclists compounded torque sufficiently to match the speed of the fastest locomotive (provided the Sextet was allowed a "flying start").[111] Squire Carter was a sales agent for the well-known line of Fowler cycles in Jackson at this time.[112]

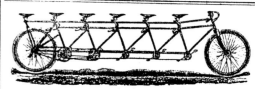
Fowler Sextet.

The above cut, the Fowler Sextet, is the largest wheel in the world, and will be on exhibition at our store, 204 West Cortland street, Tuesday and Wednesday, March 17 and 18, day and evening   All are invited to call and see this wonderful Bicycle   It will race the fastest train in the country, the Empire Express, with six professional riders some time this spring on a prepared track:

Combination Rambler Tandem.

We will show all the models of our different makes of wheels: Ramblers, Remingtons, built by the Remington Arms Co., Clevelands, Clippers and Crescents This will be a good opportunity of seeing together all the leading makes and models of wheels, and it will enable you to choose a wheel more intelligently.

No. 1 Crescent.   No. 4 Crescent.

Remember that every New Wheel we sell is protected one year against theft. Call and get full particulars. If you have a wheel and desire this protection you can have the seal affixed and wheel registered one year for two dollars.

The Jackson Bicycle Riding Academy
IN GUARD HALL,

Will open March 15. All persons buying wheels of us will be taught to ride free. To others fifty cents per lesson.
All Bicycle Sundries, Bicycle Repairing, Etc.

Cor. Cortland and Jackson Sts.   S. B. CARTER.

Fig. 40. A group of celluloid Fowler Cycle Manufacturing Co. stickpins and lapel studs, one of which pictures the Sextet; S. B. Carter held the sales agency for the well-known line of Fowler cycles in Jackson during the mid-1890s. *Author's collection*

Fig. 41. Fowler Sextet advertisement from the March 14, 1896 issue of the *Jackson Daily Citizen*, in which S. B. Carter announced that the Fowler Sextet would be displayed at his new brick bicycle store on March 17 and 18, 1896; he also touted the Jackson Bicycle Riding Academy, which provided free lessons to anyone who bought a new bicycle from the Carters. *Courtesy of the Jackson District Library*

Dorothy Adell "Della" Carter

Eighteen ninety-six was an auspicious year for the 32-year-old B. J. Carter: on July 1, 1896, he married Dorothy Adell "Della" Gillette (October 9, 1875 – May 21, 1958).[113] Charles A. Trask recounted the time he first met Della Gillette in a Christmas note he sent her many years later in 1945: "Since you have a married granddaughter [Sallie Sparks Kendall] I have been thinking back to about 1899? when Byron brought his office girl down to my Pearl street place to look at the contrivance that I had made and used to teach people to ride a bicycle. At that time I detected indications that that office girl was to become Mrs. B. J. Carter, not long after that there was a wedding trip down through southern rivers."[114]

B. J. and Della Carter's wedding announcement in the July 3, 1896 *Jackson Daily Citizen* reported that "the estimable young couple departed on the New York express for an extended bridal journey, from which they will return to reside at 214 W. Washington street."[115] In the next year, the Carters welcomed their first daughter, Rachel Lucretia Carter (October 31, 1897–November 29, 1960), mother of Sallie Sparks Kendall, who assisted the author in research for this book.[116]

Fig. 42. B. J. Carter's future wife, Dorothy Adell "Della" Gillette (right), prior to their 1896 marriage; she is pictured with her older sister, Coriette "Cora" A. Latson, née Gillett. (Della added an *e* at the end of her original surname spelling "Gillett.") *Courtesy of Sallie Sparks Kendall*

Fig. 43. Della Carter in an early 20th-century photograph. *Courtesy of Sallie Sparks Kendall*

A Prospecting Venture for Oil, Gas, and Minerals

In March 1897, B. J. Carter, always on the lookout for new business opportunities, filed articles of incorporation for the Diamond Oil Company, which was capitalized at $10,000, divided into 400 shares of stock at $25 per share. Carter formed this organization with employees Fred T. Lockwood and Fred P. Hinckley; each of the three was granted 16 shares.[117] It is unclear who held the other 352 shares; perhaps these three founders intended to seek additional investors. The purpose of Diamond Oil was to bore for oil, gas, minerals, and "other substances" and to sell them.[118] No historical materials could be found to indicate whether this prospecting venture was actually a success for Carter and his partners, although the Lockwood negatives (figs. 44–49) suggest that they at least made a serious attempt. It may be surprising to know that oil and gas exploration and drilling actively continue in Jackson County to the present day. In a February 24, 2013 MLive.com article, Brad Flory of the *Jackson Citizen Patriot* reported that oil wells in Jackson County had produced 812,856 barrels, or 34 million gallons, during the first six months of 2012, which was at least triple the output of any other Michigan county.[119]

Figs. 44–49. In March 1897 B. J. Carter formed the Diamond Oil Company to bore for oil, gas, minerals, and "other substances." These six photographs from the Lockwood negative collection show drilling towers and other oil-prospecting apparatus and are likely related to the Diamond Oil Company or to the operations of its competitors. Carter is third from the right in the first picture. *Author's Lockwood negative collection*

B. J. Carter, the Employer and Mentor

Squire and Byron Carter's rapid business expansion could only have been achieved by hiring and training talented employees. Some were brought on "green" and trained to be bicycle repairers and machinists. Others were hired away from competing Jackson machine shops and arrived with more experience and skill. In addition to printing-press and paper-cutter operators for the United States Tag Co. starting in 1895 and administrative employees, the Carters had at least one machinist working for them in 1893 and 1894, and had at least two machinists and bicycle repairers on the payroll in 1895, three in 1896, and four during the years 1897 through 1900. All Carter employees would have had the opportunity to acquire or fine-tune valuable machining skills and would have learned innovative approaches to challenging mechanical puzzles by working directly with B. J. Carter. Carter's inventive mind, mechanical expertise, and drive to succeed would undoubtedly have been inspiring. Many went on to pursue their own machine shops, manufacturing, printing, and bicycle, motor boat, and automobile parts and sales businesses and careers.

JOHN H. CARPENTER

One of the earliest Carter machine shop employees appears to have been John H. Carpenter (November 4, 1870–June 20, 1916), who had joined the Carter bicycle enterprise sometime in 1893 as a 22-year-old accomplished machinist.[120] The *Jackson Daily Citizen*, in Carpenter's February 1895 wedding announcement, thought it newsworthy to mention that he was "now connected with a bicycle manufactory at Jackson."[121] Once Carpenter joined the Carter machine shop, he also joined B. J. Carter in becoming an active cyclist.[122]

Prior to starting work with the Carters, Carpenter had worked with Charles A. Trask, in 1889 and 1890, as a machinist at the Geo. T. Smith Middlings Purifier Co., a manufacturing enterprise located at the northeast corner of the intersection of Jackson and Clinton streets.[123] A middlings purifier was a device used in the production of flour to remove the husks from the kernels of wheat. After leaving the middlings purifier business, Carpenter became a machinist for the Michigan Central Railroad in 1891.[124] After a brief "permanent" relocation to Chicago in October 1891, Carpenter returned to Jackson, first worked for the Shaw Electric Crane Co., and then joined the Carter business in 1893.[125] It appears that Carpenter had resigned from the Carters' operation by 1897, as he is not listed in the 1897 *Jackson City Directory* and, by 1900, Carpenter had moved back to Chicago.[126]

A skilled machinist, Carpenter, would resurface again in 1902, when Carpenter relocated his family from Chicago back to Jackson to accept a toolmaker position with the Jackson Automobile Company.[127] But by 1905 John H. Carpenter had parted ways with the Jackson Automobile Company and relocated to Kalamazoo.[128] Carpenter moved to La Crosse, Wisconsin, sometime before 1914 and died in 1916.[129]

Fig. 50. Fred T. Lockwood, circa 1897.
Author's Lockwood negative collection

FRED T. LOCKWOOD

Another early S. B. Carter employee, Fred T. Lockwood, joined the Carter enterprise as a machinist and bicycle repairer in 1895, when he was 22 years old.[130] Lockwood assisted in rebuilding B. J. Carter's first horseless carriage in June 1899 in order that it could be demonstrated on the streets of Jackson.[131] In March 1901, Fred Lockwood resigned from his B. J. Carter bicycle-shop position to open Lockwood Brothers, an electrical, machine shop, and bicycle-repairing business at 131 East Cortland Street.[132] Lockwood's involvement with Squire B. and B. J. Carter, as well as his later business and political accomplishments, are described more fully in Section 8.

Fig. 51. Frank N. Bradley, circa 1897.
Author's Lockwood negative collection

FRANK N. BRADLEY

Frank N. Bradley (January 19, 1866–November 16, 1920) had been a fellow cyclist and friend of B. J. Carter and Fred T. Lockwood during the 1890s and was hired first as a printer for the United States Tag Co. in 1896, and then as a clerk for S. B. Carter in 1897.[133] Bradley's tenure with the Carters was fairly short, as in November 1898 he resigned to become a print job foreman at a periodical named the *Herald* (likely the *Jackson Herald* owned by Bera J. Kingston, who would later be affiliated with the *Jackson Citizen*).[134] Bradley did not sever his contact with B. J. Carter entirely, however, as he assisted Carter with building his first gasoline carriage the following year.[135] In 1900 Bradley left the printing business altogether to be a cigar dealer with his relative by marriage, Sylvester Beckwith; they called the enterprise Bradley & Beckwith and set up shop at 253 East Main Street in Jackson.[136] By 1902 Frank N. Bradley was no longer listed in the *Jackson City Directory*, and by 1907 he had moved to Battle Creek, where he worked as a brakeman.[137] Bradley would later return to Jackson and lived there until he was 54 years old.

ARTHUR L. BUTCHER

Fig. 52. Arthur L. Butcher in 1899.
Author's Lockwood negative collection

Arthur Lewis Butcher (March 23, 1875–December 29, 1939) demonstrated ambition early, at 12 or 13 years old, when he took a job in the bookbinding works for Holland's Book Bindery in Jackson.[138] He soon moved on and learned the sheet metal trade as a "tinner" for two Jackson hardware retailers: Belden & Belden, in 1889 and 1890, and then O. H. McConnel in 1891.[139] Butcher would realize his true calling in 1892 or 1893, when he advanced to the position of machinist for Charles A. Trask in Trask's shop at 136–138 West Pearl Street.[140] In a January 6, 1940 letter Trask sent to Della Carter, he wrote, "It is about forty eight years ago that I hired him [Arthur L. Butcher] first, – he was about sixteen and as a boy he proved industrious, ingenious, and very capable, we are very sorry to hear of his death."[141] By 1896 Butcher had joined Squire B. Carter's operation, also as a machinist.[142] It appears that Butcher may have been one of the Carters' best in-house, longer-term machinists, as he was hired back by B. J. Carter after at least one resignation. Butcher is pictured steering the tiller of B. J. Carter's first 1899 horseless carriage in figure 64 and assisted in rebuilding this machine to make it operational; yet he might not have actually been a Carter employee at the time.[143] The March 14, 1898 *Jackson Daily Citizen* reported that Butcher had left B. J. Carter's shop to return to work for Charles A. Trask as "head mechanic" for a new bicycle-repair business in Bay City, Michigan, called the Cyclorium.[144] But by September 1900, Butcher had come back to Jackson and established his own business to offer "automobile frame fittings" of "special bicycle steel" and manufacturing and drop forging services, which he advertised nationally in *The Motor Vehicle Review*.[145]

After his independent 1900 "automobile frame fittings" business, Butcher was once again, in late 1901, employed by B. J. Carter and was promoted to foreman of Carter's steam-automobile manufacturing operation.[146] Carter was apparently impressed by Butcher's automobile mechanical, machining, and management talents, as Carter hired Butcher again in 1902 to be a foreman in the newly established Jackson Automobile Company.[147] Butcher's tenure at the Jackson Automobile Company was rather short, however, and by 1904 he had resigned to work as a machinist for Lockwood Brothers.[148]

His Lockwood Brothers stint was also brief—in late 1904 Butcher teamed up with another former C. A. Trask machinist, Charles A. Gage, to establish the prominent Jackson engineering and machining firm of Butcher & Gage.[149] Butcher & Gage first offered general machining work and automobile repairing at 301 South Mechanic Street, and by 1907 the enterprise had moved to 113–117 East Washington Street, where the business was expanded to make "a specialty of designing and building machinery for special purposes," including pattern making and drop-forge work.[150]

One of Arthur Butcher's notable inventions was the automatic wheel primer painting device he designed for the enormous Hayes Wheel Company of Jackson. (Hayes Wheel manufactured over four million wheels in 1916, when Butcher designed his wheel-priming machine.)[151] Clarence B. Hayes had consulted with Butcher and "told him a machine which would dip a wheel into a reservoir of paint, lift it out again, then whirl it violently to distribute the priming and get rid of the surplus, might turn the trick."[152] It was reported that Butcher studied the wheel-and-cam mechanisms of automatic linotype machines in the *Jackson Patriot* newspaper facilities and then successfully designed the machine Clarence Hayes needed, patented it in 1916, and sold the patent to Hayes Wheel.[153] When the Hayes Wheel Company secured a $3 million war production contract from the U.S. government in late 1917, a major factory expansion was required and "in order to further equip the plant for the new contract a substantial order for machinery will be placed with Butcher & Gage."[154] By all accounts, Arthur L. Butcher continued to have a successful career and died in 1939, at the age of 64.

FRED P. HINCKLEY

Frederick "Fred" P. Hinckley (July 1866–November 24, 1953), another machinist, was hired by Squire and Byron Carter in early 1897, when Hinckley was 30 years old.[155] Hinckley, who had worked as a machinist at the Geo. T. Smith Middlings Purifier Co., had teamed up with Charles A. Trask in 1890 to establish the firm of Hinckley & Trask, located at Trask's 138 West Pearl Street facility. A May 3, 1890 advertisement in the *Jackson Daily Citizen* labeled them as "practical machinists," who were "builders of vertical engines"; this ad incorrectly named Trask's partner as "Fred *D*. Hinckley."[156] Even though Trask and Hinckley had known each other for several years (Trask had been a witness to Hinckley's October 1887 wedding, and they had worked together at the Geo. T. Smith Middlings Purifier Co.), it appears their partnership lasted for less than one year, as Hinckley & Trask was not even listed in the 1890 or 1891/1892 Jackson city directories.[157] Further, Hinckley is not listed again until the 1898/1899 *Jackson City Directory*, so his whereabouts immediately before accepting his employment opportunity with the Carters are unknown.[158] Fred P. Hinckley was apparently an enthusiastic adherent of B. J. Carter's business convictions, as Hinckley, along with Carter and Fred T. Lockwood, founded the Diamond Oil Company in March 1897.[159]

After a four-year tenure as a machinist for B. J. Carter, Hinckley resigned his Carter position sometime in 1900 to accept the assignment of general superintendent for the Automatic Coaster Brake Co., a manufacturing business located at 120–124 East Washington Street in Jackson.[160] By 1902 Hinckley, with partner, Miar McLaughlin, had apparently acquired the Automatic Coaster Brake Co. and renamed the enterprise Hinckley & McLaughlin.[161] Fred P. Hinckley was again listed as a machinist in 1904 and appears to have been the longest-lived former B. J. Carter employee—he died in 1953 at the age of 88, in Jackson.[162]

Fig. 53. Lewis N. Tussing in 1896.
Courtesy of Buzzy Carter Maurer

LEWIS N. TUSSING

Lewis "Lou" N. Tussing (September 1871–1945) was hired by B. J. Carter as a bicycle repairer by 1897.[163] Tussing had acquired his mechanical skills elsewhere, and in early 1891 the 19-year-old was quoted in the *Jackson Daily Citizen* as saying, "The machinist business is a slow way to get rich."[164] Tussing took a break from the machine shop and served as a clerk at Parker & Fleming Co., a wholesale and retail grocer and baker, immediately prior to joining the Carter operation.[165] Apparently Tussing had been hanging around B. J. Carter's bicycle shop early in 1896, as he appears in the March 1896 photograph (fig. 39) that pictured the Fowler Sextet cycle. And Tussing is noted as having assisted B. J. Carter in assembling Carter's first gasoline carriage in June 1899.[166]

By 1902 Carter finally promoted Tussing from a repairer to a machinist, and then, perhaps in conjunction with the Jackson Automobile Company's July 1902 founding, the two men appear to have parted ways.[167] Tussing was listed simply as a machinist in the 1903 *Jackson City Directory*, with no employer name specified, and by 1904 Tussing, like Arthur L. Butcher, had taken a machinist position with Lockwood Brothers.[168] Prior to 1909 Tussing formed a machine shop partnership with Harry E. Sayles called Sayles & Tussing, located at 107 East Cortland Street.[169] Lou Tussing would ultimately return to selling and repairing bicycles, and he was still in this business in Jackson as late as 1943, when he was 72 years old.[170]

OTHER CARTER EMPLOYEES

Several other employees were brought on by the Carters between 1893 and 1902. As previously mentioned, when Squire B. Carter determined that a full-time bookkeeper was needed to keep track of his various businesses, he hired Emma M. Smith, in 1897.[171] And from a 1945 Christmas note Charles A. Trask sent to Della Carter, it appears Della may have been employed as an "office girl" in B. J. Carter's shop shortly before they were married in 1896.[172] By 1900, B. J. Carter had also hired a stenographer, Genevieve A. Mitchell, who was promoted to bookkeeper in 1901; she then followed Carter to the Jackson Automobile Company, in 1902, as its bookkeeper.[173] Two additional Carter machinists were William Henry Diehl (January 12, 1878–1934) and Edward Joseph Doody (born October 19, 1884). Diehl, who resigned from his bicycle repairer and machinist position with Charles A. Trask, joined B. J. Carter's machine shop in 1901, and then accepted a machinist position a year later with the Jackson Automobile Company, where he worked until at least 1908.[174] Edward J. Doody took a machinist position with B. J. Carter in 1901 but departed after less than a year; he would go on to work for the Jackson Automobile Company as a machinist and "auto tester" (1908–1912) and was later employed by the Briscoe Motor Company (later the Briscoe Motor Corporation) in Jackson.[175] A few clerks (often training positions for future machinists) joined B. J. Carter as well, including Fred W. Graver and Charles H. Keller, both in 1899 or 1900, for about one year.[176]

The list of Squire B. and Byron J. Carter's employees contained in these sections is by no means intended to be exhaustive; yet these 13 individuals serve to demonstrate the rapid expansion of business and engineering activity in the Carters' operations in the 1890s and the early 20th century.

Fig. 54. Charles A. Trask in 1899.
Author's Lockwood negative collection

Charles A. Trask: Master Machinist in Jackson and Chief Engineer for the Cartercar

It does not appear that Charles A. Trask (August 1867–October 26, 1951 [interment date]) was ever a direct employee of B. J. Carter during Carter's pre-1903 bicycle and experimental automobile days, other than occasional contract work. Trask's machining, engineering, and engine-building business ventures, however, intertwined with B. J. Carter's during this period, and several Trask employees took machine shop positions with Carter. In light of their frequent bicycle outings reported during the 1890s and several letters Trask wrote many years later to Della Carter and Della and B.J.'s son, Kenneth, B. J. Carter and Trask were friends. Trask likely built engines for B. J. Carter's first Jaxon autos, and he would ultimately work for Carter starting in December 1906, when he followed Carter to Detroit to assist in engineering and manufacturing the Cartercar.

Other than B. J. Carter's bicycle and machine shop, C. A. Trask's machine and motor-building shop was likely the most influential incubator for aspiring machinists in Jackson. Trask, the son of an English farmer, immigrated to Jackson in 1883 from Wiltshire in England's South West region when he was 15 or 16 years old.[177] His first work assignment in Jackson, from 1884 to early 1890, was alternately as a "machine hand" and machinist for the Geo. T. Smith Middlings Purifier Co.[178] During the latter years of Trask's stint there, he likely became acquainted with John H. Carpenter, who would later join B. J. Carter's shop.

Trask resigned his position with the Geo. T. Smith Middlings Purifier Co. and by May 1890, when he was 22 years old, formed a partnership with a middlings purifier firm associate and future Carter employee, Fred P. Hinckley.[179] A May 3, 1890 *Jackson Daily Citizen* advertisement for Hinckley & Trask described the partners as "builders of vertical engines," providing general repairing, machining, model making, and experimental machinery; they were also "dealers in brass goods, engine supplies, etc."[180] This first independent Trask enterprise was located at 138 West Pearl Street, where Charles A. Trask would continuously operate a machine shop and engine-manufacturing operation until January 1903. The Hinckley & Trask partnership was short-lived, as by February 1891, Trask was the only machinist listed at 138 West Pearl Street with "fine general repairing a specialty."[181] Apparently business was brisk, as in 1892 he expanded his facilities into the adjacent building and listed his address as 136–138 West Pearl Street.[182]

Fig. 55. An advertisement for Charles A. Trask's machine and engine-building shop and bicycle-manufacturing and repair facility at 136–138 West Pearl Street from *R. L. Polk & Co.'s 1896 Jackson City Directory. Courtesy of the Jackson District Library*

Fig. 56. View of an unpaved West Pearl Street, circa 1894; the façade of Charles A. Trask's machine and engine-building shop and bicycle manufacturing and repair facility at 136–138 West Pearl Street is visible on the right. *Courtesy of the Ella Sharp Museum*

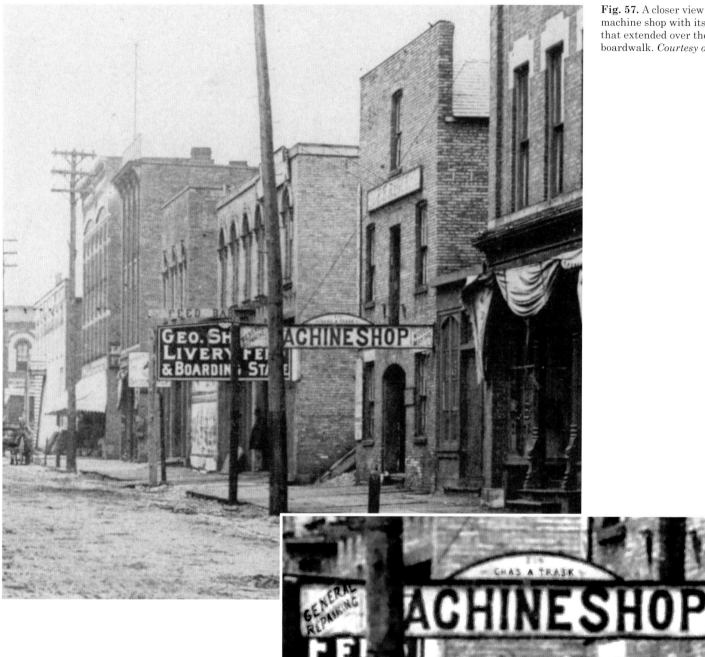

Fig. 57. A closer view of Charles A. Trask's machine shop with its prominent sign that extended over the entire depth of the boardwalk. *Courtesy of the Ella Sharp Museum*

Fig. 58. Detail of Charles A. Trask's machine shop sign. *Courtesy of the Ella Sharp Museum*

Fig. 59. Likely a photograph of the back interior of Charles A. Trask's machine and engine shop and bicycle-manufacturing and repair facility at 136–138 West Pearl Street; a Trask-manufactured gasoline engine (see fig. 129) can be seen on the wood bench along the back wall, and the building width and window style and side-wall placement seem generally to conform to the exterior Trask machine shop view in figs. 56 & 57. *Courtesy of the Ella Sharp Museum*

When he saw the bicycle's popularity growing rapidly, Trask, being an astute businessman, expanded his services to include "bicycle and tricycle repairer" sometime during 1893, when Squire B. Carter also established his first bicycle sales and repair business.[183] Not content merely to repair bicycles, Trask, in the summer of 1894, commenced manufacturing "a new machine of superior quality and remarkable strength, built from perfected models," which he branded the Rocket bicycle.[184] Trask advertised that a Rocket buyer "can have it made to your order and have a bicycle that is perfection."[185] A December 15, 1894 *Jackson Daily Citizen* article indicated that Trask had expanded his machine shop to increase his bicycle-manufacturing capabilities and that "his plant is now fully established, and will give employment next season to a large force of skilled mechanics . . . a great bicycle factory would prove a welcome addition to Jackson's industries."[186]

In addition to manufacturing the Rocket bicycle, Trask had, in 1895, begun selling other manufacturers' bicycles, including the America, Ben-Hur, Envoy, Fleetwing, Keating, Majestic, Outing, Overland, Sylph, and Viking brands.[187] Trask designed and built other bicycles as well. A February 28, 1895 *Jackson Daily Citizen* item said that Trask was building "a bicycle built for two . . . the first tandem that has been built in Jackson, and no doubt will create great interest."[188] Another *Jackson Daily Citizen* piece, on July 17, 1897, advised that Charles A. Trask had "just finished a bicycle for A. E. Putnam, of Midland, Mich., which is a novel as well as practical idea."[189] Putnam had patented this bicycle assembly in which the chain and sprocket were "entirely enclosed in sort of a gear case which is embodied in the frame. Thus protecting the delicate parts of the wheel and the sprocket and chain from dirt."[190]

Trask built at least two miniature bicycles for his children. The first was a single-seat model (figs. 14 and 15), which Trask designed and manufactured for his two-year-old son, Verne Alva Trask, in early 1898.[191] The second was a tiny tandem two-seater built for use by Verne and his younger sister, Marjorie Iva Trask, in the fall of 1899.[192] Marjorie was only 18 months old at the time.[193] The *Jackson Daily Citizen* labeled it as "the smallest tandem in the world."[194] As with Trask's earlier diminutive single-seat bicycle, the tandem cycle was equipped with 13 1/2-inch pneumatic tires; however, it was considerably longer with a 40-inch wheelbase.[195] Marjorie Iva Schley,

née Trask, described in an April 1964 letter she wrote to the *Jackson Citizen Patriot* how her father "had circulated pictures abroad of his children on the tandem bike in order to promote his business."[196]

Trask was presented with an opportunity in early 1898 to expand his bicycle-repairing business to another Michigan market. The March 14, 1898 *Jackson Daily Citizen* reported that Trask had "associated himself with C. M. Hague and [they] have opened the Cyclorium at Bay City where they will do a general line of bicycle work"; Bay City is about 135 miles from Jackson.[197] This article also mentioned that Charles A. Trask had hired his former employee Arthur L. Butcher away from B. J. Carter's shop to serve as Trask's "head mechanic" in the Cyclorium.[198] While Trask may have been growing his bicycle-repair business, it appears he decided to phase out selling bicycles a few months later. In a May 26, 1899 advertisement in the *Jackson Daily Citizen*, Trask announced: "After July 1st, I shall discontinue the sale of bicycles for this season at least and devote my entire time to my machine shop. For the next five weeks I shall sell all the wheels I can at marvelously close figures . . . I shall continue to operate the largest and best equipped repair shop in the city, which will receive my undivided attention."[199] This advertisement may have simply been a marketing ploy, although it does appear that about this time Trask started to focus more of his energies on gasoline engines for marine and stationary applications.

In addition to his bicycle business and other repair work, Trask manufactured water motors, electric fans, and special machinery and crafted "light drills," and by the mid-1890s his reputation as an expert motor builder and repairer and engineer was known outside of Jackson.[200] For example, in October 1895 he was "at Albion [Michigan], superintending some extensive repairs on the big Corliss [steam] engine at the Gale manufacturing plant."[201]

Working for Charles A. Trask must have been an attractive opportunity for young machine hands and machinists in Jackson, as the bicycle and motor design and building work would serve as excellent training. This situation would ultimately benefit B. J. Carter—several of Trask's machinists and clerks would resign and bring their newfound expertise to Carter's shop. Among them were Arthur L. Butcher, John H. Carpenter, William H. Diehl, and Fred P. Hinckley.

Fig. 60. Bicycle lapel studs and stickpins representing nearly all of the bicycle brands Charles A. Trask offered from 1893 through 1899. *Author's collection*

Even though they were competitors, Carter and Trask appear to have been reliable business associates who regularly exchanged ideas (and employees). Trask was present, for example, when Carter and his employees rebuilt Carter's first horseless carriage in June 1899 (although as Fred T. Lockwood noted in his September 1919 reminiscence in the *Jackson Citizen Patriot*, "'Charley' Trask didn't have much to do with it").[202]

It looks like Charles A. Trask may have built engines for B. J. Carter's first major motorcar venture, the Jackson Automobile Company, when Trask's new firm, The Trask-Field Gas Engine Co., leased a machine shop within the Jackson auto factory complex. The December 19, 1902 issue of the *Jackson Daily Citizen* reported, "Charles A. Trask, who has been operating a machine shop on Pearl street for nearly 13 years, has formed a co-partnership with Rayner Field, the new company to be known as the Trask-Field Gas Engine Co. They will build gas and gasoline engines exclusively, from patterns and improvements that Mr. Trask has been working on for the past five or six years. They will move into their new quarters, one of the buildings owned by the Jackson Auto Co., on Park avenue about January 15th" 1903.[203] Carter was interviewed about Jaxon car production in early March 1903 and said, "One firm of well known machinists now have an order for 100 engines and that will keep them busy."[204] It is highly likely Carter was referring to The Trask-Field Gas Engine Co., in light of its close proximity to other Jackson Automobile Company manufacturing facilities and Charles A. Trask's reputation. Trask's tenure with The Trask-Field Gas Engine Co. was fairly brief, as he either resigned or was bought out in 1904.[205]

Charles A. Trask's engineering and machining ambitions would soon be connected much more closely with B. J. Carter's friction-drive transmission endeavors. It appears Trask may have collaborated with Carter in Jackson shortly after Carter resigned from the Jackson Automobile Company in 1904 to refine and promote his newly invented and patented friction-drive motorcar transmission. Trask's daughter, Marjorie I. Schley, in her April 1964 letter to the *Jackson Citizen Patriot*, said that her father "became associated with Byron Carter of Jackson and Detroit in the manufacture of the friction-drive 'Cartercar.' He was a staunch advocate of the friction-drive car as opposed to the gear-driven car . . . We grew up thinking gears were an abomination of the Lord."[206]

Trask is not listed in the 1905 *Jackson City Directory* because he had moved to Ypsilanti by that time, where he worked first as a machinist and later established an automobile-repair business.[207] It was not long until Trask and B. J. Carter would again collaborate on automobile projects: a group of investors persuaded Carter to relocate his friction-drive-transmission automobile business, and his family, from Jackson to Detroit in the fall of 1905; Trask followed Carter there in December 1906 to design and build the Cartercar.[208] Trask would ultimately be promoted to chief of Cartercar's engineering department and factory production manager.[209] When Cartercar moved to a new factory in Pontiac, Michigan, Trask and his family relocated to 60 Williams Street in Pontiac, in late 1908 or early 1909.[210]

In March 1912, Trask resigned his positions at Cartercar.[211] A month later, the *Detroit Free Press* and *Automobile Topics* reported that Trask "is going to Europe to study the latest foreign automobile and aeroplane [engineering] practice, and will be gone about three months."[212] Trask would divide his three-month trip equally between his native England and "the Continent."[213]

As a respected member of the Society of Automobile Engineers (renamed the Society of Automotive Engineers in 1916), Charles A. Trask had earned a national reputation; after returning from Europe, his automobile design and construction observations regarding European practice were reported in major automotive journals of the day.[214] A June 15, 1912 *Automobile Topics* article entitled "Trask Discusses Foreign Practices" stated that Charles A. Trask had "inspected and analyzed automobile manufacturing conditions in a large number of foreign factories," and afterward Trask had declared "that there are at least some things that are done more carefully on the other side than in the United States."[215] He said that "wire and other forms of metal wheels are becoming more generally used on the European products . . . from an engineering standpoint, the metal, and particularly the wire wheel, is being looked upon as a decided improvement" over the poorer quality hickory that was available in Europe for wood-spoke wheels.[216] Additionally, Trask opined that "great attention is given to careful assembly by European manufacturers" and that many of these motorcar builders delegated the fitting of coachwork and bodies to firms independent of the motorcar factories.[217] Trask concluded, "Regardless of our love of the good old United States and our admiration for the keen engineering minds that this country has produced, we must admit that, in a few things at least, in their excess of energetic haste many of the Americans have momentarily lost sight of the absolute necessary attention which must be given to careful assembly and proper fitting of parts in order to turn out a sturdy, lasting, three-hundred-and-sixty-five-days-a-year automobile."[218]

While in Europe, Trask accepted the position of factory manager for the Henderson Motor Car Co., incorporated in May 1912 to be located in Indianapolis, where he soon moved his family.[219] In light of Trask's automotive design observations after his European trip, it is not surprising that the first Henderson roadster and touring car models were fitted with well-designed demountable wire wheels with a sophisticated locking mechanism and constructed in a manner to make tire changing as quick and easy as possible.[220]

His tenure at the Henderson Motor Car Co. lasted less than a year, and by the end of January 1913 Trask had resigned to join a more established Indianapolis automobile manufacturer, the Nordyke & Marmon Company.[221] Trask's new firm built the highly regarded Marmon car; its bright-yellow Marmon "Wasp" racer had taken first place in the inaugural Indianapolis 500 in 1911.[222]

Trask's daughter, Marjorie I. Schley, wrote in her April 1964 letter to the *Jackson Citizen Patriot* that her father "had seen very small cars on a trip home to England in 1912 and was convinced they would sell in the U.S."[223] In fact, these smaller automobiles, typically called cyclecars, did indeed become very popular in the United States; there was a cyclecar boom, primarily during the teens and to a much lesser extent in the 1920s, with over 150 different U.S. cyclecar manufacturers.[224]

Trask followed his convictions and built a prototype cyclecar, which he branded the Economycar.[225] *The Automobile* reported that the Economycar was "the first car to be built in Indianapolis on true cyclecar lines."[226] Trask designed the Economycar in 1912, and its prototype made an initial test appearance in the May 26, 1913 Indianapolis Decoration Day parade.[227] It was reported that by February 1914, Trask had driven the prototype Economycar with an air-cooled V-type two-cylinder engine and planetary transmission over 5,000 miles; in the meantime, Trask had formed the Economy Car

Company in Indianapolis and was seeking a suitable factory site for Economycar production.[228]

By February 1914, Trask, who had resigned from Nordyke & Marmon some time earlier, formed a partnership with experienced automobile executive Fred K. Parke (a former vice president with the Everitt-Metzger-Flanders, Studebaker, and Universal Motor Truck companies) to manufacture and sell the Economycar.[229] This new venture, called the International Cyclecar Company, was announced on February 7, 1914.[230] The International Cyclecar Company first established temporary offices in the United States Rubber Building at 1790 Broadway in New York, and shortly after in a 100,000-square-foot factory in Providence, Rhode Island.[231] According to an ad in the March 1914 issue of *The American Cyclecar*, the production-model Economycar, alternately called the "Economy cyclecar" in this same advertisement, was offered for $375 ($395 with a folding top), was built with a 36-inch tread, which was 20 inches narrower than the standard automobile tread of the day, and weighed only 470 pounds.[232] (In a March 28, 1920 letter that Charles A. Trask sent to the late B. J. Carter's then 13-year-old son, Kenneth, Trask included Economycar photographs and told the lad, "When we formed the International Cyclecar Co. in February 1914 . . . we set the price at $375.00, at that time the complete sets of parts, not assembled would have cost us $248.00 per set.")[233] Motive power in the Economy cyclecar production model was upgraded from the prototype model's engine to 12 horsepower with an air-cooled F. W. Spacke Machine Co. V-type two-cylinder engine.[234] Although plans were made to produce 6,000 units in 1914 (with "demonstrators in March" and "deliveries in April"), it does not appear that the International Cyclecar Company actually built Economy cyclecars in any quantity, because Trask resigned from the enterprise within five months of its formation.[235]

It was announced in early July 1914 that Trask had allied himself with another cyclecar designer and builder, Fred P. Mertz (not to be confused with Charles Merz, another Indianapolis cyclecar builder), president of the recently reorganized Comet Cyclecar Co., in Indianapolis.[236] Trask was designated as factory manager for this operation.[237] Illustrations of the Comet cyclecar show a machine extremely similar in appearance to Trask's Economycar design.[238] Purportedly, 20 Comet automobiles were built in the Indianapolis

Fig. 61. The 1913 Economycar cyclecar designed and built by Charles A. Trask, who is shown piloting the machine; it was powered by an air-cooled 12-horsepower V-2 Spacke engine with belt drive to the rear wheels. Trask established the International Cyclecar Co. in February 1914 to manufacture the Economycar, with an office in New York and plans for a production facility in Providence, Rhode Island. Substantial, sustained Economycar production was, however, never achieved. *Author's collection*

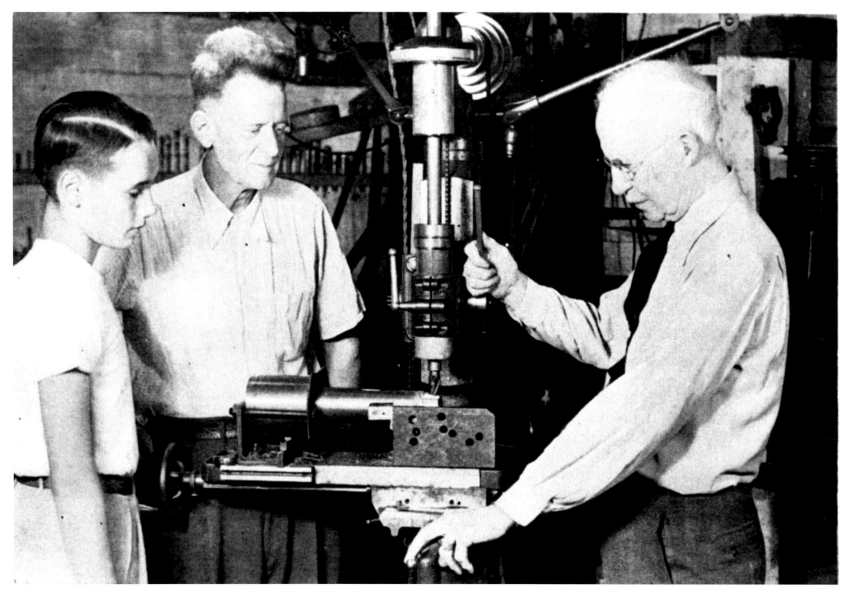

Fig. 62. This photograph from the December 1950 issue of *Popular Science* is captioned, "Teamwork paid off in production when Charles A. Trask [right], a retired engineer, began doing defense work in his basement shop in 1942. Soon swamped with jobs, he recruited neighbors and high-school boys, training them himself. Now 83, Trask is again helping Uncle Sam re-arm. Here he shows two friends in his shop how to work a small vertical milling machine. That thing he's making is an adapter sleeve for a 30-ton horizontal boring mill." *Copyright © 1950 by Bonnier Corporation, publisher of Popular Science. Reproduced with permission of Bonnier Corporation*

Comet Cyclecar Co. factory; however, as Charles A. Trask's daughter, Marjorie I. Schley, wrote in her April 1964 letter, "The 'Economycar' did not become as popular as he thought . . . and he was forced to abandon it."[239] Consistent with this account, Trask, in his March 28, 1920 letter to Kenneth G. Carter, wrote, "When I started this car I hoped the business would grow, it ought to—my car is six years old now and is in fine condition." Trask went on to say that in early 1914 "there were a lot of worthless small cars put out and I think this had a good deal to do with" the Economycar's (and Comet's) failure.[240]

Unlike B. J. Carter, who launched two major automobile companies, Charles A. Trask was unsuccessful in organizing a car company that manufactured autos in any quantity, as even the Comet Cyclecar Co. appears to have shuttered its operations later in 1914.[241] It should be noted that the field of automotive manufacturing had become considerably more crowded by 1914 (than it had been in 1905 and earlier), and competition for investors and working capital was substantially more fierce.

Trask maintained an active engineering career and continued to be an ardent promoter of B. J. Carter's and similar friction-drive transmission designs. He presented a technical article titled "Tractor Friction Transmissions" to the Indiana Section of the Society of Automotive Engineers in 1918; Trask's illustrated piece argued for the supremacy of friction-drive transmissions, provided numerous examples of truck and locomotive applications, and was ultimately published in the *Journal of the Society of Automotive Engineers*.[242] In another paper presented at a March 12, 1925 meeting of the Indiana Section of the Society of American Engineers, Trask once again made the case for the friction-drive transmission, which was then "still performing satisfactory service on various types of tractors and commercial jobs," when "he suggested that for light cars which approach cycle size the friction type might be found useful still, in spite of the fact that the type has now been abandoned for passenger cars."[243]

Charles A. Trask would serve as mechanical superintendent for the Rockwood Manufacturing Co., of Indianapolis, until he resigned in October 1920 to assume a factory-manager position with the National Metal Products Co., also in Indianapolis.[244] It appears Trask returned to Rockwood Manufacturing Co. in the late 1920s as an equipment efficiency engineer.[245] The Rockwood Manufacturing Co. was a reliable resource for loyal long-time Cartercar owners after the Cartercar Company had ceased production—the firm advertised in 1917, "If you own or operate friction-drive cars, we can supply friction fillers for repairs." Incidentally, a successor company to Rockwood called Paper Pulleys, Inc., of Columbia, Tennessee, still manufactures compressed paper pulleys and paper-faced friction-drive assemblies, available today for Cartercar owners who wish to keep their antique machines operable.[246] In closing her 1964 letter to the *Jackson Citizen Patriot*, Marjorie I. Schley, Charles A. Trask's daughter, said, "If there is a 'hero' in this piece, it is my father, who died at 83 [in 1951], after working as a mechanical engineer until the day before his death, and enjoying every bit of his work immensely."[247]

The Carter Enterprise at the End of the 1890s

When the *Jackson Daily Citizen* announced B. J. and Della Carter's 1896 wedding, it labeled B.J. as "a prominent young business man of this city."[248] This assessment was indeed valid and foretelling. Near the close of the 19th century, the northwest corner of Cortland and Jackson streets had become a bustling center of commercial activity for several seemingly unrelated businesses owned by B. J. and Squire Carter: bicycle sales and repair, a tag- and label-printing and punching operation, machining and foundry capabilities, a furniture store, a talking machine shop (selling both phonographs and Columbia Graphophones), a loan and pawnbroker office, storage facilities, and petroleum and mineral exploration and sales.[249] To add to the mix, by 1897 B. J. Carter had formed a partnership with his uncle Charles D. Carter to manufacture strawberry-planting and hulling tools under the name of the Carter Manufacturing Company, located at 204 West Cortland Street.[250] In the midst of this exciting period for the Carter businesses, Squire B. Carter turned over management of all operations to B.J., and by 1901, Squire had returned to his original vocation, farming.[251]

With this considerable business, mechanical, and machining experience as a foundation, B. J. Carter's long curiosity in and study of the emerging, still-primitive field of motorcar development would soon culminate in the construction of B. J. Carter's first automobile.

First Automobile Assembled in Jackson, Michigan

The June 26, 1899 *Jackson Daily Citizen* made an important announcement, albeit in an understated manner: "Carter & Son's bicycle shop has turned out a horseless carriage, which was seen about the streets today."[252] Ensuring that a local newspaper reporter was present at the automobile's inaugural public run to record the event may have been a scheme that B. J. Carter learned from the Detroit inventor Charles Brady King, who had sold Carter the components for the incomplete machine just 10 days earlier. Carter soon also announced his first automobile in the national press. *The Horseless Age*, the most prominent automobile journal of the day, wrote in its August 9, 1899 issue that "B. J. Carter, Jackson, Mich., has built a gasoline carriage for himself."[253]

It is somewhat perplexing that Carter's first clearly, and contemporaneously, documented automobile project was propelled by a gasoline motor, in light of his long association with steam engines. In 1899 steam-engine technology was commonplace, and steam as a motive power had been employed by a handful of automobile makers. There was also a small selection of ready-built steam engines available for purchase by auto inventors. We will likely never know why B. J. Carter chose to first build a gasoline-powered carriage. It is speculation, but perhaps it was simply a matter of opportunity in light of Carter's association with Charles Brady King. It is also plausible that Carter's acquaintance with Charles A. Trask may have encouraged Carter to work with gasoline engines for motorcars. (Trask had, by 1899, been manufacturing marine and stationary engines of various types for nearly 10 years, and Carter would have been familiar with these motor designs, so it is conceivable that the inventive Carter experimented with gasoline or steam engines for horseless carriages earlier than 1899 as well. This speculation is supported by a couple of Byron J. Carter's obituaries, which indicate, somewhat improbably, that Carter commenced motorcar engine experimentation as early as 1894, and certain unsubstantiated thirdhand accounts written several years after his death.)[254] Carter's initial dedicated (and concurrently documented) *gasoline* car and engine experiments would turn out to be fairly short-lived, and within one year, Carter would shift his primary attention to *steam*-powered carriages and engines.

The design of B. J. Carter's first gasoline automobile is not fully specified in periodicals of the day; we know, however, that most of its components had been designed, manufactured, and assembled by Charles Brady King of Detroit with 1895 and 1896 parts. King then sold the incomplete gasoline motor carriage, along with eight batteries and a spark coil, to Carter on June 15, 1899, for $616.75 (pneumatic tires were not included).[255] Two versions of the original receipt for this transaction, one hand written the other typed, still exist in the Charles Brady King Collection in the Detroit Public Library's National Automotive History Collection. It was only through the dedicated efforts of Carter and his bicycle-shop employees and associates that the unfinished King machine, after it was delivered to Jackson, was properly rebuilt, improved, and put into working order to be driven on the streets of Jackson within 10 days, on June 26, 1899.

As Fred T. Lockwood stated in his 1919 *Jackson Citizen Patriot* reminiscence, B. J. Carter "went to Detroit and bought the body, the engine, and steering gear for Carter's first gasoline automobile. We had lots of trouble assembling it. 'Art' Butcher, Byron Carter, Frank Bradley and myself did most of the work; 'Charley' Trask didn't have much to do with it . . . the machine didn't work at all well, and we brought it back to the shop and made it over—I guess we revamped it three or four times. But that started Byron Carter in the automobile business."[256]

Fortunately, Charles Brady King (February 2, 1868–June 23, 1957) was a meticulous record keeper who carefully collected and saved a comprehensive archive of his business correspondence, working documents, engineering and patent sketches and drawings (King was granted at least 64 patents during his career), photographs, and other ephemera.[257] This expansive research trove is preserved in the Charles Brady King Collection in the Detroit Public Library's National Automotive History Collection in 42 large archival storage boxes; among many interesting materials, the collection contains some specific information regarding B. J. Carter's first gasoline car. King also detailed and documented early automotive history in two books he wrote and published: *Psychic Reminiscences*, in 1935, and a memoir titled *A Golden Anniversary, 1895–1945, Personal Side-Lights of America's First Automobile Race*.[258] The National Automotive History Collection in Detroit also holds a substantial archive known as the Oliver Edward Barthel Collection papers, 1868–1955. Additionally,

Fig. 63. B. J. Carter's first documented experimental gasoline automobile, which made its inaugural run in Jackson on June 26, 1899, when the *Jackson Daily Citizen* reported, "Carter & Son's bicycle shop has turned out a horseless carriage, which was seen about the streets today"; the two-cylinder motorcar with dos-à-dos (back-to-back) seating is shown outside the Carter bicycle repair shop's west side door, with the Jackson County Jail and Jackson sheriff's office visible behind the dilapidated wooden fence. B. J. Carter and his crew had made fast work of rebuilding a machine that functioned by June 26, as only 10 days had elapsed from the day Carter purchased the incomplete motor carriage, eight batteries (visible on the front floorboard), and spark coil for $616.75 from Charles Brady King, an important automotive pioneer in Detroit. *Author's Lockwood negative collection*

Fig. 64. B. J. Carter's then former employee Fred T. Lockwood in an illustrated September 14, 1919 *Jackson Citizen Patriot* reminiscence about early automobile days in Jackson, stated that this photograph "was taken just as the old machine went out the side door of Carter's bicycle shop. 'Art' Butcher was driving it, with one hand on the tiller and the other holding on to the seat; Frank Bradley sits with him on the front seat, and the young fellow in the straw hat wearing the bicycle socks sitting on the rear seat is 'Lou' Tussing. 'Charley' Trask is standing in the doorway of the shop where the machine was assembled." *Author's Lockwood negative collection*

Fig. 65. B. J. Carter's 1899 gasoline automobile running north on South Jackson Street at the corner of West Cortland Street (the Jackson Corset Co. smokestack and a short portion of its sign are visible in the background); while the auto's driver in this photograph appears to be B. J. Carter, the original negative unfortunately does not have sufficient resolution to confirm. *Author's Lockwood negative collection*

The Reminiscences of Mr. Oliver E. Barthel, from an interview conducted in July 1952 and held in the Collections of The Henry Ford at the Benson Ford Research Center, is an illuminating historical document with several references to B. J. Carter. Oliver E. Barthel (October 3, 1877–August 1, 1969), who was Charles B. King's draftsman and engineering assistant until 1901, collaborated with Carter to design gasoline engines in 1900, and possibly in 1899 as well. The King and Barthel archives in the National Automotive History Collection, Detroit Public Library, and *The Reminiscences of Mr. Oliver E. Barthel* in the Collections of The Henry Ford serve another consequential purpose for historians: many of King's and Barthel's later writings in the twilight of their careers were efforts to set the record straight for posterity (and to garner more recognition for their own achievements), as many automotive-history writers in the

1910s to 1950s were, in King's and Barthel's assessments, carelessly misstating, mischaracterizing, and misdating information, sometimes with less-than-pure motives.

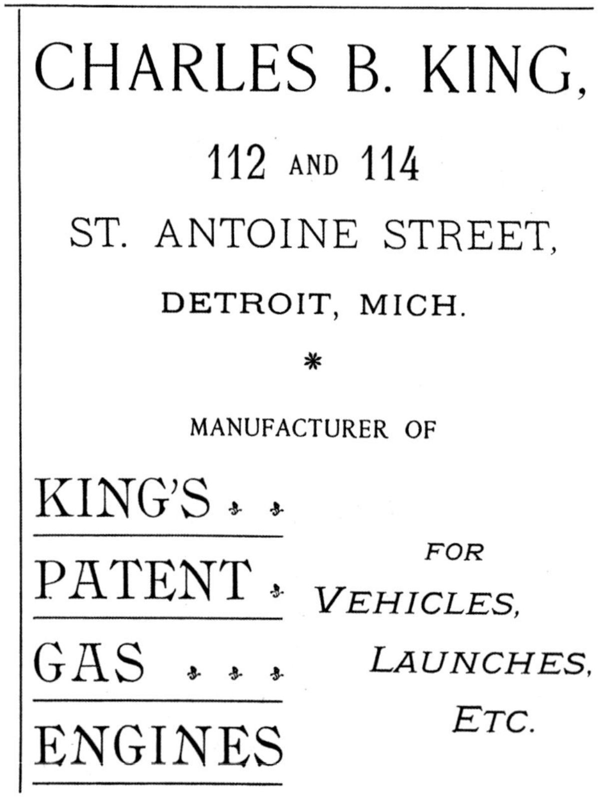

Charles Brady King was a widely known and influential gasoline-engine and automobile designer and builder in the 1890s and early 20th century. King established an engineering business in Detroit called the Charles B. King Company in the fall of 1893, at 112–114 St. Antoine Street, in the second floor premises he rented from the John Lauer Machine Shop.[259] The Lauer Machine Shop provided King the facilities to build many of his early automobile and marine engines and other inventions with Lauer's fine equipment and mechanics. As King described in his memoir, "On a custom basis I used these facilities and superintended my own work, which I kept at a high standard."[260] King, who studied engineering at Cornell University, had developed and patented the pneumatic jackhammer and had also patented a steel brake beam in 1893.[261] The manufacturing of the pneumatic jackhammer and the sale of his brake beam patent provided King the wherewithal for his primary interest, designing and building automobiles and engines.[262]

Charles B. King appears to have been acquainted with most of the key automotive pioneers in the earliest days of U.S. horseless carriage development, and he had intended to run an experimental King four-cylinder machine in America's first-ever automobile race conducted by the *Chicago Times-Herald* on Thanksgiving Day, November 28, 1895.[263] As King wrote in his 1945 memoir, "Mine [was] the only Michigan entry . . . Not completing the car in time, I withdrew my entry but was honored by being appointed an umpire."[264] King's machine also had had other problems: he had been unable to procure the correct pneumatic tires for it and he had nearly depleted his funds.[265] While serving as an umpire for the event in the last hour of the nearly half-day race (the winning driver's elapsed time for the 52.4-mile trek—Jackson Park in downtown Chicago to Evanston and back—was ultimately 10 hours 23 minutes, with an average running speed of 6.66 miles per hour), King was recruited to pilot an entrant's Mueller-Benz "motocycle" to the finish line when the driver, Oscar B. Mueller, who was the car owner's son, fell unconscious from exhaustion caused by the extreme November cold and blizzard conditions, missed meals, and by pushing his father's machine through virtually impassable stretches of muddy, snow-covered roads.[266]

CHARLES B. KING,

112 AND 114

ST. ANTOINE STREET,

DETROIT, MICH.

*

MANUFACTURER OF

KING'S

PATENT

GAS

ENGINES

FOR VEHICLES, LAUNCHES, ETC.

Fig. 66. Charles Brady King was already designing, building, and selling marine and "vehicle" gasoline engines by the time this advertisement appeared in vol. 1, no. 1 of *The Horseless Age* magazine in November 1895. *Author's collection*

These drivers (sometimes then called "conductors"), Charles B. King and Oscar B. Mueller, who regained consciousness, ultimately finished in second place, and the car's owner was awarded $1,500 for "performance in the road race and economy in operation"; it had taken King and Mueller 10 hours 47 minutes to complete the race, with an average running speed of 5.51 miles per hour.[267] Charles B. King "was offered half of this amount but declined it. He was however presented with a gold medal."[268]

Shortly after this race, in a January 18, 1896 contract, King formed a brief partnership with the legendary Duryea brothers, Charles E. and J. Frank Duryea, to manufacture the two-cylinder, four-cycle Duryea-King Motor, in Detroit, according to J. Frank Duryea's patent (no. 557,496); King would later refer to it as the "King-Duryea" motor; only one engine was actually manufactured as a sample and then sold to be installed in a circus motor wagon (fig. 81).[269] Although a debate about who constructed the first U.S. automobile has gone on for over 100 years, the Duryeas are most often credited as the builders of the first American automobile, which was road tested on September 21, 1893, in Springfield, Massachusetts; this machine is preserved today in the Smithsonian Institution.[270] Incidentally, an improved version of this history-making 1893 automobile was later manufactured by the Duryea Motor Wagon Company and won the $2,000 first prize in the 1895 *Chicago Times-Herald* race, beating the Mueller-Benz vehicle driven by Charles B. King and Oscar B. Mueller.[271]

Aside from his involvement in the first-ever American automobile race and his many inventions and patents, Charles Brady King may be most well known as the first inventor to design, build, and drive a horseless carriage on the streets of Detroit, on March 6, 1896, several months before King and Barthel's acquaintance Henry Ford

Fig. 67. Charles Brady King's horseless carriage, which he built using an iron-tired Emerson & Fisher Co. delivery wagon, and then first drove in Detroit on March 6, 1896; Charles B. King (right) sits with his hand on the steering tiller; King's draftsman and engineering assistant, Oliver E. Barthel, is on the left. The *Detroit Journal* of March 7, 1896, described King's car as having a water-cooled three-horsepower four-cylinder gasoline engine with a belt-drive transmission and an unusual equalizing gearing (i.e., a differential assembly); it was capable of running seven or eight miles per hour. King's machine was the first experimental horseless carriage built and demonstrated in Detroit—months before Henry Ford's inaugural run of his first motorcar, later in 1896. *Courtesy of the National Automotive History Collection, Detroit Public Library*

Fig. 68. Photograph of the water-cooled three- or four-horsepower four-cylinder engine, with an "open frame" configuration, that was designed and built by Charles B. King and intended as the power source for King's carriage from the horse-drawn vehicle maker, Sievers & Erdman (the carriage that King sold to B. J. Carter in 1899 but with a different motor); King had planned to run this machine in America's first-ever automobile race, the *Chicago Times-Herald* event on Thanksgiving Day, November 28, 1895, but it was not ready in time and King withdrew his entry. This four-cylinder engine was later installed in the King horseless carriage (see fig. 67), which was demonstrated a few months later in Detroit in March 1896. *Courtesy of the Charles Brady King Collection, National Automotive History Collection, Detroit Public Library*

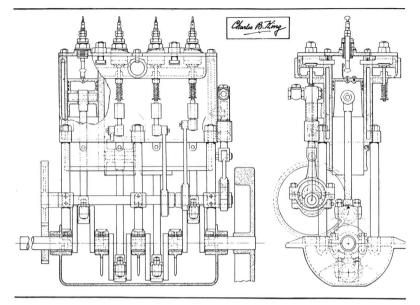

Fig. 69. Charles B. King's drawing of the 1895 four-cylinder engine, pictured in fig. 68, which reflects improvements King made to the motor's pistons and cylinders shortly after the photograph in fig. 68 was taken; in his 1945 memoir, King wrote, "After this change was made, I gave two of the original valves to Henry Ford for use on the two-cylinder engine he built for his first little car, the 'Quadricycle,'" demonstrated in mid-1896. *Courtesy of the Charles Brady King Collection, National Automotive History Collection, Detroit Public Library*

made the inaugural test run of his first car, the "Quadricycle" later in 1896."[272] The *Detroit Journal* of March 7, 1896, described King's experimental car as having a water-cooled, three-horsepower, four-cylinder engine with a belt-drive transmission and an unusual equalizing gearing (i.e., a differential assembly).[273] The motor had an "open frame" configuration, four-cycle intake, ignition, and exhaust, a 5-inch piston stroke and a 2 3/4-inch cylinder bore, was 23 inches tall, and weighed 130 pounds.[274] With an approximate overall weight of 1,300 pounds, King's horseless carriage was said to be capable of running five to eight miles per hour.[275] King's March 6, 1896 testing vehicle was constructed with an iron-tired Emerson & Fisher Co. delivery wagon (which had only arrived from the Cincinnati wagon maker on February 27, 1896) into which King installed his four-cylinder engine (i.e., the four-cylinder motor originally intended for King's thwarted 1895 *Chicago Times-Herald* race carriage).[276] Not surprisingly, the confident King made a proclamation about motor carriages in the March 7, 1896 *Detroit Journal* piece after his initial Detroit test run: "I am convinced they will in time supersede the horse."[277] King's primitive horseless carriage of March 1896 was reconstructed for a 60th-anniversary celebration in 1956, and the replica vehicle is displayed in a permanent Detroit Historical Museum exhibition called *America's Motor City*.[278]

In his 1945 memoir, Charles B. King wrote, "Another of my cars built at Lauer's was sold to Byron J. Carter of Jackson, Michigan. I had hoped to have this car ready for the Chicago Race of 1895, but could not do so for lack of pneumatic tires as well as the car not being completed."[279] An undated outline completed by King titled "Cars Built and Designed by Charles B. King—1893–1903," labeled the vehicle he sold Carter as the "Times-Herald entry" and indicated he had begun building it "sometime in July or August 1895" as "a bevel-drive car for the King four-cylinder, four-cycle engine" shown in figure 68; King had started designing the machine in 1894.[280] King and Barthel both noted that the machine King sold Carter had a friction-type transmission connected to the bevel-gear rear axle, which is intriguing in light of Carter's extensive friction-drive-transmission experiments that started in 1901 (according to later Cartercar sales literature).[281] Barthel further described Carter's machine as having a "bevel type differential gear and [a] two universal joint propeller shaft drive. The rear axle housing was tubular, and the axle shafts had Hyatt Roller Bearings. The wheels were wire spoke with rolled steel rims and single tube pneumatic tires with ball bearings in the front wheels. The steering gearing was of the worm and sector type with steering column and wheel and there was a fin and tube radiator in front for cooling. There was a dash on this car but the whip socket was missing."[282]

This description largely conforms to the photographs of B. J. Carter's first horseless carriage (figs. 63 and 64), with the exception that either Carter or King had replaced the steering wheel gear with a more simple steering tiller, the radiator is not readily visible, and the dash had been removed before the photographs were taken. Carter likely installed the steering tiller himself: Fred T. Lockwood, in his 1919 *Jackson Citizen Patriot* reminiscence, said that Carter "went to Detroit and bought the body, the engine, and *steering gear* [italics added] for Carter's first gasoline automobile."[283]

In a January 17, 1940 interview transcript, Charles B. King described the June 15, 1899 automobile transaction with B. J. Carter: "This was one of the first sales of a car in the U.S. and the first automobile sale in Detroit. Carter came to Detroit and wanted the outfit and offered a pretty good price and I let the car go before I had put it on the road."[284] As a reference point to illustrate just how early Carter's auto purchase was, the Winton Motor Carriage Co. in Cleveland had boldly claimed (dubiously, as at least two one-off machines had been sold earlier, in 1896) that they had made the first commercial sale of an American-made gasoline automobile on March 24, 1898, only 14 months before the King/Carter motorcar transaction.[285]

Another primary component of the incomplete vehicle that Carter bought from King was a substantial wood and metal carriage of a style typically called a hunting trap or dogcart, with dos-à-dos (back-to-back) seating, built by Sievers & Erdman, a prominent horse-drawn carriage and hearse builder in Detroit.[286] Sievers & Erdman was located at 294–298 Jefferson Avenue and had been established in 1875; by 1910, the firm was recognized as one of Detroit's leading producers of automobile coachwork for marques such as Cadillac and Columbia.[287]

Long before B. J. Carter acquired Charles B. King's incomplete Sievers & Erdman "Times-Herald entry," its original four-cylinder King engine had been removed (as stated above, to be used in another King horseless carriage—the iron-tired Emerson & Fisher testing wagon King demonstrated on the streets of Detroit on March 6, 1896). Documentation found by the author conflicts somewhat with whether King actually ever installed his four-cylinder engine in the *Times-Herald* entry, which he later sold to Carter. On the one hand, a statement in King's outline titled "Cars Built and Designed by Charles B. King—1893–1903" would seem to indicate that King's *Times-Herald* entry was never set up with King's four-cylinder engine: "The Times-Herald entry—dos a dos carriage built by Sievers & Erdman and *originally planned* [italics added] for use with 4-cylinder, 4 cycle/engine/rod frame . . . was ultimately equipped with one of the three [1896] King engines built following the King-Duryea engine" of early 1896.[288] Another comment in this same outline may further indicate that the King four-cylinder engine was never actually installed in the *Times-Herald* entry. In describing the testing wagon that King first demonstrated in Detroit on March 6, 1896, King stated: "The

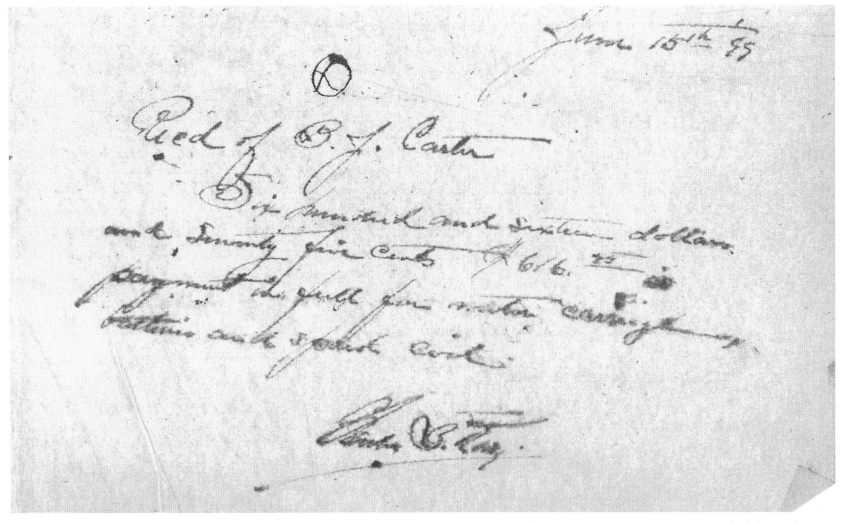

Fig. 70. A receipt in Charles B. King's handwriting from King's letterpress books, which recorded B. J. Carter's June 15, 1899 purchase of King's 1895 dos-à-dos carriage built by Sievers & Erdman and equipped with an 1896 King-built two-cylinder motor, batteries, and a spark coil, all for $616.75; no pneumatic tires were included in the deal. This receipt and the other materials shown in figs. 68–80 are all preserved in the expansive Charles Brady King Collection in the Detroit Public Library's National Automotive History Collection. *Courtesy of the Charles Brady King Collection, National Automotive History Collection, Detroit Public Library*

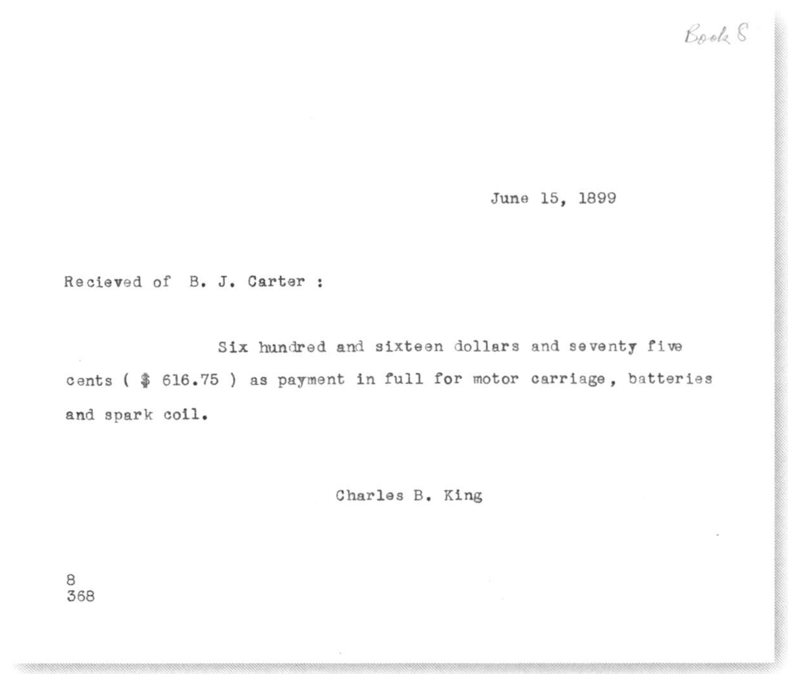

Book 8

June 15, 1899

Recieved of B. J. Carter :

Six hundred and sixteen dollars and seventy five cents ($ 616.75) as payment in full for motor carriage, batteries and spark coil.

Charles B. King

8
368

Fig. 71. The typewritten version of B. J. Carter's automobile-purchase receipt prepared by Charles B. King's stenographer. *Courtesy of the Charles Brady King Collection, National Automotive History Collection, Detroit Public Library*

rod-frame, 4-cylinder, 4-cycle engine built originally for the Times-Herald entry, was *first* [italics added] installed in this [1896 testing wagon] vehicle"[289] On the other hand, a biographical sketch penned by King preserved in the Detroit Public Library's Oliver Edward Barthel Collection states that the *Times-Herald* carriage "as sold to Carter, formerly had in it the four-cylinder engine, and was the one I had hoped to drive in the Chicago Times-Herald Race. However, the four cylinder engine had been sold previously to Charles G. Annesley and this two-cylinder engine took its place."[290] Although interesting, in the end this historical query is not essential to understanding how King ultimately powered B. J. Carter's first automobile.

It is unambiguous that Charles B. King had designed, built, and installed an 1896 King water-cooled two-cylinder gasoline engine in the "Times-Herald entry" carriage by the time B. J. Carter purchased it from him on June 15, 1899. King stated in his 1945 memoir that the three similar two-cylinder engines he built in 1896, of which one was Carter's, "were of my own design."[291] Further, the Detroit Public Library's Charles Brady King Collection includes a list King prepared in his own hand, which is titled "First Engines built and tested at Lauer's Shop are numbered as follows."[292] In this list, King assigned numbers 5-A, 5-B, and 5-C to his three 1896 two-cylinder engines, with No. 5-A shown as the motor in B. J. Carter's machine.[293] King sold engine No. 5-B to Professor W. H. Pickering, a Harvard University astronomer, (shipped on September 7, 1896, for a horseless carriage Pickering intended to build himself), and No. 5-C was purchased by the Kalamazoo Railroad Velocipede and Car Company in April 1896 to power a motorized handcar.[294] King's three 1896 two-cylinder gasoline engines were of a horizontal configuration, water cooled, and designed with four-cycle

B. J. Carter
Jackson, Mich.
June 15 To One Motor Carriage $616.75
" 15 By Cash 8 Batteries and Spark coil. $616.75
616.75 616.75

Fig. 72. The journal entry in Charles B. King's 1899 accounting ledger, which added a detail about the number of batteries (eight) B. J. Carter received with his horseless carriage; Carter paid the $616.75 purchase price in cash. *Courtesy of the Charles Brady King Collection, National Automotive History Collection, Detroit Public Library*

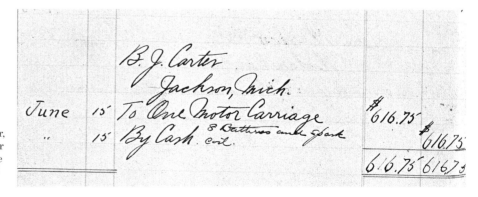

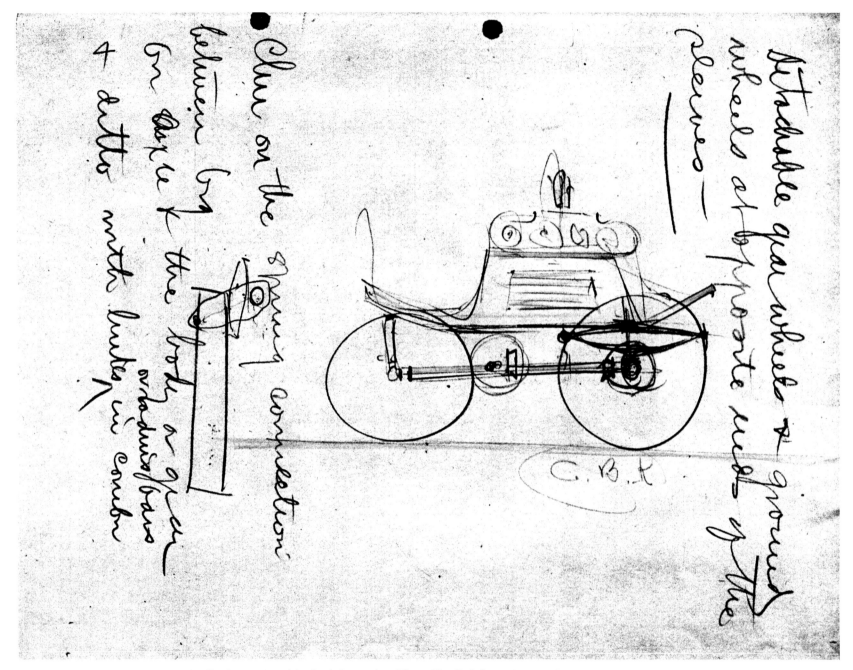

Fig. 73. An undated sketch initialed by Charles B. King of the dos-à-dos carriage King sold to B. J. Carter in 1899; the wood-and-iron carriage had been built by Sievers & Erdman, a Detroit horse-drawn vehicle maker, and was modified by King to accept the four-cylinder gasoline engine (see fig. 68) and a running gear in July or August 1895. Charles B. King had intended to compete with this vehicle in the *Chicago Times-Herald* automobile race on November 28, 1895, but the machine was not completed and proper tires could not be located in time, and King had to withdraw his entry from the race. Interestingly, the car still did not have tires when it was sold to B. J. Carter (as noted in a summary written by King that listed all the cars and motors he had sold). When Carter purchased the machine, its original 1895 four-cylinder engine had been replaced by an 1896 water-cooled two-cylinder motor built by King. *Courtesy of the Charles Brady King Collection, National Automotive History Collection, Detroit Public Library*

Fig. 75. A photograph from the September 1896 issue of *The Motocycle* shows the water-cooled two-cylinder four-cycle 3 1/2-horsepower (with inlet valves in the heads) engine manufactured by Charles B. King for Professor W. H. Pickering, a Harvard University astronomer who was building his own car. King had manufactured three of these two-cylinder engines by April 1896, and one of them was installed in the motor carriage King sold to B. J. Carter on June 15, 1899. *Courtesy of the Charles Brady King Collection, National Automotive History Collection, Detroit Public Library*

Fig. 74. Another view of the two-cylinder engine built by Charles B. King for Professor W. H. Pickering when it was temporarily installed, for experimentation purposes, in the same iron-tired test wagon King had first demonstrated on the streets of Detroit on March 6, 1896 (then with the four-cylinder engine seen in fig. 68). *Courtesy of the Charles Brady King Collection, National Automotive History Collection, Detroit Public Library*

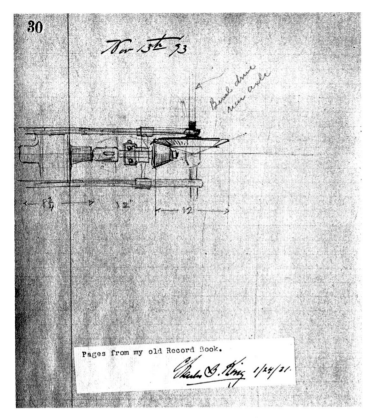

Fig. 76. A sketch by Charles B. King dated November 13, 1893, from King's "old Record Book," which shows a bevel-gear rear-axle assembly similar to the one installed in the motor carriage King sold B. J. Carter. *Courtesy of the Charles Brady King Collection, National Automotive History Collection, Detroit Public Library*

Fig. 77. An undated photograph showing the rear axle, bevel-drive gear assembly, springs, and wire wheels as were installed in B. J. Carter's 1899 gasoline car. *Courtesy of the Charles Brady King Collection, National Automotive History Collection, Detroit Public Library*

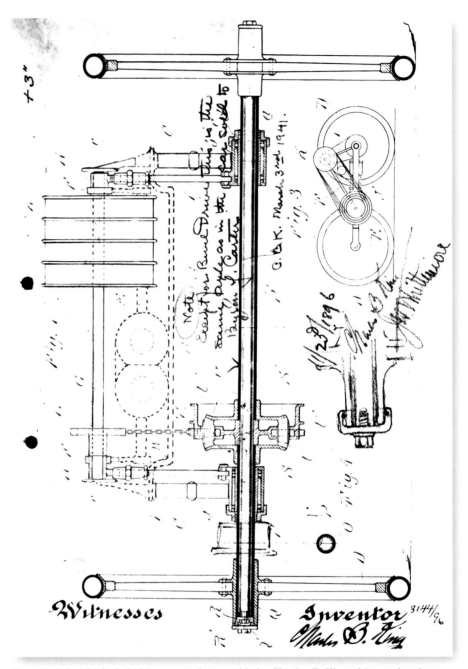

Fig. 78. A sketch of a belt-drive rear-axle assembly by Charles B. King, this one dated November 23, 1896; on March 3, 1941, King added the note, "Except for [the missing] bevel drive this is the same axle as in the car sold to Byron J. Carter." *Courtesy of the Charles Brady King Collection, National Automotive History Collection, Detroit Public Library*

July 17, 1899

B. J. Carter Esq.

    Jackson, Michigan

Dear Sir :

        The rear wheels were pressed on in a wheel press and on this attached in a similar manner to car wheels. No keys or pins are used.

        Your information is so meager that we are unable to give you further information in reference to carburetor without a personal examination. The carburator should work well as it is.

        Your engine is running too fast. It should turn from four to five hundred under load.

                Yours truly,

                    Charles B. King

8
390

Fig. 79. In this July 17, 1899 letter sent by Charles B. King to B. J. Carter, King addressed Carter's continued carburetor problems in the gasoline carriage he had bought from King and then rebuilt. Unfortunately, the author could not find the letter Carter sent to King that solicited this response. *Courtesy of the Charles Brady King Collection, National Automotive History Collection, Detroit Public Library*

10/ 16/ 99

B. J. Carter Esq.

    Jackson Mich.

Dear Sir :

        The mixer that you have is amply large enough for your engine. It is the same as used by us on our 6 H.P. engines with Cylinders 5½" x 8¼".

        Examine the valve and see that it is tight. The position of the mixer makes no difference.

        The mixer should be supplied with warm air sucked from near the exhaust pipe, cold weather affects mixture.

        The writer can come out and look the engine over for $ 5.00 a day and expenses.

                Yours truly,

                    Charles B. King

8
496

Fig. 80. This October 16, 1899 letter sent by Charles B. King to B. J. Carter indicates that Carter's challenges with his automobile's carburetor (or mixer) persisted. It is interesting to read that King was willing to travel to Jackson to assist Carter with engine adjustments for five dollars per day plus expenses. Unfortunately, the author could not find the letter Carter sent to King that solicited this response. *Courtesy of the Charles Brady King Collection, National Automotive History Collection, Detroit Public Library*

intake, ignition, and exhaust (inlet valve in the head and exhaust valve in the side); the flywheel was 18 inches in diameter, and the engines had a 4 1/2-inch cylinder bore and a 6-inch piston stroke and produced 3 1/2 "actual" horsepower.[295]

By August 1896, Charles B. King had begun trial runs with his newly designed two-cylinder engine after temporarily installing Professor Pickering's motor in King's March 1896 Emerson & Fisher Co. testing wagon (by this time, King had removed his four-cylinder motor from this iron-tired vehicle). The *Detroit Free Press*, in its August 16, 1896 issue, reported favorably on King's pioneering endeavors with his two-cylinder engine and "horseless wagon," which was "the invention of Charles B. King, of this city": "A good many people have been rather startled for a day or two past by seeing a wagon come tearing along the street at a lively rate, dodging people and teams . . . The speed attained by the testing wagon is twenty miles an hour."[296]

The September 1896 issues of *The Horseless Age* and *The Motocycle* also praised King's new two-cylinder engine as "one of the simplest and most efficient motors yet produced" for horseless carriages and stated that "all of the working parts are large and of ample proportions. The motor is capable of making extended runs without attention."[297] Both magazines included a photograph of the engine, and further described it: "No carburetor or gasolene pump is employed . . . its weight, complete with fly-wheel, is 230 pounds, and it develops over three and one-half actual horse-power at the brake. A signal whistle is added for the convenience of the motorman."[298] This description was not entirely accurate. Charles B. King, in a narrative titled "Charles B. King and Lauer's Shop," with slightly different versions in the Detroit Public Library's Charles Brady King and Oliver Edward Barthel collections, said that Carter's and the other two 1896 King two-cylinder motors "each had a float-feed carburetor and an automatic [sight-feed] oiling system."[299] Additionally, Charles B. King's July 17, 1899 and October 16, 1899 letters to B. J. Carter (figs. 79 and 80) indicate that Carter's machine was fitted with a carburetor, or a "mixer," as they were frequently called in early auto days.

These letters demonstrate that B. J. Carter and Charles B. King remained in contact for several months after Carter purchased the gasoline motor carriage components from King. King's letters to Carter are very direct, with a slight hint of exasperation; this may simply have been King's writing style, or perhaps it indicates that King was growing a bit weary of Carter's persistent questions and apparent challenges with making his horseless carriage function properly. Although it is guesswork, these letters may provide insight into why Carter was soon working with King's engineering assistant, Oliver E. Barthel, instead of with King directly. Carter and Barthel's working relationship designing engines is discussed further in Section 19.

It is impossible to pinpoint when B. J. Carter first became aware of and interested in horseless carriage technology. From Charles B. King's account of Carter's apparent eagerness when he bought King's *Times-Herald* entry, one gets the impression that Carter had been searching for suitable auto components and an engine to purchase for some time. One can infer that Carter had known of Charles B. King's automobile experiments through reading about them in national journals such as *The Horseless Age* and *The Motocycle*, or perhaps Carter had met King during one of Carter's many trips to Detroit, long before he bought King's machine. Carter was also likely aware of King from newspaper accounts of the historic November 28, 1895 *Chicago Times-Herald* race. It is a bit confounding that contemporaneous pre-1899 documentation could not be found to establish that B. J. Carter built a horseless carriage of his own sooner than 1899, given Carter's excellent machine shop and access to Charles A. Trask's engines and Trask's own well-equipped machine shop. Finances, a persistent issue for Carter in his early auto years, may have been the problem; in the 1890s, motor carriages, other than those built by blacksmiths, mechanics, and tinkerers, were limited to privileged individuals who had the means to buy one. The $616.75 Carter paid King, albeit for an incomplete machine, was considerably less expensive than just about every other gasoline carriage on the market in 1899. Some examples of 1899 and 1900 gasoline model prices include Haynes-Apperson at $1,350–$1,500, Loomis at $750–$1,200, Orient (actually a De Dion-Bouton Motorette rebranded for the U.S. market) at $850, Packard at $1,200, St. Louis at $1,200–$1,600, Stearns (by late 1901) at $3,000, and Winton at $1,000.[300] Access to and availability of a manufactured horseless carriage in the late 1890s could also have been obstacles for Carter; production was often unreliable with delayed deliveries, and the supply of gasoline carriages was quite tight, as gasoline-automobile production quantities before 1900 were remarkably small, and there were only a handful of reputable builders. My guess is that the incomplete, unfinished state of the 1899 King vehicle was also highly appealing to the inventive Carter as an experiment, as opposed to a fully manufactured and operational automobile from an established builder. Carter's first selected car was also powered by a more advanced two-cylinder engine when many of the gasoline carriages in this period only had one-cylinder power plants.

A comment in Fred T. Lockwood's illustrated 1919 *Jackson Citizen Patriot* reminiscence about B. J. Carter's automobile experimentation may shed some light on what triggered Carter's first serious auto interest. Lockwood said that Carter was inspired to build his first horseless carriage after he had examined a Stanley steam car in an 1898 parade "stunt" promoting the Hi Henry minstrel-show troupe, which had arrived in Jackson for its stage show.[301] (The Stanley brothers had built their first steam automobile in 1897, so it is plausible that one may have been demonstrated in 1898.)[302] Lockwood said, "The automobile game in Jackson was born one day when Hi Henry's minstrels showed in town. It all dates back to a parade of white-hatted performers who marched down the street ahead of a brass band, with a 'horseless carriage' bringing up the rear . . . 'Lou' Tussing, Frank Bradley, 'Charley' Trask, and myself were then working in Byron Carter's bicycle shop . . . As that machine [Stanley steam car] went chugging down the street, Byron Carter, Tussing, Bradley, Trask, and myself all jumped our jobs in the bicycle shop and followed it like a lot of kids in an effort to see how the thing worked. After the parade it was taken down to the Michigan Central freight depot, and there we looked it up again, went all over it and wondered if we couldn't make something like it ourselves. Byron Carter kept thinking of the 'horseless carriage' in the minstrel parade and pretty soon after the minstrels coming, he went to Detroit and bought the body, the engine, and steering gear for Carter's first gasoline automobile."[303]

Lockwood's recollection makes for a colorful story; a newspaper search, however, surfaced only one similar *Jackson Daily Citizen* account, which reported that the "famous" Hi Henry had indeed run a steam automobile in its Jackson minstrel parade (the article called it "Hi Henry's Locomobile Parade"); however, this parade occurred on April 17, 1900, nearly one year *after* B. J. Carter had run his first gasoline auto on the streets of Jackson.[304] That said, it is certainly possible

that Lockwood did not recall correctly the details of the parade he mentioned. While there were numerous minstrel-show parades reported in pre-June 1899 Jackson newspapers, none of the newspaper articles referenced an automobile, horseless carriage, or similar machine.

Instead Lockwood could have been recalling the July 12, 1897 circus parade and big top shows in Jackson put on by the John Robinson and Franklin Bros. Circus. The day before the "Great John Robinson and Franklin Bros.' Enormous Shows" came to town, the *Jackson Daily Citizen* proclaimed, "It is a wonderful sight to see the wonderful 'horseless carriage' in trial test of speed at every performance and in the great double parade."[305] There is a Charles B. King connection to the John Robinson and Franklin Bros. automobile, as it was powered by the *gasoline* (not *steam*, as in Lockwood's reminiscence) two-cylinder Duryea-King Motor that King had built in early 1896.[306] This rubber-tired motor carriage (fig. 81) with the Duryea-King engine was actually constructed and assembled by the Emerson & Fisher Co. for the John Robinson and Franklin Bros. Circus to promote the circus "in their street parades and also for the opening march in the ring."[307] As noted earlier, the Emerson & Fisher Co. had supplied a different delivery wagon (iron-tired) to Charles B. King, which he used for his testing machine demonstrated in Detroit on March 6, 1896.[308] In an article titled "The Emerson & Fisher Motor Wagon," the May 1896 issue of *The Horseless Age* reported that "the wagon which the Emerson & Fisher Co., of Cincinnati, O., recently constructed for [the John Robinson and] Franklin Bros.' circus is modeled somewhat after the Duryea motor wagon. The motor employed is the Duryea King motor, made by Charles B. King, of Detroit, Mich., and the gearing and body is the product of the Emerson & Fisher Co.'s factory. The Emerson & Fisher Co., are prepared to build both gasoline and electric vehicles."[309] The article's illustration is shown in figure 81. King had given his Duryea-King Motor "a short run in the test-wagon on April 11th, 1896. It was then shipped to Cincinnati two days later for installation in the Emerson-Fisher car" used for the circus.[310] King indicated he "went to Cincinnati and spent a week to see that all was properly installed and operative," and the John Robinson and Franklin Bros. Circus took delivery of the car while on the road with performances; it was then reported that the motor carriage "will be exhibited through the country."[311]

Fig. 81. Illustration from the May 1896 issue of *The Horseless Age* of the rubber-tired motor carriage constructed and assembled by the Emerson & Fisher Co. for the John Robinson and Franklin Bros. Circus, to promote the circus in parades and opening ceremonies in the ring; this machine was powered by the Duryea-King Motor, which Charles B. King manufactured in early 1896. It is likely that this horseless carriage made an appearance in Jackson on July 12, 1897, during the John Robinson and Franklin Bros. Circus parade and two big-top performances that day. *Courtesy of the National Automotive History Collection, Detroit Public Library*

After the John Robinson and Franklin Bros. Circus completed its July 12, 1897 parade and two performances for large crowds in Jackson, the *Jackson Daily Citizen* provided detailed post-event accounts; vexingly however, a horseless carriage was not mentioned in these reports.[312] We may never know for certain whether B. J. Carter had the opportunity to view a motor carriage during these July 12, 1897 circus events in Jackson.

Overall, it seems highly unlikely that B. J. Carter's automotive interests were triggered by any one event or experience. Instead his fascination with horseless carriage experimentation probably arose early and over time through discussions with his peers, including Charles A. Trask, Charles B. King, and Oliver E. Barthel; newspapers, technical publications such as *The American Machinist*, and bicycle and automotive journals and magazines; at least three *Jackson Daily Citizen* articles regarding the historic November 28, 1895 *Chicago Times-Herald* race, including descriptions of the horseless machine built for the race by Michigan's own Baushke Carriage Works in Benton Harbor but which was not ready in time to compete; and Carter's general mechanical experience, inclinations, and talents. By the late 1890s, motorized carriages were not quite so alien as they initially had been, and they were referred to even in the general nontechnical newspapers with some frequency.[313] The December 26, 1897 issue of the *Cleveland Plain Dealer* in an article titled "Looking Back Over 1897" stated, "Horseless carriages have ceased to be the butt of the cartoonist's pencil and the joke writer's pen. In three great cities of the world, London, Paris and New York, motor carriages have become such a familiar sight as to be an object of curiosity to none but country visitors."[314] Similarly, the *Jackson Daily Citizen* had reprinted a professor's paper in its September 20, 1897 issue titled "The Horseless Carriage, It Is as Yet a Somewhat Imperfect Mechanism," which opined that steam would likely be the best automotive power source and that "the motor carriage of the future will probably imitate the bicycle in its rubber tires and ball bearings; it will have a very respectable weight, and it will require a smooth road."[315]

Once B. J. Carter actually got started, in mid-1899, in the "automobile game," as Fred T. Lockwood called it, the pace of Carter's work on horseless carriage and engine inventions and his bold entrepreneurial efforts to establish a secure, profitable automobile-manufacturing business would pick up speed quickly. The early 20th century would prove to be an auspicious (and ultimately tragic) time for the talented, ambitious, and motivated Carter, and he would attain a certain level of fame in the automotive world.

The Erroneous Butcher & Gage Attribution

B. J. Carter's 1899 gasoline automobile has been repeatedly and incorrectly credited as having been manufactured by Butcher & Gage. A March 1952 article from *The Flying A* magazine, a promotional publication from Jackson's Aeroquip Corporation, and a March 23, 1952 *Jackson Citizen Patriot* article are the earliest published sources of this error that the author found.[316] Both articles show the photograph of B. J. Carter's machine with three passengers (see fig. 64) and state that the experimental horseless carriage had been built by Butcher & Gage.[317] In this photo, Arthur L. Butcher, a Carter employee around the time Carter's first car was assembled and photographed in 1899, is the person holding the steering tiller. As previously mentioned, Arthur Butcher's well-respected engineering and machining firm, Butcher & Gage, was not established until late 1904, more than five years after Carter's first gasoline car was built, run on the streets of Jackson, and photographed in 1899. The author could find no documentation in automotive journals and Jackson's newspapers that Butcher & Gage ever manufactured any automobiles of their own in the firm's earliest days, after its 1904 formation.

Coe Smith Reeves, Another Jackson Automotive Pioneer

B. J. Carter was not the only Jackson citizen who built a horseless carriage around 1900. (Of course as the 20th century progressed, there would be myriad other Jackson bicycle repairmen, carriage builders, machinists, blacksmiths, speculators, and industrialists who would construct experimental vehicles and, in some instances, manufacture and market them with varying degrees of success.) The May 17, 1901 *Jackson Daily Citizen* stated that "Cole [sic] Reeves, electrician has constructed an automobile which was in operation about the city yesterday afternoon. Mr. Reeves made all the parts of the machine, which worked admirably."[318] The talented Coe Smith Reeves (May 15, 1865–April 1, 1933) offered electrical-engineering services with "motors and dynamos a specialty," including electric-locomotive expertise, along with bicycle repairing and nickel plating and enameling services at 157 West Pearl Street, just down the way from Charles A. Trask's machine shop.[319] Reeves has been credited in several post-1945 accounts as building the first automobile in Jackson, in 1897 or 1898; however, based on the 1901 *Jackson Daily Citizen* piece, it appears that May 1901 is more accurate, two years after B. J. Carter's first gasoline carriage was demonstrated.[320] Coe S. Reeves' daughters Mary B. Reeves Glaspie and Luella Reeves recounted some history about their father's horseless carriage in a March 17, 1946 *Jackson*

Citizen Patriot article: "Father used to drive the car home to lunch, and it attracted so much attention that we felt very conspicuous. Once, the noise made by the machine scared a team and the horses ran away, breaking the harness and doing other damage." Glaspie recalled that her father made the car "with the help of Art Weisser," and "that the muffler resembled a tomato can full of holes. The frame was made of pipe and the body was made by the Fuller Buggy Co. with a dashboard just like an ordinary buggy. The three-wheeler was equipped with bicycle wheels and tires. The body was painted red and green" and "the gas tank was under the seat."[321]

The *Jackson Citizen Patriot* article continued, rephrasing Mary B. Reeves Glaspie's comments: "During the time that he had the car, Reeves sought constantly to improve it. He put headlights and a tail lamp, burning acetylene gas, on the machine. Later he added a fourth wheel which made the vehicle ride much easier."[322] Reeves ultimately sold the car to "a Mr. Scofield" from Jackson.[323] A March 1952 article from the Aeroquip Corporation's *The Flying A* magazine, based on interviews with survivors of Jackson's early automobile years, indicates that this 1901 machine was the only horseless carriage that Reeves built.[324]

Fig. 82. Another clever Jackson automotive pioneer, Coe S. Reeves, built a three-bicycle-wheeled horseless carriage, which was outfitted with a carriage body from the Fuller Buggy Company; his son, Dayton E. Reeves, is the passenger. Coe S. Reeves, an electrician at 157 West Pearl Street, has sometimes been credited as building and running this machine in Jackson in 1897 or 1898. It appears that Reeves' car was built a bit later, as the May 17, 1901 issue of the *Jackson Daily Citizen* reported that "Cole [*sic*] Reeves, electrician has constructed an automobile which was in operation about the city yesterday afternoon. Mr. Reeves made all the parts of the machine, which worked admirably." *Courtesy of William S. Jackson*

Early Gasoline-Engine Manufacturing Endeavors and Work with Oliver E. Barthel

Even though B. J. Carter had already accomplished a considerable feat by completing, assembling, and demonstrating his first horseless carriage on June 26, 1899, he quickly launched another ambitious automotive venture. By early November 1899, within four months of the inaugural run of his first motorcar, Carter had actively entered the field of designing and building gasoline automobile engines (although there is anecdotal evidence in certain Carter obituaries and other later sources that he was experimenting with horseless carriage engines even before this date). Carter placed a small classified advertisement in the November 8, 1899 issue of *The Horseless Age* that read, "For Sale. Hydro-Carbon [gasoline or benzene] Motor, light weight for motor vehicle. Also Baldwin chain, milled sprockets, friction clutches, etc., B. J. Carter, Jackson, Mich."[325] This ad was ambiguous as to whether Carter was actually building gasoline engines; however, another magazine piece a month later eliminated this ambiguity. *The Motor Vehicle Review*, in its December 12, 1899 issue, in an item titled "Will Build Motors," reported that "B. J. Carter, of Jackson, Mich., will put on the market gasoline engines, with one, two or three cylinders. The motor is air-cooled and has been used successfully in vehicles built for testing purposes."[326] It was not long before Carter began offering his gasoline engines in combination with other integrated automobile assemblies suitable for building complete cars. An advertisement labeled "3-Cylinder, Air Cooled Motor For Sale" appeared in the March 28, 1900 issue of *The Horseless Age*.[327] This advertisement described the gasoline motors as being "of light weight, giving ample power and simple in construction, also Transmission Gear and Compensating Gear; all attached and ready to receive the rear axle, giving two speeds ahead and backward. B. J. Carter, Jackson, Mich."[328]

Carter soon also designed and built his own *water*-cooled gasoline engines (as noted earlier, the King engine in Carter's first automobile was coincidentally water cooled). In 1900, and possibly in 1899 as well, Carter collaborated with Charles B. King's draftsman and engineering assistant Oliver E. Barthel regarding the design of a water-cooled gasoline engine that Carter intended to construct. Carter had likely been introduced to Barthel during one of Carter's visits to Charles B.

King's Detroit shop. In a 1939 narrative completed at the request of Milo M. Quaife, PhD, secretary-editor for the Detroit Public Library's Burton Historical Collection, Barthel said that after Charles B. King had sold Carter the *Times-Herald* entry machine (equipped with King's two-cylinder motor), "I was later engaged by Mr. Carter to design an engine for this [June 1899] car."[329] Barthel added in his July 1952 *Reminiscences* that Carter's 1899 auto "became the forerunner of the Carter friction-drive car," which seems like a bit of a stretch (even though the running gear in this 1899 King/Carter motor carriage was apparently equipped with a friction-drive transmission of sorts).[330]

Like Charles B. King, Oliver E. Barthel had contributed to and witnessed many of the earliest U.S. horseless carriage engineering developments. Barthel joined the Charles B. King Company engineering shop in November 1894 (at the age of 17) as a "draughtsman, engine and tool tester, and general office man" and, by the end of his long engineering career, Barthel would be granted 36 patents.[331] In Barthel's December 1939 narrative for Dr. Quaife, he said that "Mr. King was a graduate of Cornell University and took the trouble to help me in my efforts to complete my engineering studies."[332] Barthel would work for King for nearly seven years until 1901, when King sold this company.

In May 1901 Barthel set up his own engineering and machine-design business, and one of his first clients was Henry Ford. Ford arranged for Barthel to spend half his time with Ford's machinists, mechanic Edward "Spider" S. Huff, and a blacksmith to engineer, design, build, and test Ford's first racing car, which would come to be known as the "Sweepstakes" racer. By way of background, Henry Ford's first motorcar company, The Detroit Automobile Company, formed in mid-1899 and incorporated as of January 1, 1900, built only a few vehicles and then went bankrupt a year later, losing $86,000 of investment capital.[333] The five Detroit businessmen who purchased The Detroit Automobile Company's assets at the receiver's sale in early 1901 engaged Henry Ford to continue his work, which soon included building a race car to create publicity for the new enterprise. This was achieved in part on October 10, 1901, by the "Sweepstakes" racer at the Grosse Pointe, Michigan, sweepstakes race, when Ford's race car, with Henry Ford at the wheel, triumphed over the established automobile manufacturer Alexander Winton in his own record-

Fig. 83. Oliver E. Barthel (right) with Henry Ford behind the wheel of Ford's 1901 40-horsepower two-cylinder "Sweepstakes" race car; Barthel was the principal designer for this machine, with several other engineers and machinists working on various components and the actual manufacturing. The "Sweepstakes" name was established at the October 10, 1901 Grosse Pointe, Michigan, sweepstakes race, when Ford's race car, which he drove, beat Alexander Winton, who was piloting his own record-breaking race car. The Sweepstakes race car had attained speeds of 72 miles per hour in test runs prior to this race (the official 1901 world speed record had been 65.79 miles per hour). The Sweepstakes race car exists today in the collections of The Henry Ford Museum. *From the Collections of The Henry Ford, ID# THF23067*

breaking race car. Soon after this race, the five original businessmen investors and Ford formed the Henry Ford Company, on November 3, 1901. Oliver E. Barthel was hired as a full-time designing engineer for the new venture, which was to manufacture and market a small car. As Barthel said, "Mr. Ford, however, had the racing fever and could not settle down to a production plan." After Henry Ford secretly had Barthel working on designs for a second, larger race car against the wishes of one of the key Henry Ford Company investors, "Mr. Ford was retired from the company and was given the unfinished design and approximately $900 for his interest, and it was agreed to change the name of the company discontinuing the use of his name." The new brand of this enterprise would ultimately be the Cadillac Automobile Company (after 1905, called the Cadillac Motor Car Company). Barthel departed shortly after Ford did, but before Cadillac was fully launched.[334]

Barthel then organized what was first called the Mohawk Automobile Company, and then the Barthel Motor Co., "but was not successful in getting sufficient finances to continue even though both cars that were built proved entirely successful."[335] Barthel would later take relatively short assignments with the Ford Motor Company, Oldsmobile, and other motorcar and marine-motor enterprises and would lead a long, notable engineering and designing consulting career, retiring in 1955.[336]

Over a year before Oliver E. Barthel joined Henry Ford's race car engineering team in 1901, B. J. Carter and he worked together on water-cooled gasoline-engine designs, possibly starting as early as mid-1899, shortly after Carter bought the *Times-Herald* entry machine from Charles B. King, but more likely in 1900. According to Barthel's *Reminiscences* of July 1952, he visited Carter in Jackson to discuss the project: "Carter was the mechanic in charge of the machine shop in Jackson Prison. When I went there to arrange to design the engine for him, I went on an Easter Sunday to Jackson Prison and made my deal with Mr. Carter to design his engine for him. I came back to Detroit and designed the engine at home."[337]

Yet the author could find no information or newspaper accounts that support Barthel's statement that B. J. Carter had a role in the Jackson Prison's machine shop, either as head mechanic or as an instructor.

The imposing Jackson Prison, alternately called the Michigan State Penitentiary or State Prison of Southern Michigan at Jackson, was reported as confining 809 convicts in 1899.[338] This prison was where many of Jackson's largest 19th-century industries got their start, including the Withington & Cooley Manufacturing Co. and the Austin, Tomlinson & Webster Manufacturing Co., which made the widely advertised Jackson Wagon.[339] Jackson Prison's convict labor shops and industrial machine and workshops were sophisticated for their time and well equipped for bending, cutting, shaping, forming, drilling, and polishing metal and other materials.[340] Everything, including turning lathes, presses, huge trip hammers, and woodworking equipment, was powered by enormous steam engines through overhead line shafts with elaborate pulley-and-belt systems.[341] Products manufactured in the Jackson Prison included farm tools, carriages, wagons, marble monuments, shoes, shirts, furniture, binder/bailer twine, barrels, and later, canned goods, license plates, and road signs.[342] The Jackson Prison shop's machining equipment and tooling would likely have had advanced capabilities with tighter engineering tolerances beyond those of the machining equipment and tooling in B. J. Carter's small-scale bicycle machine shop.

In light of how specific Barthel's *Reminiscences* are about the Jackson Prison, perhaps Carter had indeed accepted some sort of short-term assignment (during the winter, outside of the regular bicycle sales season) as a manager or supervisor at the Jackson Prison machine shop. This sort of opportunity could have permitted Carter to avail himself of the prison shop's more technically advanced equipment for machining and constructing his first gasoline engines. Barring some new documentation coming to light, we will probably never be able to confirm this.

A small sampling of correspondence from B. J. Carter to Oliver E. Barthel exists (figs. 84–86): two letters addressed to Barthel at Charles B. King's 112 St. Antoine Street machine shop, dated May 29, 1900, and June 15, 1900, and a third letter, dated June 25, 1900, to Barthel's Detroit residence at 111-18th Street.[343] Based on the timing of these letters and their content, Barthel's "Jackson Prison" meeting on "Easter Sunday" with Carter would most likely have occurred on Easter Sunday, April 15, 1900, and not in 1899. Because these letters are a bit difficult to read, certain excerpts are reprinted here, exactly as

B. J. CARTER,

Bicycles AND Phonographs

and Sundries.   and Supplies.

JACKSON, MICH.

May 29, 1900.

Mr. O. E. Barthel,
          112 StAntoine St. Detroit,
                    Dear Sir:--In reply to yours of the 25th I would
say that I can not see how you can give the Engine the Smooth appearance you mention without carrying the water jacket full length of
Cylinder or having two thicknesses of metal at crank end of cylinder
and that this will add weight and it would seem to me would have a
tendency to heat the cooling water still more, this being true it
would seem to me best to have the jog at end of water space and to
carry the water space about the length of the stroke, now of course
if I am not correct in my surmises above I would be pleased to hear
from you further with a rough sketch showing your idea of the matter
I desire to build a perfect engine if possible and will be pleased to
    have you advise and opinion on any of the details,
          Awaiting your further replies in this matter, I am
                              Respectfully,

P S. The Locomobile came in last night and as it was shipped in pieces
boxed it took some time to assemble it which has occupied quite a little of my time but we have it running in fine shape now,

Figs. 84–86. Three historic letters B. J. Carter sent to Oliver E. Barthel in mid-1900 regarding gasoline engine design and Carter's early steam car observations. *Author's collection, courtesy of Ronald G. Bean*

B. J. CARTER,

Bicycles AND **Phonographs**
and Sundries.   and Supplies.

JACKSON, MICH.

June 15, 1900.

Mr. Oliver E. Barthel,
      112 StAntoine St. Detroit,

          Dear Sir:--In looking over the drawings you sent
last I do not see any provisions for the sparking outfit as we talked
it over, to be operated from the two to one gear on opposite side
from the exhaust cam, possibly you have made the provisions for this
and hope so as I would not think of depending on the Jump " Spark and
yet I hope it is much better than the other style we talked over,

      I hope you will be able to send the balance of the drawings or
al least enough to keep the pattern maker busy as he has all made
that you have sent except the fly wheel and I think I will have a casting made off of the King Engine wheel I have here which is very near
the dimensions of your drawing wheen it is turned up.

      I have been using a lot of Money this week and can much better
send you the amount asked for next week some time and I hope this will
be entirely satisfactory to you,

      I went down in Ohio this week and brought a Locomobile home by
road and had a fine ride, made 65 miles over very bad sandy and hilly
roads after two o'clock and was here for supper.

      Come to Jackson and I will take you out for a nice ride,

                    Respectfully,

                        B. J. Carter.

B. J. CARTER,

Bicycles *AND* Phonographs

and Sundries.   and Supplies.

JACKSON, MICH.

June 25, 1900.

Mr. O. E. Barthel,
        111 18th St. Detroit,
                Dear Sir:--I was out of the city all last week
which is the reason that I did not send you the remittance I said I
would send you,   I went down in Kentucky and bought a Locomobile
and run it through to test it thoroughly on all kinds of roads and
to give stem power a good test as well and to learn as far as possible what is wanted in this line as far as possible and the steps I
made and being detained a considerable by rain I was gone longer than
I expected to have been gone,   I had a fine run , Sunday I made
140 miles over bad roads ony having thirty miles of gravel road .
        I herewith inclose you my check for Twenty Five Dollars as reques-
ted, I would like very much to have you come to Jackson if you can
find the time to do so.
                                Respectfully,
                                B. J. Carter.

written by Carter. These letters provide one a sense of the industrious Carter's drive to rapidly develop a superior product in the new field of automotive engineering and motor design; Carter's curiosity, ingenuity, intelligence, and creativity are abundantly evident.

B. J. Carter sent the May 29, 1900 letter in response to a May 25, 1900 letter from Barthel. Carter was seeking certain engineering and gasoline-motor design guidance: "I desire to build a perfect engine if possible and will be pleased to have your advise [sic] and opinion on any of the details." In this letter Carter refers to specifications for a water-cooled gasoline motor with a "smooth appearance," which had been proposed by Barthel. Carter did not think Barthel's "smooth" engine design could be achieved "without carrying the water jacket full length of cylinder or having two thicknesses of metal at crank end of cylinder and that this will add weight and it would seem to me would have a tendency to heat the cooling water still more." Carter respectfully proposed an alternate design to the experienced engineer Barthel: "It would seem to me best to have the jog at the end of the water space and to carry the water space about the length of the stroke, now of course if I am not correct in my surmises above I would be pleased to hear from you further with a rough sketch showing your idea of the matter."[344]

Barthel subsequently sent B. J. Carter several engineering drawings for the gasoline motor Carter was then building, and on June 15, 1900, Carter wrote, "In looking over the drawings you sent last night I do not see any provisions for the sparking outfit as we talked it over, to be operated from the two to one gear on opposite side from the exhaust cam, possibly you have made the provisions for this and hope so as I would not think of depending on the Jump Spark and yet I hope it is much better than the other style we talked over. I hope you will be able to send the balance of the drawings or at least enough to keep the pattern maker busy as he has all made that you have sent except the fly wheel and I think I will have a casting made off of the King Engine wheel I have here which is very near the dimensions of your drawing when it is turned up." Carter also said he had been "using a lot of money this week" and asked Barthel for a one-week extension to pay Barthel's drafting fees. Carter closed his June 15, 1900 letter by inviting Barthel to "come to Jackson and I will take you out for a nice ride" (in a Locomobile steam car Carter had just purchased in Ohio).[345]

In Carter's June 25 1900 letter to Barthel, he apologized: "I was out of the city all last week which is the reason that I did not send you the remittance I said I would send you." Carter enclosed a $25 check in this third letter and mentioned he had been conducting road tests on another Locomobile that he had just purchased from a seller in Kentucky. Once again, Carter closed his letter to Barthel with an invitation: "I would like very much to have you come to Jackson if you can find time to do so." It appears that Barthel accepted one of Carter's invitations and made at least one more visit to Jackson. In his 1952 *Reminiscences*, Barthel said: "Later I went back to Jackson and gave the designs to Carter. Carter worked it up in his machine shop there. It was built in Jackson Prison."[346]

These three letters are the only correspondence between B. J. Carter and Oliver E. Barthel that the author could find; they provide some glimpse into the mind of B. J. Carter as he was striving to design and build high-quality practical gasoline engines and automobiles at the dawn of the 20th century.[347] Carter's letters to Barthel were also prophetic in that they included references to some of his earliest experiments with steam carriages and his observations about steam as a motive power for automobiles. Within four months, he would engineer and build his first Carter steam carriage.

Automobile Sales and Service at 204 West Cortland Street and Carter's Eccentric Associate, Professor L. A. Harraden

Designing automobiles and selling his own gasoline engines was still essentially a sideline for B. J. Carter in early 1900. For the bulk of his revenue he sold phonographs, operated the United States Tag Co., and continued his established bicycle sales and repair operations; Carter then added a small automobile sales and service business. Carter first sold other manufacturers' horseless carriages and by October 1900 would offer a steam carriage of his own design and construction for sale.

Fig. 88. In addition to B. J. Carter's automobile advertisements, he consistently ran a variety of bicycle sales and repair advertisements in the *Jackson Daily Citizen* throughout most of 1900. In early 1899, B.J. had taken over management and advertising for the substantial bicycle business from his father, Squire, and also started offering phonographs and Columbia Graphophones for sale. *Courtesy of the Jackson District Library*

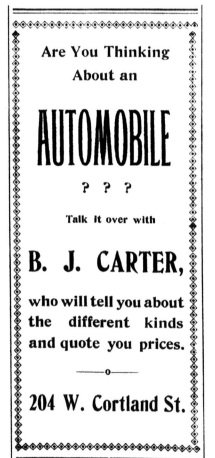

Fig. 87. B. J. Carter ran this advertisement, generally for other manufacturers' cars, in the *Jackson Daily Citizen* for most of June and July 1900. *Courtesy of the Jackson District Library*

Carter's earliest horseless carriage sales appear to have been Locomobile steam cars built by the Locomobile Company of America. In his May 29, 1900 letter to Oliver E. Barthel, Carter wrote that "the Locomobile came in last night, and as it was shipped in pieces boxed it took some time to assemble it which has occupied quite a little of my time but we have it running in fine shape now."[348] That same day the *Jackson Daily Citizen* stated that a Professor L. A. Harraden (the pen name of Stewart M. Watson [1871–1954]) had taken delivery of a motor carriage "from the Stanley factory at Bridgeport, Conn., a fine automobile which attracted much attention about the city today"; the car cost $900.[349] The eccentric Professor Harraden was "a noted hypnotist" who earned a considerable income from publishing scientific and educational books and tracts

including *Harraden's Hypnotic Journal*.[350] A problem with this *Jackson Daily Citizen* account is that Stanley steam cars were actually built in Watertown, Massachusetts, in 1900, but *Locomobile* steam carriages were, by 1900, built in *Bridgeport, Connecticut*.[351] Therefore, it seems fairly certain that the Locomobile B. J. Carter assembled on May 28, 1900, and described in his letter to Oliver E. Barthel, was the same horseless carriage sold to Professor L. A. Harraden, and not a Stanley steam car as written up the next day in the *Jackson Daily Citizen*.

This conclusion is supported by a January 5, 1941 *Jackson Citizen Patriot* interview with Stewart M. Watson (who by then was no longer using the Professor L. A. Harraden pen name). Watson recounted that when his first car, a Locomobile, arrived, he "took it immediately to

Fig. 89. Professor L. A. Harraden (right) in the 1900 Locomobile steam car he bought new for $900; this hazy image is from a January 5, 1941 newspaper interview with Harraden. The machine was delivered to B. J. Carter disassembled in crates on May 28, 1900. Carter stayed up much of the night putting it together and, as reported in the *Jackson Daily Citizen*, Professor Harraden ran it the next day on the streets of Jackson. The professor is accompanied by A. J. MacAvinche (left) of Chicago. *Copyright © 1941 by MLive Media Group, publisher of The Jackson Citizen Patriot. Reproduced with permission of MLive Media Group*

Fig. 90. Professor L. A. Harraden (pen name of Stewart M. Watson), hypnotist, pioneer Jackson motorist, and B. J. Carter's associate, is pictured on the cover of one of his hypnotism lesson books, which he published in 1900. *Author's collection*

Byron Carter who operated a bicycle shop," and that Lewis N. Tussing and Fred T. Lockwood were there as Carter's employees at the time.[352] In this article, Watson said that "Byron Carter was an inventive genius . . . he went over every part of the new machine, and announced that he believed he could make a car just as good. The following year Carter had accomplished the task."[353] Watson also claimed, not quite accurately, that he was the first buyer of a Carter steam carriage but correctly added that Floyd Mitchell, proprietor of the Jackson News Co. and a loan broker, was another purchaser of a Carter-built steam carriage.[354] Further, Watson said in this same 1941 *Jackson Citizen Patriot* interview that he was Jackson's first automobile owner when he bought his Locomobile in 1900, which is inaccurate in light of B. J. Carter's prior ownership of the gasoline carriage he completed and drove in June 1899.[355] To add to the confusion of dates, Watson indicated that his Locomobile had been ordered at "the first automobile show in New York Nov. 3, 1900," which is not possible, as this event occurred five months *after* Watson actually took delivery of his Locomobile in Jackson.[356] Given that 40 years had elapsed between Watson's *Jackson Citizen Patriot* interview and his Locomobile and Carter steam-carriage purchases and that we know Watson sometimes embellished, these timing mix-ups are not surprising. Nonetheless, it is clear that Stewart M. Watson was indeed among B. J. Carter's earliest automobile customers.

In the same 1941 *Jackson Citizen Patriot* article, Watson praised Carter, the "inventive genius" for his repair skill: On a trip to Gregory, Michigan, Watson's old hometown, Watson had "'scorched' a boiler [on his Locomobile], had to hire a team to haul the car to Stockbridge where he chartered a flat car from the Grand Trunk railroad, had his car run upon and anchored to the flat car and then hauled to Jackson."[357] Watson recounted, "Byron Carter put it back into running order . . . It was a good half days work to get a boiler out of a car."[358]

The prosperous Watson was a very enthusiastic early motorist in Jackson, and, after the Locomobile, he purchased a Carter-built steam carriage and also a succession of three gasoline automobiles he listed in his 1941 interview: a one-cylinder Winton, a 1901 11-horsepower Stearns (which he bought from B. J. Carter in February 1901), and a two-cylinder "Silent Northern," which Watson said he drove for about 10 years.[359] Both Carter and Watson diligently stayed abreast of the latest motorcar and engine developments, and it was reported on September 20, 1900, that "Prof. L. A Haradin [*sic*] and B. J. Carter have gone to Chicago to attend the automobile show."[360] This particular 1900 exhibition must have been an ad hoc affair, because Chicago's first official car show is generally considered to be the First Annual National Automobile Exhibit conducted six months later during March 23–30, 1901, where nearly 20 manufacturers displayed vehicles.[361] Like Carter, Harraden was also quick to embrace other new technologies; on February 13, 1900, the *Jackson Daily Citizen* reported that Harraden had ordered "six graphophones for use in his stenographic department"; Carter sold Columbia Graphophones in his bicycle shop at this time and may have been the source for Harraden's recording phonographs.[362]

In his January 1941 *Jackson Citizen Patriot* interview, Stewart M. Watson claimed one more first: he was the first Jackson motorist to feel the sting of the law for a traffic violation when he received a speeding ticket from Jackson's police sergeant on March 21, 1902, with an associated $15 fine for exceeding Jackson's six-mile-per-hour speed limit.[363] It was not long until Fred T. Lockwood was also reported as having violated Jackson's speed limit, in July 1903.[364]

It is an interesting side note that B. J. Carter also stored and repaired automobiles for visitors to the City of Jackson, and his shop was referred to as a "horseless carriage hostelry" in an April 27, 1901 *Jackson Daily Citizen* piece.[365] This article stated that an evangelist, "H. C. Blandford and wife, of London, England . . . are touring this country with a De-Dion Bouton [De Dion-Bouton] motorette carriage, manufactured in Paris, and arrived in Jackson yesterday overland from Detroit. A three and one-half horsepower gasoline engine furnishes the 'get-up, Bill' and it climbs over hills and sand with ease. The machine was given a stall in B. J. Carter's horseless carriage hostelry during the stay in the city."[366] Not only did Carter store the Blandford's horseless carriage, H. C. Blandford also hired him to fix the machine because it had been damaged en route to Jackson.[367]

First Automobile Races

B. J. Carter's earliest automobile activities extended to racing, as he piloted a car in Jackson's first-ever automobile race on July 4, 1900, at the Jackson Fair Grounds (as the location was then called). There were four entries in this auto race, two from Jackson and two from Detroit.[368] One of the two cars from Jackson was owned by Wiley R. Reynolds Jr., treasurer of Parker & Fleming Co., (and driven in the race by B. J. Carter), and the other was owned by Professor L. A. Harraden.[369] According to the *Jackson Daily Citizen*, the automobiles "went a dead heat" at a little over 23 miles per hour.[370] The make of Reynolds' car is unknown today, but Professor Harraden's machine in this race was almost certainly the Locomobile steam car that had been delivered and assembled by B. J. Carter a little over a month earlier.

Soon after running a machine in Jackson's first automobile race, Carter entered a horseless carriage of unknown make in the September 26, 1900 automobile race at Albion. He competed against at least one other auto owner, Fred P. Hinckley, then an employee of Carter's and a coinvestor in the Diamond Oil Company in 1897.[371] Carter was reported to have won the race.[372]

Carter's Automotive Ambitions Shift from Gasoline-Propelled Machines to Steam Carriages

Shortly after B. J. Carter's engineering work with Oliver E. Barthel on gasoline engines in mid-1900, Carter appears to have shifted his focus almost entirely to designing and building steam-driven cars. It is uncertain why Carter returned to steam as the mode of automotive power versus starting with steam in the first place (given his long familiarity with steam-powered devices). Perhaps his aspirations to build the "perfect" gasoline engine, as he mentioned in one of his letters to Barthel, had been set too high, and he was dissatisfied with the pace of development of his gasoline motors. Or perhaps sales of his gasoline engines had been too slow to justify additional production.

Soon after assembling Professor L. A. Harraden's Locomobile in May 1900, Carter acquired another Locomobile. In Carter's June 15, 1900 letter to Barthel, he wrote, "I went down in Ohio this week and brought a Locomobile home by road and had a fine ride, made 65 miles over very bad sandy and hilly roads after two o'clock and was here for supper." Ten days later, Carter, in another letter, told Barthel about another Locomobile he had just purchased: "I went down in Kentucky and bought a Locomobile and run it through to test it thoroughly on all kinds of roads and to give steam power a good test as well and to learn as far as possible what is wanted in this line . . . and the steps I made." Carter added that "being detained a considerable by rain I was gone longer than I expected to have been gone. I had a fine run, Sunday I made 140 miles over bad roads only having thirty miles of gravel road."[373]

The Barthel letters demonstrate that the ambitious Carter had been working on designs for both types of engines in tandem; yet between the fall of 1900 and mid-1902, he would dedicate his inventive work primarily to steam-powered carriages. Carter's experiments with steam as a motive power were done with a purpose: in a little over three months after his June 25, 1900 letter to Barthel, he would design, build, test, and demonstrate the first of several clever Carter steam carriages.

The 1900 Carter Steam Carriages

It is plausible that the machine B. J. Carter piloted to win the aforementioned Albion automobile race was actually his first steam carriage, which he designed and built for himself. Sixteen days after the Albion race, on October 12, 1900, the *Jackson Daily Citizen* wrote, "Byron J. Carter has just completed a locomobile that runs easy and fast; in fact, it is one of the finest ever seen in Jackson. Mr. Carter superintended the construction of the entire rig, and has reason to feel proud of the result of his labors. It has been sold to a gentleman in Lansing, the consideration being $1,000."[374] This appears to be the earliest newspaper reference to B. J. Carter's $1,000 steam carriage with Stanhope-style coachwork, which he introduced by the fall of 1900 (see figs. 91, 93–96). Incidentally, the lowercase term "locomobile" used in the *Jackson Daily Citizen* article was used generically at this time to describe steam cars and was coined from "locomotive" and "automobile." Locomobile, when capitalized, would not apply here, as it would represent a steam automobile manufactured by the Locomobile Company of America.[375] B. J. Carter delivered this Carter steam carriage to its new owner, E. Bement & Sons of Lansing, on November 7, 1900.[376]

Carter's first elegant and delicate-looking steam carriages, with a J motif formed by the wood moldings on each side of the bodies, were further described in the January 1, 1901 issue of *Cycle and Automobile Trade Journal* as being built "according to the designs of B. J. Carter, which are equipped with large, new balanced valve engines, with large, easily adjusted bearings, and the smaller parts of forged steel. The boiler is ample for the engine and is fired by automatic burner. The body is a graceful Stanhope with Victoria top, high, roomy, comfortable seat and a curved, grained leather dash. The operating levers are on the right side of the seat, and the steering is by a centrally placed curved lever. It has 32-inch wire wheels, standard track and long wheel base. The price is $1,000 complete."[377] The January 9, 1901 and February 27, 1901 issues of *The Motor Age* specified that the engines in Carter's Stanhope-style steam carriages produced 2 3/4 horsepower and that prices for the carriages would range from $750 to $1,000, which means that Carter was manufacturing and offering more than one type or model.[378] It is not absolutely clear whether Carter actually engineered and built the steam engines for his first

steam carriages or whether he purchased the motors ready-made from another manufacturer. The January 1, 1901 *Cycle and Automobile Trade Journal* article seems to validate the former theory, stating that Carter's steam Stanhopes were built "according to the designs of B. J. Carter."[379] Additional information will need to surface to confirm whether Carter actually engineered the engines for the steam cars he manufactured in 1900.

Carter offered his 1900 steam carriages nationally within a month of the test auto's maiden run, when he placed a simple advertisement in *The Motor Vehicle Review* that ran from November 8, 1900, through January 3, 1901 (fig. 92). With this expanded exposure, Carter took the opportunity to offer a broad array of other automotive items: a Locomobile steamer, model No. 2, an air-cooled three-cylinder gasoline engine (from a March 28, 1900 classified ad in *The Horseless Age* it looks like Carter had been trying to sell this same engine or one like it for at least seven months), steam boilers, engines, and burners, complete automobile running gears (chassis), and any parts machined or "in the rough."[380]

In addition to the initial sale of a Carter steam carriage to E. Bement & Sons of Lansing, Carter also sold other 1900 Carter steam carriages to Professor L. A. Harraden and Floyd Mitchell.[381] (Carter and Mitchell had known each other since at least the mid-1890s, when they were both members of the Jackson Wheelmen cycling club.) Professor Harraden described his Carter steam carriage as "virtually the same design [as Harraden's 1900 Locomobile], although more substantially put together."[382]

An extant photo of Fred T. Lockwood and his wife in a steam carriage, from the Lockwood negatives, may picture yet another Carter steam-carriage model from 1900 (fig. 98), perhaps the version offered by Carter for $750. Lockwood's machine appears to have the same running gear as was used on the Carter steam carriage with Stanhope-style coachwork (note the unusual perforated chain sprocket on the rear axle and nearly identical bicycle-tube frame configuration, as found on the Carter Stanhope model). And Lockwood's car closely resembles a Carter steam carriage photographed later in front of B. J. Carter's bicycle shop (fig. 99). If B. J. Carter built this machine for Lockwood, then Carter chose an alternative body style far simpler, and

668

Fig. 91. A photograph from B. J. Carter's family papers of Carter's first steam carriage, which the October 12, 1900 issue of the *Jackson Daily Citizen* noted he had "just completed." This picture may have been taken a few days earlier, as the steam carriage is not 100 percent assembled (i.e., the cylindrical, horizontal draft flue visible in figs. 93–95 had not yet been installed over the boiler across the back deck lid). The January 1, 1901 *Cycle and Automobile Trade Journal* described the machine as "a steam Stanhope" built "according to the designs of B. J. Carter" with a new 2 3/4-horsepower balanced-valve steam engine. The horseless carriage had a graceful Stanhope-design body with a Victoria-style top, a grained-leather dash where the primary steam gauges were mounted, and a centrally placed curved tiller for steering the horseless carriage. This Carter steam carriage's price was $1,000. This picture was taken on West Cortland Street in front of the Jackson Corset Co. factory opposite Carter's bicycle shop and a short distance west. *Courtesy of Sallie Sparks Kendall*

less expensive, than the body installed on Carter's Stanhope-style steam carriages. This particular alternative body style was similar, but not identical, to the wooden bodies found on certain Locomobile, Mobile, and Stanley steam carriages of the day.[383] Professor L. A. Harraden's Carter steam carriage probably also resembled Lockwood's Carter steamer: Harraden later mentioned that his Carter machine was "virtually the same design" as his 1900 Locomobile.[384] A 1993 book entitled *The History of Business and Industry in Jackson, Michigan* contends that this photograph (fig. 98) shows a steam carriage built by Lockwood Brothers; however, the book does not provide a source to verify this information.[385] That said, steam-carriage engines, running assemblies, bodies, and other parts could be purchased from various national suppliers at this time, so it is plausible (but unlikely) that Lockwood Brothers, rather than B. J. Carter, built this machine.

It did not take long before B. J. Carter experienced his first accident with a Carter steam carriage. The October 15, 1900 *Jackson Daily Citizen* (only three days after it announced B. J. Carter had "just completed" and demonstrated his first Stanhope-style steam carriage) reported that B. J. Carter and Bera J. Kingston, former proprietor of the *Jackson Herald*, and at the time of this accident, a *Jackson Citizen* advertising solicitor, were making a trip to Michigan Center in a Carter steam carriage on Sunday, October 14, 1900.[386]

Kingston's presence during this accident probably caused Carter some angst, as Carter was likely using this journey to promote and gain publicity for his newly built steam carriage within the ranks of the *Jackson Citizen*, the city's main newspaper. Carter's steam carriage had passed a horse and buggy occupied by a couple, and the horse "took fright and endeavored to run away. As the horse started to run the wheels on the side went over the embankment, upsetting the buggy. For a moment it looked as if a serious accident had happened," but, fortunately, the man and woman in the buggy were not badly injured.[387] The newspaper article concluded, perhaps in an effort to redeem Carter a bit, by stating that Carter and Kingston were able to catch the horse and stop it from running off and that "a broken wheel and a broken top and some excitement was all that happened. As a rule very few horses are afraid of [steam] locomobiles."[388]

CARTER

Steam Carriages

Elegant in Design,
Substantially Built.

—ALSO—

Complete Gears

or any parts, machined or in the rough.

——

Boilers, Engines, Burners,
and other parts.

——

B. J. CARTER,

JACKSON, MICH.

P. S. A No. 2 Locomobile for sale, also a 3-cylinder Hydro-Carbon Air Cooled Carriage Motor.

Fig. 92. Advertisement for Carter steam carriages that was run in *The Motor Vehicle Review* from November 8, 1900, through January 3, 1901; it is interesting to note that Carter also offered for sale a Locomobile steam car and a three-cylinder air-cooled "Hydro-Carbon" (gasoline or benzene) engine in this national ad (from a March 28, 1900 classified advertisement in *The Horseless Age*, it looks like Carter had been trying to sell this same engine for at least seven months). *Courtesy of Gregory R. Loftness*

Fig. 93. A side view of B. J. Carter's 1900 steam Stanhope from the Lockwood negatives; figs. 93–96 were captured on the same day by the Lockwood camera in front of Jackson Fire Station No. 1, which was located on West Cortland Street, opposite B. J. Carter's bicycle shop and about a block west of it. *Author's Lockwood negative collection*

Fig. 94. Another side view of the 1900 Carter steam carriage with a Stanhope-style body, which shows details of the dash gauges and controls. *Author's Lockwood negative collection*

Fig. 95. The 1900 Carter steam carriage with its Victoria top folded down. *Author's Lockwood negative collection*

Fig. 96. Front view of the 1900 Carter steam carriage; the metal bicycle-tubing frame built for this machine is clearly visible. This photographic negative unfortunately shows a double-exposure partial image of a side view of this automobile as well. *Author's Lockwood negative collection*

Another encounter six months later between an automobile and scared horse pulling a wagon was reported at the intersection of Cortland and Jackson streets, near Carter's shop; in this case the motorcar's driver was not identified.[389] The May 20, 1901 *Jackson Daily Citizen* informed readers that the agitated horse ran off and threw the wagon's driver to the pavement, "where he alighted on his head receiving a severe scalp wound. One of his arms was also badly sprained."[390] The horse had then broken loose from the wagon and "proceeded to Main street, where it fell and came very near sliding under a passing street car. The horse had its forelegs quite badly bruised, the skin being scraped off."[391] The existence of these sorts of dangerous accidents and resulting serious injuries created considerable conflict between the legions of citizens who still relied on long-proven horse transportation and those who advocated for the new, sometimes noisy automobiles, which typically belched steam or oily exhaust and often startled horses.

Fig. 97. The City of Jackson's Fire Station No. 1, circa 1894, where Fred T. Lockwood's photographs of B. J. Carter's 1900 Stanhope-style steam carriage (figs. 93–96) were taken. *Courtesy of the Ella Sharp Museum*

Fig. 98. Fred T. and Florence E. Lockwood in an auto that is believed to be another style of a 1900 Carter steam carriage, perhaps the $750 model mentioned in the January 9, 1901 issue of *The Motor Age*. (It has the same running gear as the Carter steam carriage with Stanhope-style coachwork, which cost $1,000, but with a simpler body installed; note the unusual perforated chain sprocket on the rear axle, also seen in photographs of Carter's steam Stanhope model [figs. 91, 93–95]). The Lockwood's automobile also closely resembles a Carter steam carriage photographed sometime later in front of B. J. Carter's bicycle shop (see figs. 99 & 111). This photograph (fig. 98) was a taken in front of Mr. and Mrs. Lockwood's home at 1011 Wildwood Avenue. *Author's Lockwood negative collection*

Fig. 99. Another model of a 1900 Carter steam carriage very similar to the Lockwoods' Carter steam carriage shown in fig. 98; this photograph, which was taken in front of the Carters' 204 West Cortland Street bicycle shop, is a close-up view from fig. 111. The identities of the two men aboard the steamer are unknown. *Courtesy of Sallie Sparks Kendall*

Carter Urgently Needs a Cash Infusion to Launch Steam-Carriage Manufacturing Operations

As a result of his all-consuming efforts to design engines and to build and sell horseless carriages, B. J. Carter soon found himself needing a significant capital investment (in addition to the revenues from his bicycle and automobile sales and repair, phonograph shop, and United States Tag Co.) before he could pursue his automobile-building ventures more fully. It would appear that the ambitious Carter had already been in contact with potential investors when his first steam carriage was mentioned in the *Jackson Daily Citizen* on October 12, 1900. In a small piece the next day, which B. J. Carter undoubtedly prompted (perhaps with the aid of Bera J. Kingston), the newspaper provided the first indication that investors might be interested in manufacturing and marketing Carter's steam car: "It is stated that overtures are being made to a Jackson man to join in a project at Grand Rapids for the manufacture of locomobiles. A gentleman from that city was in Jackson yesterday and said a $50,000 stock company would be organized provided satisfactory arrangements could be made with this Jackson gentleman to commence business in that city. If it would be a good thing for Grand Rapids, why should not Jackson people investigate this project and keep the industry here?"[392] B. J. Carter had now started his adept series of maneuvers to motivate Jackson moneymen to support and keep his automobile manufacturing business in the City of Jackson. Carter, however, could not have anticipated, in October 1900, just how much time would pass and how frustrated he would become before well-heeled Jackson investors would actually step forward and take up his cause.

Carter's next move to publicly jumpstart investor interest occurred only two days later, when his brother-in-law announced that he would provide financial support for Carter's motor-carriage venture. The October 15, 1900 *Jackson Daily Citizen* proclaimed that "Byron J. Carter and Frank F. Muns have formed a partnership for the manufacture of automobiles in this city. Mr. Carter has just perfected one of the most practical and perfect patterns ever produced in that line, and it is now the intention to push the manufacture of them. The demand so far has been more than manufacturers could supply."[393]

Frank F. Muns, who resided in Jackson, was married to Birdie S. Muns, née Miller, the half sister of B. J. Carter's wife, Della; he was a foreman at Smith & Adams, a Jackson picture-frame and wood-molding maker.[394] Della had boarded with Frank and Birdie Muns before she married B. J. Carter, and the Munses had hosted B. J. and Della Carter's wedding ceremony at their residence on July 1, 1896.[395]

Little is known today of what became of this partnership between Muns and Carter, but Carter's continued and persistent pursuit of more funding would indicate that the inner-family partnership did not solve Carter's money woes, and it may have simply been a publicity stunt by Carter to drum up more investor interest at that time.

The information Carter submitted for the 1900 United States federal census shows that he was renting his residence at 214 West Washington Street (where Della and he had lived since their 1896 wedding, next to his parents' home, now at 216 West Washington Street).[396] Given that home ownership would have demonstrated financial stability and accomplishment, and the fact that Carter was head of a young family, one can assume this situation was disappointing for Carter, who was by then in his late 30s. Despite Carter's confidence in his ideas and inventions, he was also probably anxious and uncertain as to whether financial backers would ultimately come forward and launch a dedicated Carter steam-carriage manufacturing operation.

In a transaction likely made to raise funds, Carter sold his established United States Tag Co. business, in November 1900, to R. T. Allen, who moved the business to 120 South Mechanic Street.[397] During this time of seemingly tight finances, B. J. Carter nonetheless expanded his bicycle and automobile premises a bit when he took over the small ramshackle building with galvanized tin siding at 206 West Cortland Street; given its appearance in figures 24, 25, and 111, it probably did not cost much.[398]

Even though B. J. Carter in 1900 and 1901 offered for sale and serviced several other manufacturers' automobiles and also built gasoline engines and steam carriages of his own design, there is no mention of his automotive activities in the 1900/1901 *Jackson City Directory*. For that matter, no other automobile manufacturers were listed in this city directory either. However, by 1902, the *Jackson City*

Directory included Byron J. Carter, at 204–206 West Cortland Street, under the new directory heading, "Automobile Mnfrs."[399] (Given the directory's printing schedule, this would mean Carter was promoting himself as an automobile manufacturer in Jackson by 1901, consistent with the national attention his first steam carriages had received in *The Motor Vehicle Review*, *Cycle and Automobile Trade Journal*, *The Horseless Age*, and *The Motor Age* starting in late 1900 and during much of 1901.)[400] Incidentally and not surprisingly, B. J. Carter was the sole automobile manufacturer listed in the 1902 *Jackson City Directory*, and his longer-term occupations as a bicycle dealer and machinist were designated as well.[401] Carter would have used the "Manufacturer of Automobiles" business or calling card (fig. 100) as he courted possible investors for his proposed venture to build his new steam machines in quantity at the beginning of the 20th century.

Fig. 100. B. J. Carter's business or calling card when he was seeking investors for his proposed steam-carriage enterprise 1900–1902; this card predates Carter's involvement with the Jackson Automobile Company and The Motorcar Co., of Jackson. *Courtesy of Sallie Sparks Kendall*

Grand Rapids Businessmen and Others Express Interest in Moving Carter's Automobile Company

As a follow-up to the minor mention in the October 13, 1900 *Jackson Daily Citizen* about a potential out-of-town investor, the newspaper soon sounded a more pronounced alarm when B. J. Carter informed the *Jackson Citizen* that serious discussions were under way with W. Smalley Daniels, a highly successful bicycle agent from Grand Rapids, Michigan, to form a new enterprise called the Michigan Automobile Company, which would entail moving all of Carter's auto manufacturing operations to either Detroit or Grand Rapids. In an article titled "The Michigan Automobile Company," the October 23, 1900 *Jackson Daily Citizen* proclaimed: "Among the many visitors attracted to Jackson this fall to see the new steam automobile manufactured by B. J. Carter, has been a young businessman, of Grand Rapids, who has been thoroughly investigating all new makes of automobiles heard of in this part of the country. After critical examination and a half-day's test, he pronounced it the most improved and best steam carriage on the market and predicted much for it. Yesterday this gentleman, who the 'Citizen' learned was W. S. Daniels, of the firm of Jarvis & Daniels, large sporting goods and bicycle jobbers of Grand Rapids, returned here and it now develops that he has interested himself with Mr. Carter in the formation of what is to be known as the Michigan Automobile Co., for the purpose of actively engaging in the manufacture of Mr. Carter's automobile. Further information could [not] be gained as to the intention of the new company, although it is understood there is capital in this city [Jackson] ready for the formation of a large factory. The inclination of the gentlemen is to locate in a larger field preferably at Detroit or Grand Rapids."[402]

Carter and Daniels also skillfully shared the news of the proposed new Michigan Automobile Company with the *Grand Rapids Herald*. The Grand Rapids newspaper, in its December 2, 1900 issue, struck an excited tone similar to that of the *Jackson Daily Citizen* when it reported the possible relocation of Carter's steam-carriage business from Jackson to Grand Rapids. The *Grand Rapids Herald* described Carter's motor carriage as "steam-propelled and is of a new pattern" without "many of the objectionable features of the steam carriages now on the market."[403] The article continued, "The Clipper bicycle plant [in Grand Rapids], which is now for rent, has been mentioned as a very desirable building which could easily, with small cost, be converted to meet the requirements of successful automobile manufacture. The Carter machine is already a success, two years of experimental work having been passed and there is the usual outlay of money to come for that purpose. Business men in Jackson are ready to form a company for the manufacture of the machine, but the promoters of the scheme prefer to locate in a large city, where there will be a heavy local trade. The city of Elkhart, Ind., has offered a factory of 300 foot frontage and a stock company with a paid up stock in the amount of $25,000, and the Studebaker Wagon company of South Bend, Ind., are also negotiating for the right to manufacture the Carter machine. The matter will be brought before the local board of trade at once and effort made to establish a company in this city [Grand Rapids] to begin operations at once."[404]

On a national basis, preliminary (and premature) announcements were made in *The Horseless Age* (December 12, 1900 issue), *Cycle and Automobile Trade Journal* (January 1, 1901 issue, illustrated with a Lockwood photograph from the series in figures 93–96), and *The Motor Age* (January 9, 1901 issue) that the Michigan Automobile Company had already been established and would be located in the former Clipper bicycle factory in Grand Rapids.[405] *The Motor Age* article recited most of the December 2, 1900 *Grand Rapids Herald* piece and repeated that approval (and likely some funding) would need to be obtained from the Grand Rapids "board of trades" to convert Grand Rapids' vacant Clipper bicycle plant "to meet the requirements of a successful automobile manufacture."[406]

Despite all the positive publicity and promotion, a venture to expand the manufacture of Carter's first 1900 Stanhope-style steam carriages in Grand Rapids, Jackson, or elsewhere never got off the ground. Perhaps Carter, Daniels, or the Grand Rapids board of trade businessmen got cold feet once they calculated how much money would actually be required to convert and equip the former Clipper bicycle plant with all necessary machinery to manufacture the Carter steam carriage. It also appears that no investor in Jackson stepped forward with a serious funding approach either. Another possibility is that the various potential investors wanted to see demonstrations of Carter's vastly improved steam carriage with a newly designed three-cylinder engine, which was, by then, already in development on Carter's drafting table.

The 1901 Carter Steam Carriages with Radically Improved Engine and Lubrication Systems

Almost a year after B. J. Carter demonstrated his first Stanhope-style steam carriage, the August 5, 1901 *Jackson Daily Citizen* enthusiastically announced a new, improved Carter steam machine:

> B. J. Carter, of this city, has just completed an automobile which is constructed throughout with automatic devices for regulating a horseless carriage the way it should be. It is a combination double-seated carriage, is almost noiseless, and at all times under perfect control of the "driver." The improved driving power is self-activating, for instance, when the steam reaches a certain point the fire under the boiler is lessened or increased automatically, with high or low pressure steam, and when the water reaches a certain point in the guage [*sic*] a pump is automatically started, and stops when sufficient water is in the boiler. And that is only a part of the many devices the carriage is supplied with, the machinery also being self-lubricating, so that the operators of the auto have little to look after, as they silently glide along over the hills and dales. Saturday evening four autos were in parade on Main Street, and Mr. Carter's new machine was numbered with them, and attracted considerable attention. The first run was to Kalamazoo and return, about a week ago, just for exercise, and within a month Mr. Carter expects to make an overland trip to Buffalo and return with his new carriage. On good roads the new auto can travel 25 miles an hour with ease.[407]

Carter had now manufactured and demonstrated the first 1901 improved, self-lubricating Carter steam carriage, and on January 18, 1902, he applied for a U.S. patent (no. 722,206) for his newly designed three-cylinder steam engine (figs. 101 and 102).[408] On January 1, 1903, *The Motor World* published a significantly delayed article about this improved "Carter's Runabout" built by "the Carter Automobile Company, Jackson, Mich."[409] (Apparently this piece had been written many months earlier but was not finally published until nearly six months after Carter had moved on to establish a new, different motorcar enterprise, the Jackson Automobile Company). *The Motor*

World article informed, "The vehicle is equipped with a three cylinder engine possessing some novel features. A rotary valve constructed on the same principle as the slide valve is used, which will keep seated at all times; wear will not affect the valve in any degree. There are no stuffing boxes . . . The carriage has a low water alarm as well as a gauge glass and try cocks, a steam air pump and a 11-16 inch bore to boiler. The feed pump has two six gallon tanks of gasolene, with separate cut outs, which sets under front hood, or seat."[410] This first model of Carter's improved steam carriage had capacity for four passengers, two in the driver's seat and two more in a precarious fold-out second seat at the front of the machine. The body was described as "hung very low, a construction made possible by the fact that the shaft runs through the engine with driving sprocket on the side instead of through the centre. By so placing it the [drive] chain [to the rear axle] passes alongside the boiler instead of under the firebox."[411] The J motif formed by wood moldings on the 1900 Carter steam Stanhope bodies was also employed on Carter's improved-steam-carriage bodies. With a few subsequent modifications, the improved 1901–1902 Carter three-cylinder steam carriage would form the design for the Jaxon Steam Surrey announced in mid-1902.

Coincidentally, a month earlier, Carter's longtime cycling friend and the owner of the Jackson News Co., Floyd Mitchell, had been listed as owning "a machine . . . made by B. J. Carter, of Jackson" in a *Jackson Daily Citizen* article.[412] Given the timing, Mitchell's Carter steam carriage was likely a 1900 model, because Carter's improved two-seat 1901 model was probably not yet completed and ready for sale when this June 1901 newspaper article was published.[413] Mitchell, in his Carter steam carriage, was reported as making the 66-mile trip from Jackson to Kalamazoo in six hours (11 miles per hour, on average).[414]

One of Carter's inventions, which he likely installed on the Carter three-cylinder engine in his improved 1901 steam carriage, was the Carter Automatic Cylinder Lubricator. The March 1, 1902 *Cycle and Automobile Trade Journal* stated, "B. J. Carter, Jackson, Mich., manufactures a Cylinder Lubricator which has been in use on various makes of automobiles for about a year past" (i.e., starting in 1901).[415] This exceptional lubricator, designed to provide cylinder oil to steam engines, held one quart of oil and was described as entirely automatic, working only when the engine was in motion. In an effort to raise much-needed revenue, Carter would soon advertise his Automatic

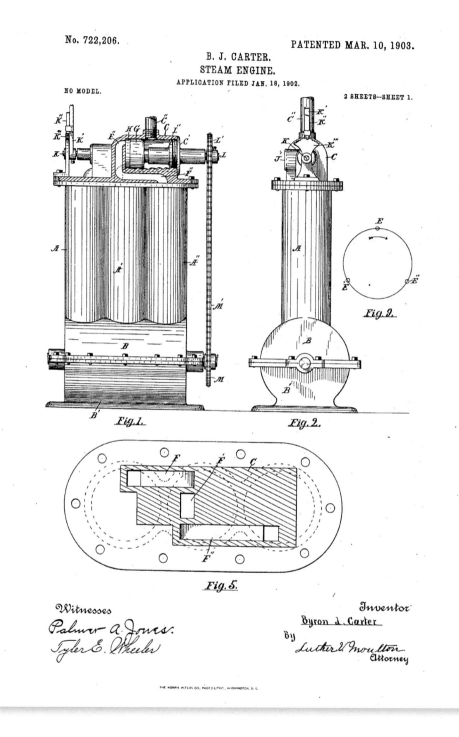

Fig. 101. Sheet 1 of the patent drawing for B. J. Carter's improved six-horsepower, three-cylinder rotary-valve steam engine with automatic lubrication, first mentioned in the August 5, 1901 issue of the *Jackson Daily Citizen*; this U.S. patent (no. 722,206), which was filed January 18, 1902, and granted March 10, 1903, formed a substantial part of Carter's contribution to establishing the Jackson Automobile Company. *Courtesy of Buzzy Carter Maurer*

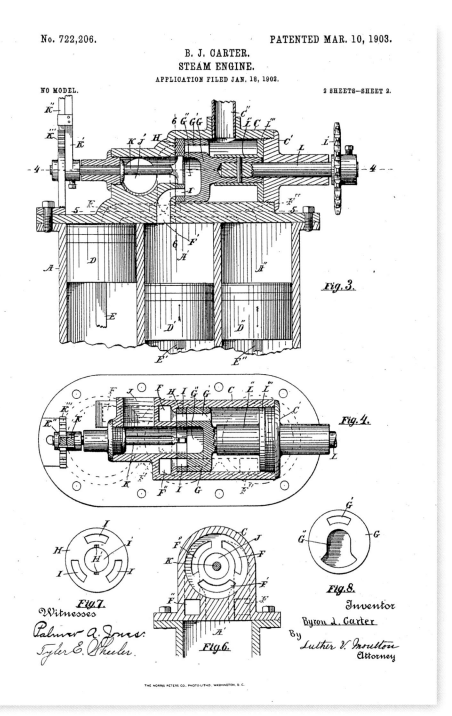

Fig. 102. Sheet 2 of the patent drawing for B. J. Carter's improved steam engine filed January 18, 1902, granted March 10, 1903, and assigned to the Jackson Automobile Company. *Courtesy of Buzzy Carter Maurer*

Fig. 103. An extant improved three-cylinder steam engine (front view) designed and built by B. J. Carter sometime between the summer of 1901 and July 1902, when the Jackson Automobile Company was founded; a galvanized sheet-steel cylinder jacket/heat shield, likely with an asbestos lining, covers the three steam cylinders. The small device in the lower left is a boiler feed pump and the block chain, which travels vertically along the left side of the engine, drives the overhead rotary steam valve mechanism. The original chain sprocket on the right side of the engine for the rear-axle drive was likely replaced at some point with a belt pulley in order that the engine could be used for other purposes with a belt drive. Or perhaps the belt pulley is an original feature: as advertised in *The Horseless Age* in 1902, these steam engines could be purchased separately from Carter for other applications, at a cost of $100. *Courtesy of Todd and Faith Holton*

Fig. 103a. Brass identification tag riveted to the galvanized sheet-steel cylinder jacket/heat shield on B. J. Carter's improved three-cylinder steam engine, which shows "No. 57"; it seems highly unlikely that Carter manufactured 57 complete Carter steam carriages equipped with this improved engine between the summer of 1901 and July 1902, so serial numbering may have been started at 50 to inflate production numbers artificially (an April 26, 1902 *Jackson Daily Citizen* article indicated that Carter's production capacity was only one steam car per month). Carter advertised his improved steam engines for sale separately at $100 in 1902, which could account for a higher than expected number of motors manufactured. The brass tag also states "Patents Applied For," which probably indicates this particular motor was built after January 18, 1902, when Carter filed his federal patent application for this three-cylinder steam engine design. *Courtesy of Todd and Faith Holton*

Fig. 104. Photograph of B. J. Carter's improved steam engine (back view), which shows how the galvanized sheet-steel cylinder jacket/heat shield was attached; the two cast-iron supports at the top permit the engine to pivot on a horizontal rod when the engine is at work. *Courtesy of Todd and Faith Holton*

Fig. 105. A factory photograph from B. J. Carter's family papers of an incomplete improved Carter steam carriage during the manufacturing process in 1901 or early 1902; this machine had not yet been painted or upholstered, and the engine, boiler, and other drive mechanisms had not been installed. It only has one seat (versus the two fore-and-aft seats on the first improved Carter three-cylinder steam carriage, as described in the August 5, 1901 issue of the *Jackson Daily Citizen*). *Courtesy of Buzzy Carter Maurer*

Fig. 106. A factory photograph printed in *The Motor World* of an improved Carter steam carriage after completion, also with a single seat and a plain front dash in place of the folding auxiliary front-seat assembly on the original improved Carter steam carriage model. *Courtesy of Gregory R. Loftness*

Fig. 108. Side view of the same improved Carter single-seat steam carriage owned by Phillip T. Watkins after he had installed kerosene driving lamps on the front dash. This photograph was taken in 1928; it is unknown whether this automobile still exists today. *Author's collection*

Fig. 107. Front view of a late 1901 or early 1902 improved Carter steam carriage, a single-seat model, photographed in the 1920s, when the antique machine was owned by Phillip T. Watkins (left, in a top hat) of Lansing, Michigan. Mr. Watkins holds a high-wheel Ordinary bicycle alongside the auto. *Author's collection*

Cylinder Lubricator nationally in *The Horseless Age* and *The Automobile and Motor Review* in mid-1902.[416]

Carter focused on other efforts to raise capital as well, and, as evidence of his commitment to building autos, even offered his business real estate for sale, as a potential site for Jackson's planned new Carnegie library. Andrew Carnegie, who had devoted his life to large-scale philanthropy with a special emphasis on local libraries, had donated $70,000 to the City of Jackson for the construction of a new library building. The July 2, 1901 *Jackson Daily Citizen* stated that several parties had offered various real estate holdings under "bid" to the Jackson City Common Council for the new library site.[417] Among them was B. J. Carter, who submitted "land on the northwest corner of Jackson and Cortland street[s]," offered at $12,000.[418] It is unclear from this description whether this offer included both the 204 West Cortland Street bicycle shop and the adjacent wood-frame structure that the Carters had used for their various businesses. However, in light of the scale and size of the new Jackson library, which exists today, it would seem likely that the library construction project would have required all of B. J. Carter's property, including 204 West Cortland Street. As it transpired, B. J. Carter's land offer was not accepted, and the impressive Jackson District Library–Carnegie Branch building was completed in 1906 on West Main Street.[419]

One may never understand why Carter offered to sell his property, because his 204 West Cortland Street facilities and machinery were essential to Carter's burgeoning automobile-manufacturing operation. Perhaps Carter had gained a level of confidence that his soon-to-be-demonstrated improved 1901 steam carriage would impress the Grand Rapids businessmen or other investors and they would ultimately fund Carter's enterprise and possibly move it elsewhere. Or perhaps Carter had concluded his 204 West Cortland Street facilities were inadequate and had identified another location in Jackson to which he would relocate, if it made financial sense. Three months earlier Carter had attempted to negotiate a real estate deal with the Jackson County Board of Supervisors to swap land Carter owned behind the nearby county jail for an 880-square-foot parcel owned by Jackson County, which was adjacent to Carter's wood-frame building and fronted on Jackson Street. This proposed land swap would have allowed Carter

to expand his manufacturing facility northward along South Jackson Street. However, Carter's offer was rejected by the county, creating a setback for Carter's expansion plans, which may account for his likely frustration and willingness, three months later, to sell the entire parcel in the northwest corner of West Cortland and South Jackson streets as a library site.[420]

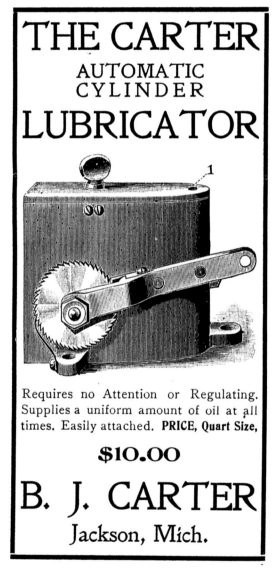

Fig. 109. An advertisement for the Carter Automatic Cylinder Lubricator for steam automobiles from the June 14, 1902 and certain later issues of *The Automobile and Motor Review*; a similar ad ran in June and July 1902 issues of *The Horseless Age* and also offered Carter's improved three-cylinder steam engines for sale at $100. A Carter automatic cylinder oil pump, similar to this model, would be installed on the Jaxon Steam Surrey engines. *Courtesy of Gregory R. Loftness*

Stymied Attempts to Drive Carter Steam Carriages to the 1901 Pan-American Exposition

B. J. Carter was not just a tinkerer who designed and built horseless carriages in his machine shop—he was also a creative and active promoter who handily controlled publicity. Shortly after piloting his first gasoline automobile on the streets of Jackson, in 1899, Carter realized that potential investors and users of his engines and motorcars would need proof that his products were durable, reliable, and well designed, and he faced ever fiercer competition as the pace of automotive development grew exponentially after 1900. A 375-mile run to the 1901 Pan-American Exposition in Buffalo with Carter's new, improved steam carriage would have seemed like just the sort of demonstration that could strengthen Carter's reputation as an automotive inventor and builder. In fact, Carter boldly expressed his intentions to drive to Buffalo "within a month," when he orchestrated the August 5, 1901 *Jackson Daily Citizen* announcement of his first double-seat steam carriage with a radically improved three-cylinder engine.[421]

The Pan-American Exposition was a world's fair that ran from May 1 through November 2, 1901; it commemorated a century of material, cultural, and mechanical progress in the Western Hemisphere. At night the exposition was alight with thousands of electric lightbulbs, and there was a prominent 389-foot illuminated Electric Tower on the grounds, all powered by turbine generators at Niagara Falls. Total attendance was more than eight million.[422]

Today the Pan-American Exposition is remembered primarily because President William McKinley was shot by an anarchist in the Pan-American's Temple of Music on September 6, 1901. McKinley was transported by the exposition's electric automobile ambulance, built by the Riker Motor Vehicle Company, to the exposition's small, ill-equipped hospital for an inadequate surgical attempt to remove two bullets

(only one was successfully extracted).[423] Following this medical treatment, McKinley was again transported in the Riker electric ambulance to the Buffalo home of John G. Milburn, president of the exposition's board of directors, in order that McKinley could further rest and recuperate. Despite an initial optimistic prognosis from the doctors, President McKinley died eight days later. McKinley's assassin was promptly tried, found guilty, and sentenced to death, and was executed on October 29, 1901, in another new technology, the electric chair.[424]

A significant display of automobiles and various motorcar sporting events were offered at the Pan-American Exposition. And in conjunction with the exposition, the Automobile Club of America intended to conduct a motor vehicle tournament and international speed contest starting September 16, 1901.[425] Numerous motorists aspired to attend the exposition by driving their automobiles there, particularly those who lived in the Northeast. These motorists often

Fig. 110. The 1901 Pan-American Exposition's electric ambulance built by the Riker Motor Vehicle Company; this ambulance transported the wounded President William McKinley after he was shot at the exposition by an anarchist on September 6, 1901. *Author's collection*

formed caravans with other motorists, driving together in touring groups to attend the exposition. There was even a group of four Jackson cyclists who announced plans to ride their bicycles to the Pan-American Exposition, leaving June 30, 1901.[426] The fate of their journey is unknown. And throughout much of 1901, the *Jackson Daily Citizen* reported the many names of Jackson citizens who attended the exposition by train.

Given the exposition's prominence, it was a highly visible opportunity for B. J. Carter to prove that his new, improved steam carriages were capable of maneuvering the deeply rutted wagon trails and rough terrain between Jackson and Buffalo, a distance of approximately 375 miles following a route south of Lake Erie. It is uncertain when Carter departed Jackson for Buffalo with his two Carter steam cars and who, exactly, piloted the second Carter steam carriage. However, this second Carter carriage driver was likely Floyd Mitchell who, as reported in the June 26, 1901 *Jackson Daily Citizen*, had just purchased one of Carter's new steam machines (likely a 1900 model) in June 1901.[427] Mitchell was reported in the *Jackson Daily Citizen* as having returned with Carter to Jackson from the Buffalo exposition "and the east" around September 17, 1901.[428] In addition to Mitchell, we know that Professor L. A. Harraden and passenger, L. B. Cowley, a Jackson shoe and boot merchant, had accompanied B. J. Carter back from the exposition, all arriving in Jackson in their automobiles by September 17, 1901.[429] According to the 1941 *Jackson Citizen Patriot* interview with Harraden, it sounds as if he also may have been driving a new Carter steam carriage during this ill-fated trek to the exposition (Harraden also owned a new Stearns motorcar at this time).[430] President McKinley was shot on September 6, 1901, and died on September 14, 1901, so it is plausible that Carter and the Jackson horseless carriage tour group may have been at the Pan-American Exposition during these tragic events.

The attempted long-distance test drive to Buffalo had been a very arduous journey for Carter and the drivers of the other machines from Jackson. One of Carter's obituaries from the *Jackson Citizen* stated that Carter and the pilot of the second Carter steam carriage, likely Floyd Mitchell, encountered "continual rains and bad roads which led the adventurers to give up the trip at Painesville, OH," a distance of

215 miles from Jackson, where they put their machines in storage.[431] Carter and the other driver made the remainder of their trip to Buffalo by train.[432] Harraden, in his newspaper interview nearly 40 years later, indicated he had had a similar experience and had been forced to leave his auto behind as well, "because the roads were so bad and the mud so deep, the Jackson men finally decided at some place in Ohio that the hardships were too great . . . put cars in storage, climbed aboard a train, and continued the trip to Buffalo."[433]

After visiting the Pan-American Exposition, B. J. Carter and the driver of the other Carter steam car (presumably Floyd Mitchell) returned to Painesville, Ohio, by train to retrieve their vehicles. They then drove the Carter steam carriages back to Jackson, returning by September 17, 1901, along with Professor L. A. Harraden, who was possibly in a third Carter steam carriage, and his passenger, L. B. Cowley.[434]

Even though B. J. Carter's attempted journey to Buffalo with his new steam vehicles was unsuccessful, this trip, some amateur racing, ample publicity, and his patent pending for the improved three-cylinder steam engine filed on January 18, 1902, drew heightened attention to Carter's automotive achievements. The stakes were now higher for the citizens of Jackson to prevent Carter's motorcar manufacturing operations from moving to another city.

A Second Scare that Carter's Automobile Operations Might Relocate to Grand Rapids

B. J. Carter clearly had advocates working within the ranks of the *Jackson Citizen*, which had previously covered and promoted his various automobile inventions and efforts. In an April 26, 1902 article titled "Why Not Keep It?" the reporter who wrote the piece declared:

> Jackson Business Men Might Yet Save Carter Automobile Plant From Going to Grand Rapids. Jackson is in imminent danger of losing its hold on a fine automobile plant unless some one takes hold of a movement looking for the retention of the B. J. Carter establishment on Cortland Street, and its enlargement. Mr. Carter has identified himself with automobile construction since the machine became more than a mere experiment and has succeeded in improving and remodeling his primitive machines to a high degree of efficiency. His work has been a credit to Jackson.[435]

This *Jackson Daily Citizen* news item went on to inform (clearly with prompting from Carter) that Carter had perfected a self-lubricating steam carriage with excellent speed results in its test runs and that the Carter steam cars "have attracted universal admiration" and, in what sounds like an exaggerated claim, that quite a number of the cars had been placed in successful operation in various parts of the country. The reporter added:

> Mr. Carter has only a small plant here, and it has a capacity of but one machine a month. At that, he has reduced the economy of the building to the lowest possible figure . . . the local plant has been unable for some time to fill its orders, which have been coming much faster than the plant has been capable of supplying them. . . . He has looked abroad for some desirable location where he might find capital that would justify him erecting a more pretentious plant and one that will conform with the excellence of his machine. Several days ago he took a carload of his machines to Grand Rapids for inspection among the business men of that city, whom he has asked to invest their money in an automobile plant in that city.[436]

These Grand Rapids businessmen were described as "enthusiastic." The article further advised: "His [Carter's] idea is to erect a plant large enough to give employment to 350 skilled automobile workmen. These men are desirable in any community, as they command big wages." The piece indicated that the suggested name for the proposed new Grand Rapids steam-car enterprise would be the Clipper Auto Car Company, capitalized at a likely overstated $400,000 "to manufacture automobile parts as well as the complete machines, the plant at Jackson already having an established business in both of these lines . . . The business seems to have a splendid future and Mr. Carter is naturally desirous of securing the necessary capital and a good location. He will act as supervising architect for the proposed plant in Grand Rapids."[437]

The reporter wrote that an option had been secured for the vacant Clipper bicycle plant and that the new steam carriages would likely be branded "Clipper." J. Elmer Pratt, formerly associated with the Grand Rapids Cycle Co., which manufactured the Clipper bicycle, would be employed as superintendent of the Grand Rapids steam-carriage factory, if the new auto business were established. Pratt had expressed an intention to hire a number of former Clipper bicycle employees and agents for the new steam-car company.[438]

Shortly after, the May 8, 1902 issue of *The Motor World* confirmed J. Elmer Pratt's involvement in the proposed Clipper Auto Car Company, in Grand Rapids, "to take over the business of B. J. Carter, of Jackson, Mich., manufacturer of steam automobiles."[439] This magazine article repeated the claim that the new Clipper steam-carriage venture would be capitalized at $400,000.[440] Two days later, *Automobile Topics*, for unspecified reasons, seemed to cast doubt on the wisdom and value of the proposed Clipper Auto Car Company venture: "J. Elmer Pratt of Grand Rapids, Mich., who was once considered one of the most level-headed men in the bicycle industry, is connected with the organization of a company for manufacturing steam vehicles in Grand Marais [presumably Grand Rapids], Mich., under patents owned by B. J. Carter of Jackson, in the same State."[441]

Conversely, the *Jackson Daily Citizen* reporter in the April 26, 1902 article was very enthusiastic about the prospects of a larger Carter steam-carriage enterprise in Jackson and reminded that

Fig. 111. This photograph of three Carter steam carriages was taken sometime between August 1901 and mid-1902. Carter and his father, Squire, occupy the main seat on the 1901 improved Carter steam carriage at the center of this lineup. The machine on the right is a 1900 Carter steam carriage with a Stanhope-style body, and the auto at the far left is also a 1900 Carter machine (fitted with a body far simpler than those installed on Carter's steam Stanhope models, and nearly identical to the body installed on Fred T. Lockwood's steam carriage seen in fig. 98). This photograph may have been taken during one of Carter's demonstrations to investors who were potentially interested in acquiring and expanding Carter's steam-automobile manufacturing company. It may also be an image captured just before B. J. Carter, Floyd Mitchell, Professor L. A. Harraden, and L. B. Cowley departed for the Pan-American Exposition in August or early September 1901 (however, that seems unlikely, as the bearded Professor Harraden does not appear anywhere in this photograph). *Courtesy of Sallie Sparks Kendall*

Jackson already had an established connection across the nation for distributing B. J. Carter's steam carriages with the nine rail trunk lines that converged in the City of Jackson.[442]

In a slightly melodramatic conclusion, the April 26, 1902 *Jackson Daily Citizen* article read: "It seems a pity that Jackson should let such a project go without putting up a hand to save it to the town. There is no doubt that this is a big business future in the manufacture of the popular automobile, and that Jackson which has presented the world with a new and improved model, should lose the results of the efforts of one of her citizens who has become discouraged with the outlook here for promoting his plans."[443]

It seems very likely that the cagey Carter may have written or directed much of this article, and one gets the impression that he may have been artfully bluffing and truly wanted his enterprise to remain in Jackson, where he and his father had conducted businesses for over 17 years, and where B. J. Carter had started a family.

After detailed searches of the 1900, 1901, and 1902 Grand Rapids newspapers and city directories, the author could find nothing that proved Carter steam carriages were ever actually manufactured by the Michigan Automobile Company, Clipper Auto Car Company, or any other Grand Rapids business entity, either under the name "Carter," "Clipper," or "Michigan." As further evidence that a Grand Rapids venture to build Carter's steam carriages never materialized, the May 8, 1902 issue of *The Motor World* had it that B. J. Carter's manufacturing plant for improved Carter steam engines and Carter steam carriages was then still located in Jackson, and the Jackson Automobile Company would be established a little over two months later, which precluded a Grand Rapids relocation.[444]

The Michigan Automobile Company name did, however, resurface in Grand Rapids in early 1902, when W. Smalley Daniels, who had been interested in manufacturing B. J. Carter's steam Stanhopes in 1900, sold his share in the substantial sporting goods and bicycle enterprise, Jarvis & Daniels, and formed another company.[445] The resulting Michigan Automobile Company entity owned by Daniels commenced offering other manufacturers' autos as a sales agent (car dealer) on April 1, 1902; however, Daniels' new firm was

described as an "automobile repository" and apparently possessed no car manufacturing facilities.[446] In a somewhat ironic turn, Daniels' Michigan Automobile Company advertised for sale a Carter improved three-cylinder steam carriage with a folding front seat in February 1903.[447] The ad indicated that the machine was "almost new," was equipped with a "Carter ratchet lubricator" (fig. 109), and had originally cost $1,500.[448] It is unknown whether W. S. Daniels played a role in the second push (in April 1902) from Grand Rapids investors, who had plans to establish the Clipper Auto Car Company to manufacture Carter's improved three-cylinder steam carriages. If so, perhaps the Carter steam machine he was selling had been acquired as a demonstrator vehicle to evaluate the merits of Carter's improved steam carriage.

While no Carter steam-car production or other business records have been found, it is apparent from surviving photographs and 1900–1902 newspaper and magazine accounts and ads that B. J. Carter was not only seeking investors during this time—he was simultaneously manufacturing and selling his improved steam carriages in very small quantities, and he was offering his patent-pending improved three-cylinder steam engines for sale separately. In certain June and July 1902 issues of *The Horseless Age*, Carter advertised "The simplest and best inclosed [sic] AUTO STEAM MOTOR on the market. No stuffing boxes or packing. $100.00."[449] These same ads also offered Carter's Automatic Cylinder Lubricator, another invention and revenue source Carter had introduced in 1901; Carter also advertised his Automatic Cylinder Lubricator in *The Automobile and Motor Review* starting in June 1902 and continuing into October 1902, three months after the Jackson Automobile Company commenced its business.[450] In addition, the Carter bicycle business and machine shop would have provided essential income. However, in light of B. J. Carter's tenacious, but unsuccessful, two-year search for financiers in Jackson or elsewhere to invest in his expansive steam-carriage manufacturing ambitions, it is very easy to understand how frustrated and discouraged Carter would have been at this point.

Things were about to improve for B. J. Carter in 1902, which undoubtedly turned into an exciting year for him. After his long slog to obtain investors, Carter would finally secure reliable financing for a large-scale automobile-manufacturing operation in the City of Jackson.

The Jackson Automobile Company

In mid-1902, B. J. Carter finally succeeded in launching his automobile enterprise in a substantial way. Two prominent Jackson industry leaders, George Adelman Matthews and Charles Lewis, were convinced that Carter's inventions and aspirations could form the basis for a successful horseless carriage venture, and they stepped forward to fund his automotive manufacturing operations. This new industry would be called the Jackson Automobile Company, which was incorporated on July 19, 1902, with its new articles of association recorded on July 23, 1902.[451] According to the Jackson Automobile Company's articles of association, its purpose was "to manufacture, buy and sell mobiles and automobiles of every kind of propelling power and vehicles of all kinds; also to manufacture, sell and buy any and all parts of mobiles, automobiles and vehicles."[452] The new enterprise was capitalized at a relatively modest $24,000, with 2,400 shares of common stock at a par value of $10 per share split evenly among the three founders (800 shares each).[453] These 2,400 shares of capital stock represented the entire stock issuance for the new corporation and, accordingly, there were no additional shares of stock available for other investors to purchase.[454] It was reported in the *Jackson Daily Citizen*, "There is no stock for sale. These three well known manufacturers are the whole thing, so far as stock is concerned, and in other respects their names stand as a synonym for enterprise and business success in whatsoever they may undertake."[455] The July 24, 1902 *Jackson Daily Citizen* predicted, "In the face of this, it is easy to assume that this company has a great future, and it means that more than ever Jackson will be brought to the front of the inventive world, and spread still further her reputation as a manufacturing city."[456] A soon-to-be-major automotive industry had now been created in the City of Jackson, and the 1903 *Jackson City Directory* listed the Jackson Automobile Company as the city's sole motorcar manufacturer.[457]

Fig. 112. Byron J. Carter, circa 1905. *Author's collection*

Fig. 113. George A. Matthews in 1895.
Author's collection

Fig. 114. George A. Matthews in 1904.
Courtesy of Kenneth F. Soderbeck

Fig. 115. George A. Matthews, circa 1912.
Courtesy of the Ella Sharp Museum

Fig. 116. An 1895 engraving of the factory of the Fuller Buggy Company, which was owned by George A. Matthews; as was often the case, these early engravings exaggerated the building's size (the actual Fuller Buggy Company plant had only two floors, not three). This now demolished building was located on the north side of East Main Street at what was then Ann Street (the City of Jackson's eastern city limits). Incidentally, the second Jackson Automobile Company factory, purchased on November 30, 1907, was located opposite the Fuller Buggy Company plant on East Main Street. *Author's collection*

Fig. 117. Charles Lewis in 1895.
Author's collection

Fig. 118. Charles Lewis, circa 1902.
Courtesy of the Ella Sharp Museum

Fig. 119. Charles Lewis, circa 1910.
Author's collection

Fig. 120. Charles Lewis owned the Lewis Spring and Axle Co., located on Leroy Street between North Horton Street and the Michigan Central Railroad tracks. The Lewis Spring and Axle Co. was Jackson's largest employer by 1910, when this engraving was made. In addition to its main buildings on Leroy Street, Lewis Spring and Axle also occupied the original Jackson Automobile Company factory at Park Avenue and Park Place shown on the left side of this image. By 1912, the firm controlled 320,000 square feet in Jackson plus a Detroit facility. *Courtesy of Gregory R. Loftness*

Charles Lewis (April 10, 1853–February 24, 1912), whose Lewis Spring and Axle Co. was incorporated on September 24, 1897, and for a time was Jackson's largest employer, was appointed as the Jackson Automobile Company's president.[458] George A. Matthews (November 23, 1852–May 13, 1914), who owned the substantial Fuller Buggy Company, incorporated on August 1, 1889, served as secretary and treasurer for the new Jackson Automobile Company.[459] Both were Jackson businessmen with impeccable reputations and substantial investment capital, who served as board directors for prominent Jackson banks.[460] The *Jackson Daily Citizen*, in its article announcing the Jackson Automobile Company's formation, described Matthews and Lewis as "well known in businesses which are already no small factor in the industries of Jackson."[461] More comprehensive biographies of Messrs. Matthews and Lewis are contained in Appendix B.

George A. Matthews and Charles Lewis each appear to have contributed at least $8,000 in cash to launch this new venture; B. J. Carter's investment was most likely not in cash but rather would have been the value of his then pending patent for the improved three-cylinder steam engine, his established automotive engineering and manufacturing talents and experience, and the business goodwill he had created with his inventions, steam carriages, and engine manufacturing efforts. Somewhat unusually, however, the Jackson Automobile Company's 1902 annual report did not list or attribute any value to Carter's patents, business goodwill, or patterns, drawings, and formulas; instead this annual report simply listed personal property, without further detail, valued at $2,000.[462] This year-end 1902 asset valuation may have reflected the fact that B. J. Carter's improved steam engine patent, filed January 18, 1902, had not yet been formally issued by the U.S. Patent and Trademark Office (the patent was not officially granted until March 10, 1903).[463]

Carter, now 38 years old, was named first vice president and manager for the Jackson Automobile Company.[464] The July 24, 1902 *Jackson Daily Citizen* labeled Carter as "the well known automobile maker, on Cortland street" and enthusiastically praised him: "So far as Byron J. Carter is concerned, when it comes to automobiles or vehicles of that kind it is well known that for years past he has been an unremitting student, inventor and expert machinist of the first class. To him, of course, will belong the mechanical part of this business to a very large

degree. For years past he has had unwavering faith in the auto as a modern vehicle for business and pleasure, and that faith leads him to the belief that in Jackson there is a splendid opening for one of the largest industries it has ever had. It will mean the bringing into the city of mechanical experts who must be to the forefront in this modern invention, and such men as these are always welcome in a community and materially add to the strength and stability of any manufacturing city. Mr. Carter is no idle dreamer, but he is sanguine that he has a machine which is now one of the best in the land, because for years he has been seeking to perfect such a vehicle."[465]

After the Jackson Automobile Company's articles of association had been filed on July 19, 1902, preparations for motorcar manufacturing were soon under way and the August 15, 1902 issue of *The Automobile Review and Automobile News* reported, "a building suitable for the purpose will be secured at once and preparations have been made to manufacture automobiles designed and heretofore built by B. J. Carter."[466] The August 23, 1902 *Jackson Daily Citizen* informed that "the Jackson Automobile Co. Friday morning [August 22, 1902] obtained the deed to the Heyser sash-door factory" complex with a main structure "66 feet wide, 300 feet long, and comprised of a large basement and two upper floors" on Park Place and Park (now Hupp) Avenue.[467] This group of buildings had formerly been occupied by S. Heyser & Sons, a wood sash, door, and window-blind milling business and lumberyard established in 1870, which had purchased the property in the northeast corner of Park Avenue and Park Place in May 1884.[468] The Heyser mill, as it was known, was not prime property, as it had been heavily damaged by fire on September 23, 1899, was then rebuilt, and was once again destroyed by fire only one year later, on October 11, 1900, when "the main building burned completely, about all that remains being the walls, and the offices at the west end" "of the once fine structure."[469] Apparently, the second fire was more than Silas Heyser, the 73-year-old lumber mill owner, could endure and he died of heart failure on December 31, 1900; his plant was not rebuilt until it was taken over by the Jackson Automobile Company one and a half years later.[470]

In his September 14, 1919 *Jackson Citizen Patriot* reminiscence about the Jackson Automobile Company's start, Fred T. Lockwood provided the following uncharitable assessment of the Heyser buildings that

Fig. 121. An 1895 engraving of the S. Heyser & Sons wood-sash, door, and window-blind milling business and lumberyard, at Park (now Hupp) Avenue and Park Place; the Heyser mill, as it was known, was not a very attractive property when the Jackson Automobile Company acquired it in August 1902. The main buildings had been heavily damaged by fire in October 1900, and most of the roof had caved in. It was only after much reconstruction that this complex could serve as the first Jackson Automobile Company manufacturing plant starting in late 1902. The Trask-Field Gas Engine Co. commenced business in one of the Jackson Automobile Company's ancillary buildings in January 1903. *Author's collection*

the new auto enterprise had purchased: "The Heyser factory had been occupied by a sash, door, and blind business. Some time previously it had all but been destroyed by fire, but part of the roof, in the rear of the building, was capable of shedding rain, and this was partitioned off from the burned portion with rough lumber, and here Mr. Carter and a few men went to work."[471] A September 20, 1902 *Jackson Daily Citizen* article was consistent with Lockwood's later account: "The work on the building of the new automobile company is progressing nicely. It was formerly the plant of the Heyser mills, which all but the walls and office was destroyed by fire about two years ago. It has required a considerable amount of work to clean out the debris that had fallen inside the walls. A number of bricklayers have been at work on the structure, and placed the walls in excellent shape. The window frames are in and carpenters are now at work constructing the frame for the roof."[472] In addition to general structural restoration, the *Jackson Daily Citizen* reported that "some big changes are being made in the interior of the building, preparatory to the placing in there of a large amount of machinery."[473]

Even before Jackson Automobile assumed occupancy of their future factory, the enthusiastic founders had begun purchasing and taking deliveries of automobile-manufacturing equipment and machinery. The July 28, 1902 *Jackson Daily Citizen* reported, "Byron J. Carter and Charles Lewis of the Jackson Automobile company, are today in Chicago, buying machinery for the new plant."[474] Two days later, the *Jackson Daily Citizen* reported that "Byron Carter and Charles Lewis are back from Chicago, where they have been buying machinery for the Jackson Automobile company. They have purchased a quantity of the kind, which will be at once put into operation, and there is need of them. Mr. Carter is just finishing a new auto, and informs The Citizen that he has a demand which has made it necessary for him to put on a number of new hands, which are all as busy as they can be. The prospect for a big business in automobiles is growing every day, and it is only a question of supply at present. The machinery which is to be shipped here will, part of it, be put into the factory on Cortland street, and as soon as the deeds for their new factory are made and signed, they will at once enter into possession and then a further increase will be made in the number of employes [*sic*]."[475]

Apparently, the Jackson Automobile Company founders were permitted to start fit-out work in the Heyser property even before the deed was signed in late August, as an August 12, 1902 *Jackson Daily Citizen* piece reported, "A number of machines to be used by the Jackson Automobile Co. was taken to their future plant yesterday . . . it is expected that in a few days negotiating will end in a deed of the place being made over to the mobile company."[476] And it appears that some initial construction work may have already started as well: the August 23, 1902 *Jackson Daily Citizen*, which announced that the deed had finally been signed, also reported, "There are already 20 men at work in the new plant, and it is likely that the present Byron Carter bicycle shop will be taken there."[477] Among these new employees was John H. Carpenter, an accomplished machinist who had worked for the Carters from 1893 through 1896. It was reported on August 1, 1902 that "J. H. Carpenter, of Chicago, with his family, has removed to Jackson. Mr. Carpenter has taken a [toolmaker] position with the Jackson Automobile Co."[478] Other Carter employees who joined the new Jackson Automobile Company venture were Arthur L. Butcher, as foreman, Genevieve A. Mitchell, as bookkeeper, and William H. Diehl as a machinist.[479]

Fig. 122. Engraving of the factory and other associated manufacturing buildings from the 1907 Jackson Automobile Company sales catalog; pictured are the main assembling facilities at Park Avenue and Park Place, two Lewis Spring and Axle Co. buildings along the top, and in the lower left, the then new E. C. Clark Motor Company plant on Leroy Street. E. C. Clark was established by George A. Matthews, Charles Lewis, and motor designer Ernest Chauncey Clark in August 1905 to build two-cylinder Jackson engines. By 1908, E. C. Clark would engineer and manufacture Jackson's advanced-design four-cylinder motors with overhead camshafts and valves. *Author's collection*

By mid-September 1902, B. J. Carter's original manufacturing operations and equipment at 204 West Cortland Street had been entirely relocated to the new Jackson Automobile Company plant on Park Avenue.[480] Lockwood Brothers, the business owned by the Carters' former employee Fred T. Lockwood and his brother, Arthur L. Lockwood, promptly leased and took possession of Carter's vacated 204 West Cortland Street building, as reported in the September 20, 1902 *Jackson Daily Citizen*, and in turn closed Lockwood Brothers' smaller leased facility at 131 East Cortland Street.[481] The newspaper wrote that "increasing business made it necessary for Lockwood Bros. to remove . . . to the store recently occupied by B. J. Carter, 204 West Cortland street. They have added largely to their line of electrical [and telephone] supplies, besides increasing facilities for machine work, bicycle repairing, etc. They also sell the [one-cylinder, curved-dash] Oldsmobile, a gasoline 'buggy' that is gaining in popularity every day, on account of its practical utility and lowness in price."[482] It was also written in 1902 that Lockwood Brothers "make a business of building engines for steamboats and have several orders ahead at present."[483] Even though Fred Lockwood was an Oldsmobile sales agent at this time, and presumably might have driven an Oldsmobile, the *Jackson Daily Citizen* on August 19, 1903 reported, "Fred Lockwood and wife came from Detroit Monday [August 17, 1903] in a new Ford automobile in five hours and fifteen minutes. The distance by road is about 80 miles."[484]

Fig. 123. A view of the former Jackson Automobile Company factory, circa 1913, when it was occupied by the Standard Electric Car Company; this enterprise manufactured the Standard Electrique enclosed coupé automobile, which traveled along nearly silently under battery power. *Courtesy of the Ella Sharp Museum*

Fig. 124. The main floor of the second-largest building in the Jackson Automobile Company factory complex, at Park Avenue and Park Place, circa 1917, when the facility was occupied by The Hackett Motor Car Co. (successor to the Argo Motor Company, Inc.); this structure is all that remains today of the original Jackson Automobile Company factory buildings. *Author's collection*

Fig. 125. B. J. Carter's automobile facility at 204 West Cortland Street, around the time Carter moved his manufacturing operations to the new Jackson Automobile Company factory and leased this building to Lockwood Brothers in September 1902; a late 1901 or early 1902 Oldsmobile (left) and a 1902 Winton car (right) are parked in front of Carter's shop. The "S. B. Carter Bicycles" sign from 1896 had been repainted to read "B. J. Carter Automobiles." *Author's Lockwood negative collection*

Fig. 126. A Lockwood Brothers advertisement for secondhand automobiles from the June 25, 1904 *Jackson Daily Citizen*, which shows the 204 West Cortland Street address; this was likely one of the last advertisements Lockwood Brothers ran at this address, as the Lockwood business soon relocated nearby to 210–212 West Cortland Street so that B. J. Carter could move back into the building after resigning from the Jackson Automobile Company. *Courtesy of the Jackson District Library*

It is no wonder that the *Jackson Daily Citizen* concluded that B. J. Carter, as manager and superintendent of this complicated Jackson factory setup effort, "has his hands full at the present time."[485] Carter's burden during these months was made much heavier when calamity struck his family: B. J. and Della Carter's second daughter, Barbara J. Carter, who had been born on May 6, 1901, died on October 16, 1902, at the age of 17 months, 10 days.[486]

In early December 1902, a reporter from the *Jackson Daily Citizen* paid a visit to the new Jackson Automobile Company factory and submitted the following: "Inquiry at the office of the Jackson Automobile Co. today shows that they are now in full swing at their new plant. The old Heyser building contains some valuable machinery, erected by B. J. Carter, superintendent and manager. There are 30 men at work fully, and while they are not actually soliciting orders, they are as busy as a hive of bees. Preparations are being made for an immense trade next year, and Jackson ere long will be known as an automobile center."[487]

The new Jackson Automobile Company also appears to have affiliated itself with Charles A. Trask, B. J. Carter's longtime business associate and competitor. The December 19, 1902 issue of the *Jackson Daily Citizen* reported, "Charles A. Trask, who has been operating a machine shop on [136–138 West] Pearl street for nearly 13 years, has formed a co-partnership with Rayner Field, the new company to be known as the Trask-Field Gas Engine Co. They will build gas and gasoline engines exclusively, from patterns and improvements that Mr. Trask has been working on for the past five or six years. They will move into their new quarters, one of the buildings owned by the Jackson Auto Co., on Park avenue about Jan. 15th [1903] and will employ a good force in the manufacture of fine engines, which they will place on the market."[488]

The new address for The Trask-Field Gas Engine Co. was 367–371 South Park Avenue.[489] It is uncertain how much motor-manufacturing contract work The Trask-Field Gas Engine Co. actually completed for the Jackson Automobile Company; however, in a March 4, 1903 *Jackson Daily Citizen* interview, B. J. Carter provided a clue, "Not only are we using our own force of men in turning out machines at our own factory, but we are compelled to place orders for parts of the machines with foundries and machine shops in the city. One firm of well known machinists now have an order for 100 engines and that will keep them busy."[490]

The Jackson Automobile Company certainly did not keep The Trask-Field Gas Engine Co. busy on a full-time basis, as the March 7, 1903, June 11, 1903, July 9, 1903, and September 4, 1903 *Jackson Daily Citizen* newspapers mentioned the completion of three Trask-Field projects to build large gasoline-engine-powered yachts for Jackson

Fig. 127. Fred T. Lockwood, motoring in a late 1901 or early 1902 curved-dash Oldsmobile (1901-style no-truss front axle with 1902-style staggered-spoke wheels) along Wildwood Avenue in front of the Ames-Dean Carriage Co. factory, near Wildwood's intersection with North Wisner Street; Lockwood Brothers held an Oldsmobile sales agency at this time. The Ames-Dean Carriage Co. facility was located on the north side of Wildwood Avenue, a little over a block west of Fred T. Lockwood's residence. *Author's Lockwood negative collection*

Fig. 128. With the Ames-Dean Carriage Co. plant in the background, Fred T. Lockwood is shown driving a 1902 15-horsepower two-cylinder Winton, which, when new, would have cost a princely $2,000. Lockwood's front-seat passenger in the derby hat is William Sparks, the future father-in-law of B. J. and Della Carter's daughter, Rachel L. Carter, who married Sparks' son Clifford M. Sparks on May 12, 1920. This *two*-cylinder Winton motor carriage is most likely not the same machine that was owned by Professor L. A. Harraden, who stated in a 1941 newspaper interview that he had once owned a *one*-cylinder Winton. *Author's Lockwood negative collection*

citizens, including one for Trask himself, during 1903.[491] In the September 1903 issue it reported that "the business is quiet just now, but he [Trask] keeps the shop going right along, and next season may develop a boat-building industry of some magnitude in Jackson."[492] Business at The Trask-Field Gas Engine Co. must have improved by January 1904, when Leonard H. Field, prominent Jackson department store owner (and father of Trask's partner, Rayner Field), acquired the Albion Engine and Motor Co. and announced that the Albion business operations would be moved to Jackson and combined with The Trask-Field Gas Engine Co.[493] Charles Lewis "also aided in securing the Albion Engine Co. to locate here [Jackson], which gives 50 men employment."[494] Sometime that year, Trask either resigned from The Trask-Field Gas Engine Co. or was bought out by the Fields. (Trask is not even listed in the 1905 *Jackson City Directory*, as he had relocated to Ypsilanti in 1904, where he set up shop as a machinist.)[495]

JAXON
GAS AND GASOLINE
ENGINES
BUILT BY
The Trask Field Gas Engine Co.,
367-371 S. Park Ave., JACKSON, MICH.

STATIONARY AND MARINE,
AN ENGINE WITH A MARK
OF EXCELLENCE.

Fig. 129. A 1903 advertisement for The Trask-Field Gas Engine Co., which was located at 367–371 South Park Avenue (in a building leased from the Jackson Automobile Company); The Trask-Field Gas Engine Co. had commenced business in this location in early 1903. Given this timing and its location within the Jackson Automobile Company factory complex, it seems likely Trask-Field manufactured the engines B. J. Carter had designed for the new Jaxon Steam Surreys and one-cylinder gasoline Jaxon Light Touring Cars. *Author's collection, courtesy of Ronald G. Bean*

After L. H. Field's Albion Engine and Motor Co. acquisition, The Trask-Field Gas Engine Co. was reorganized, first as the Jackson Engine and Motor Co., and then incorporated January 26, 1906, as The Field-Brundage Co., with Rayner Field as its secretary and treasurer, and former Albion stockholder William D. Brundage as vice president; Charles A. Trask's name was not among the list of officers for either of these new gasoline-engine manufacturing companies.[496] The 1905 *Jackson City Directory* indicated the Jackson Engine and Motor Co. and The Field-Brundage Co. operations had by then been moved out of the Jackson Automobile Company factory complex and relocated to 104–116 Belden Avenue.[497]

Likely as another parts supplier to the Jackson Automobile Company, Squire B. Carter took a break from full-time farming in 1903 and became a businessman again, as the proprietor of a gasket company.[498] His enterprise was called the Jackson Gasket Co., a manufacturer "of Fine Cloth-Covered Gaskets," and was located at 140 West Pearl Street.[499] This gasket company was a short-lived venture for Squire, as he was once again listed as a farmer in the 1905 *Jackson City Directory*.[500] Squire B. Carter's departure from manufacturing automobile parts probably coincided with his B.J.'s resignation from the Jackson Automobile Company in May 1904.

The Jackson Automobile Company's annual report for calendar year-end 1902 was filed with the Michigan Secretary of State on April 17, 1903. This annual report is unremarkable and light on detail; it indicated that the original $24,000 capitalization was still intact, that personal property, most likely equipment, was valued at $2,000, and that the company was carrying $3,000 of debt.[501] Unfortunately, for research today, only a balance sheet was included, and no revenue and expense information was shown in the annual report.

Fig. 130. This photograph of a well-equipped early 20th-century machine shop, at an unknown location, is part of the Lockwood negatives. Although it is conjecture, it may show The Trask-Field Gas Engine Co., which was located on the grounds of the Jackson Automobile Company starting in January 1903, as the proximity of buildings in the Jackson factory complex at Park Avenue and Park Place was similar to the proximity of buildings shown in this photograph. This image does not show Charles A. Trask's machine shop on West Pearl Street or any of Lockwood Brothers' operations on Cortland Street, as Pearl and Cortland streets are much wider than the passage in front of the machine shop shown here, and the window sizes and installations are inconsistent with those facilities. *Author's Lockwood negative collection*

In the Midst of Launching the Jackson Automobile Company, Carter Opines on the Bicycle's Future

A new sentiment had begun to surface in 1902 regarding bicycles. With all of the new motorized innovations, some felt that the days of the bicycle's popularity were numbered and "that the bicycle has reached the zenith of its popularity and will soon be a thing of the past."[502] Even though B. J. Carter had just launched a promising automobile enterprise in July 1902 and had stopped newspaper advertising for his bicycle store by the end of March 1902, he was still an enthusiastic fan of the bicycle business, with which he had long been associated.[503] An August 12, 1902 *Jackson Daily Citizen* article printed this quote from B. J. Carter (less than one month after the Jackson Automobile Company had been established): "Some few years ago the wheel was a fad, and to some extent it was a costly fad, or craze. Every year in even standard wheels of great note, there would be some important change in its belongings, some addition to its parts or supposed improvements. These all had a tendency to make the wheels more perfect, but the fad was a costly one, because the man or woman who was a cyclist, wanted the latest and best. This increased the number of wheels in a very marked manner, and it led to new styles and big sales. Now, the wheel is nearly perfect and there is not the changing of styles there was some three years ago, but so far as the sale of wheels goes it has reached a more normal and steady condition, and there are lots of wheels being bought yet. Again, the wheel is not so much a craze or fad, as it is a business commodity and almost necessity."[504]

B. J. Carter was asked to reinforce the notion that the bicycle business was not dead. "No," Carter said. "It is in a prosperous condition, and was never more in a normal state as an article of modern locomotion . . . as a means of locomotion the wheel or bicycle will yet remain for many years. The only thing which could supplant it would be something with a motor attachment, and that may come yet, so that it will be within the reach of ordinary people, and could be manufactured or operated by the unskilled."[505]

Carter's words were prophetic: (1) safety bicycle design had largely been standardized by the late 1890s and bikes are manufactured in very similar form today, and remain popular across the globe, and (2) successful and economical motorcycles were developed and marketed prior to 1910.

Jaxon Steam Surrey Production is Finally Under Way

At the beginning of 1903, the Jackson Automobile Company was off and running and had commenced dedicated production of a revised version of B. J. Carter's improved three-cylinder steam carriage first introduced in August 1901, now with subtle but distinct modifications to the Carter steam carriage's coachwork and with wood-spoke wheels versus the Carter carriage's wire wheels (although some very early Jackson steam cars still retained these wire wheels as standard equipment). The Jackson steam carriage was branded as the Jaxon Steam Surrey. Even though the Jaxon cars were announced in mid-1902, they were all considered to be and were labeled as 1903 models.[506] Like most car manufacturers do today, the Jackson Automobile Company offered "next year's" models starting early in the fall or late summer of the previous year. This practice continued throughout the Jackson Automobile Company's 20 years of production.

The exact date when the first Jaxon Steam Surrey was built and demonstrated is uncertain; however, a January 1, 1905 *Cycle and Automobile Trade Journal* article that recounted the history of the Jackson Automobile Company reported that a Jaxon Steam Surrey had been manufactured and "was on the road in late 1902."[507] A December 15, 1902 article in *The Automobile Review and Automobile News* reported, "The Jackson Automobile Company, Jackson, Mich., will have sample machines ready for the Chicago [automobile] show [February 16–24, 1903] if not before. Their large factory is now in full operation and the output will soon be a large and important factor in the trade."[508] The January 31, 1903 issue of *The Automobile* provided a little more detail: "The Jackson Automobile Co., of Jackson, Mich., has given the trade name Jaxon to the new cars, both steam and gasoline, which it is now building; the former being ready for delivery and the latter to follow in a couple of weeks."[509] Elsewhere in this same issue of *The Automobile*, under "Various Trade Items of Interest," the magazine wrote, "The Jackson Automobile Co., of Jackson, Mich., is building steam vehicles, which are ready for delivery now, and gasoline cars that will be ready about February 15."[510] As it turned out, this projected date for actual production of Jaxon gasoline machines was overly optimistic; it looks as if Jaxon gasoline models were not produced in any quantity until the summer of 1903.

Fig. 131. Jaxon trade name logo used by the Jackson Automobile Company during its first two years of motorcar production. *Author's collection*

An article in the March 5, 1903 issue of *The Iron Trade Review* provided some specific information regarding Jaxon Steam Surrey production quantities: "The Reliance Gauge Column Co. has recently placed on the market the Reliance low water alarm for steam carriages and is meeting with the most flattering success in this department. A number of manufacturers of steam carriages have adopted this new alarm as a part of their standard equipment, the company's last order being from the Jackson Automobile Co., Jackson, Mich., for 50 columns to equip the same number of steam carriages which that company is running through in one lot."[511]

The Jaxon Steam Surrey was offered in two models known as "A" and "B." The most obvious difference between the two models was the inclusion of the extra folding front seat on Model "A," and its omission on Model "B," which instead had a main passenger seat that was several inches wider than the main seat of the Model "A" for a bit more seating capacity.[512] A 10-gallon gasoline tank and the "repair kit" were located within the dash compartment.[513] Both machines were powered by Carter's patent-pending (until the patent was granted March 10, 1903) six-horsepower, three-cylinder (bore and stroke of 2 1/2 x 3 1/2 inches) rotary-valve steam engine with automatic lubrication and a Reliance low-water alarm.[514] A Studebaker-Burnell Company burner heated the boiler in both models; it was reported to be "of simple and

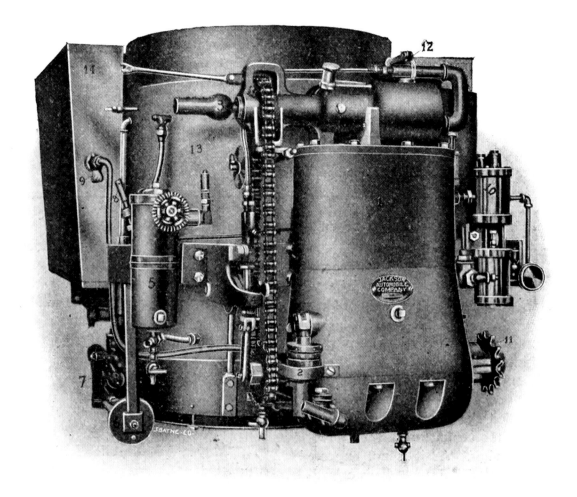

MACHINERY EQUIPMENT OF THE JAXON STEAM AUTOMOBILE.

1—Inclosed Steam Motor, all parts working in oil. 2—Boiler Feed Pump. 3—Reverse Connection. 4—Automatic Cylinder Lubricator which pumps cylinder oil from a two quart reservoir to valve and pistons automatically and requires no attention except to fill reservoir when required, feed is adjustable. 5—Low Water Alarm and Water Column. 6—Automatic Fire Regulator. 7—Generator and Pilot Light. 8—Valve operated from end of seat to steam air pump. 9—Valve operated from end of seat regulating water to boiler. 10—Steam Air Pump. 11—Drive Sprocket fitted to taper shaft and very easily changed to a larger size for high speed or a smaller size for a very mountainous section. 12—Self Closing Throttle. 13—Large Steam Generator lagged with asbestos and covered with zinc. 14—Water Tank 30 gallons capacity fitted with a tank filler and ten feet of suction hose.

Fig. 132. An engraving of B. J. Carter's patented six-horsepower three-cylinder rotary-valve steam engine components, which powered the 1903 Jaxon Steam Surrey; the boiler, pumps, water and oil storage tanks, and automatic oilers are visible on the sides of and behind the engine. *Author's collection*

Fig. 133. A photograph of the Jaxon six-horsepower three-cylinder steam engine from the January 1, 1903 issue of *The Motor World*; the block chain, which traveled vertically along the left side of the engine, drove the overhead rotary steam valve mechanism. Sometime during Jaxon Steam Surrey production, this block-chain arrangement was replaced by a more precise tower-shaft apparatus with bevel-gear drives at each end of the shaft, which alleviated the need for sporadic chain tightening to compensate for chain wear and stretching. *Courtesy of Gregory R. Loftness*

Fig. 134. The Jaxon steam engine disassembled to illustrate its pistons, crankshaft, and overhead valve assembly. *Courtesy of Gregory R. Loftness*

Fig. 135. *The Jacksonian*, a periodical for Jackson auto dealers, issued in May 1920 by the Jackson Motors Corporation, featured this photograph of a Jaxon Steam Surrey Model "A" (this early Jaxon model still retained the wire wheels that had been standard equipment on B. J. Carter's earlier steam carriages). *The Jacksonian* indicated that this Jaxon steamer still ran in 1920 and demonstrated the durability of Jackson cars. *Author's collection*

Fig. 136. Engraving of the Jaxon Steam Surrey Model "A," with the front auxiliary folding passenger seat in the closed position; the Model "A" was initially priced at $975, had a 72-inch wheelbase, 30-inch wood-spoke wheels, and a 19-inch-diameter fire-tube boiler with a Reliance low-water alarm. *Author's collection*

Fig. 137. Engraving of the Jaxon Steam Surrey Model "A," with the precarious folding front passenger seat in the open position, which provided additional seating capacity. *Author's collection*

Fig. 138. The only known surviving Jaxon Steam Surrey, a Model "A," owned by Lloyd and Judi Ganton as part of the Gantons' Ye Ole Carriage Shop museum in Spring Arbor, Michigan; Lloyd Ganton has dedicated considerable energy and resources to assembling an impressive automobile collection, which includes representative examples of nearly every motorcar manufactured in Jackson (there have been over 20 auto builders in Jackson since 1899). *Courtesy of Lloyd and Judi Ganton*

Fig. 139. Engraving of the Jaxon Steam Surrey Model "B," which had only one main passenger seat and no auxiliary folding front seat; the single seat on the Model "B" was several inches wider than the main seat of the Model "A" to accommodate three passengers, which necessitated the addition of chamfered wood blocks glued on the sides of the Jaxon Model "B" body to support the wider seat. The Model "B" used the same three-cylinder steam engine as was installed in the Model "A," but it had a shorter wheelbase at 65 inches, smaller 29-inch wood-spoke wheels, and a lower-capacity 17-inch-diameter fire-tube boiler with a Reliance low-water alarm. The Jaxon Steam Surrey Model "B" was priced at $800. *Author's collection*

scientific construction and can be started quickly. The fire may be automatically regulated."[515] Water capacity was 35 gallons.[516] Models "A" and "B" were apparently painted black with brown trimmings and moldings.[517] The side body moldings on both Jaxon Steam Surrey models formed a J motif, a carryover from Carter's steam carriages.

Original illustrations of the 1903 Jaxon Steam Surrey show wooden-spoke artillery wheels to replace the wire wheels installed on B. J. Carter's improved steam carriage of 1901; it appears, however, that some of the very first Jaxon steamers were still equipped with wire wheels. The Model "A" was initially priced at $975, had a 72-inch wheelbase, 30 x 3-inch Dunlop tires, and a 19-inch-diameter fire-tube boiler containing 525 copper tubes.[518] The smaller Model "B" was priced at $800, had a 65-inch wheelbase, 29 x 2 1/2-inch tires, and a 17-inch-diameter fire-tube boiler containing 440 copper tubes.[519]

The February 3, 1903 issue of the *Jackson Daily Citizen* reported that "The Jackson Automobile Co. are in it for keeps. According to an interview today with The Citizen they are arranging for an exhibition of their machines at Detroit from the 7th to the 14th, and on the 14th to 21st they will show at Chicago. At the first place they will have three of their machines and at the latter they will send a car load. It is their intention to have representatives at both places. They have a full force of men at work and are preparing for a big season's business."[520]

Likewise, *The Automobile* of February 21, 1903, in describing the Detroit and Chicago automobile shows, reported, "Two Jaxon steam carriages are displayed in the [Detroit Light Guard Armory] basement by the Jackson Automobile Co., of Jackson, Mich. They have never been shown before. The makers have also just completed a water-cooled and an air-cooled gasoline car that have been shipped to Chicago for the exhibition at the Coliseum show. No Jaxon gasoline cars are being shown" in Detroit.[521] A reporter from *The Motor World* attended the Detroit automobile show and noted that the Jackson Automobile Company exhibited "the Jaxon steamer, a clever machine, reflecting a great deal of credit on B. J. Carter, its designer, who is in attendance."[522]

The February 9–14, 1903 Detroit Tri-State Automobile and Sportsmen's Show at the Light Guard Armory was an elaborate and somewhat peculiar event, and unlike any car show of today.

Promotional pieces written in the *Detroit Free Press* stressed that there would be exhibits of motorcars, nearly 250 dogs in a "bench show," and sporting goods including firearms, ammunition, and trap and target shooting events inside the building, as well as canoes, launches, marine engines, and a taxidermy display of skins, heads, stuffed specimens, and "relics of the hunt" worth over $30,000.[523] Thirty-two different automobile and motor-device manufacturers, including the Jackson Automobile Company, and dealers were represented at the show with over 100 styles of motorcars exhibited.[524] *The Motor World* somewhat condescendingly reported that the Detroit show "opened tonight [February 9, 1903] to the strains of the Metropolitan Orchestra and the baying of the dogs that comprise the Bench Show, which is included in the affair. The decorations, generally speaking, are tasteful, and with cars, dogs, guns, and the like in evidence it cannot be said that the show lacks variety or that there is not plenty to be seen."[525]

Not surprisingly, the large number of dogs and shooting competitions created clashes with the automobile exhibitors and event performers. William E. Metzger, a Detroit automobile pioneer and prominent salesman, was interviewed by the *Detroit Free Press* and said, "I have not heard a word of criticism regarding the exhibits or the show, except the bench show. The barking of dogs and the noise in the shooting gallery is wearing on the nerves of the men who must be here all day long. Next year the dogs will be placed in the basement, if we conclude to have a bench show in connection with the automobile and sportsman's exhibition."[526] This article also reported, "The vocal soloists appeared Monday night, but gave it up as a bad job yesterday because of the noise made by the dogs. The management went to considerable expense to obtain this feature for the entertainment of the patrons of the show, but it will be cut out during the remainder of the week."[527]

Chicago's February 14–21, 1903 Third Annual Automobile Exhibition at the Coliseum Building turned out to be a much tamer affair. The Jackson Automobile Company had only exhibited its Jaxon Steam Surreys at the Detroit show, but two new Jaxon gasoline models made their debut at the Chicago event along with a single Jaxon Steam Surrey.[528]

A Jaxon runabout with a one-cylinder gasoline engine, designed by B. J. Carter, had been announced by the end of 1902. (Jackson's first brochure [fig. 140] for this Jaxon model called the motor "our own special design," and several of Carter's many obituaries published a few short years later confirmed that Carter had indeed designed Jackson's "single-cylinder runabout which became very popular.")[529] The Jackson Automobile Company's first gasoline car brochure also touted the fact that "practically all parts of the 'Jaxon' are built in our own factory by our own skilled mechanics from our own special designs, which have taken years of experience to get to their present high state of perfection."[530] Despite this promising start, active manufacturing and successful placement of the one-cylinder Jaxon runabout on the market would prove to be quite challenging for the Jackson Automobile Company, and it would take several months to occur.

Likely based on an optimistic conversation with someone at the factory, the November 26, 1902 issue of *The Horseless Age* reported, "The Jackson Automobile Company, Jackson, Mich., are building a single cylinder gasoline carriage, which embodies a number of new features, including a new governor."[531] Perhaps the magazine was referring to a gasoline car prototype that the Jackson Automobile Company was constructing. The January 31, 1903 issue of *The Automobile* provided an update when it reported, "The Jackson Automobile Co., of Jackson, Mich., is building . . . gasoline cars that will be ready for delivery about February 15."[532] Likewise, *The Automobile* of February 21, 1903 reported that the Jackson Automobile Company had "just completed a water-cooled and an air-cooled gasoline car that have been shipped to Chicago for the exhibition at the Coliseum show" February 14–21, 1903.[533]

A prototype gasoline Jaxon one-cylinder runabout was first exhibited nationally at Chicago's Third Annual Automobile Exhibition, and, as evidenced by the figure 141 photograph, the machine could still not drive under its own power even if the motor had been operable (the rear-axle sprocket has no drive chain installed).[534] Even the fenders were missing. It must have been a real scramble to make this display model ready for the Chicago show. In fact, it appears that only one of these one-cylinder gasoline runabouts had been built, as another was not available for display one week earlier, on February 9, 1903, when the Detroit Tri-State Automobile and Sportsmen's Show opened; Jackson had only exhibited its Jaxon Steam Surrey models at the Detroit show.[535]

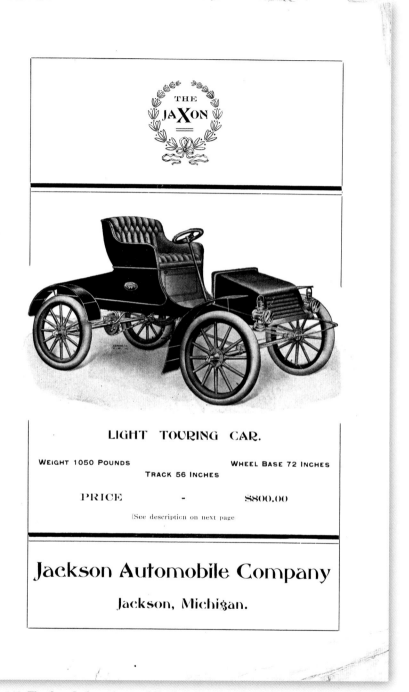

Fig. 140. The first Jackson Automobile Company gasoline-car sales brochure of 1903, which illustrated and described the two Jaxon gasoline-engine models offered with confusingly similar names: the water-cooled one-cylinder Jaxon *Light Touring Car* and the air-cooled two-cylinder Jaxon *Light Runabout. Author's collection*

Fig. 141. Photograph of the water-cooled seven-horsepower one-cylinder Jaxon gasoline car displayed at Chicago's February 14–21, 1903 Third Annual Automobile Exhibition; it was apparently a rush job to prepare this machine for the automobile show, as the Jackson factory assembly team did not even take (or have sufficient) time to install the drive chain (the car could not have been driven into the Chicago Coliseum under its own power). The engine on this model was designed by B. J. Carter and was mounted lengthwise amidships under the front seat to align its crankshaft, transmission, and chain-drive sprocket with the drive sprocket on the auto's rear axle. *Courtesy of Gregory R. Loftness*

This water-cooled one-cylinder Jaxon gasoline runabout, called the
Jaxon Light Touring Car in the first Jackson Automobile Company
gasoline-car brochure, available to prospective buyers at the Chicago
automobile exhibition, was priced at $800, and then by March 1, 1903,
the price was reduced to $750.[536] The machine was powered by a seven-
horsepower single-cylinder motor of Carter's design (by August 1,
1903, the same motor was rated at six horsepower), placed lengthwise
horizontally amidships under the front seat, the engine had a 5 x 6-inch
bore and stroke.[537] 25 miles per hour could be attained using the car's
foot throttle (an innovation when most autos were only equipped with
hand-lever throttles).[538] The Jaxon Light Touring Car's tube-and-fin
radiator was "very neatly placed under the front of the hood" with
water circulated by means of a rotary pump.[539] Power was transmitted
to the rear axle via a planetary transmission and center drive chain.[540]
The machine weighed 1,050 pounds, had a 72-inch wheelbase, and
was equipped with wood-spoke wheels with 28-inch or optional 30-inch
Dunlop tires.[541] This single-seat runabout could be ordered with an
optional rear tonneau for more passenger capacity; the wood body was
varnished maroon and it was upholstered with trimmings of "fine hand-
buffed leather."[542] The Jaxon gas car steering wheel was designed so "the
hand wheel tilts out of the way for mounting."[543]

A second smaller Jaxon gasoline runabout, which *The Automobile
Review and Automobile News* called "type C," was also exhibited at
the 1903 Chicago automobile show.[544] It too was likely a prototype
that had been hastily completed in the Jackson factory just in time for
the Chicago show. The automobile was described as a light runabout
weighing 650 pounds and costing $650, with an air-cooled two-cylinder
five-horsepower (bore of 3 3/16 inches and a 4-inch stroke) horizontally
opposed Brennan engine mounted crosswise under the front hood, with
two cooling fans, one for each ribbed cylinder head.[545] Motive power was
transmitted to the rear axle via a planetary transmission and shaft
drive with a bevel-gear differential, with a foot throttle to regulate
speed. It was reported that "the maximum speed claimed is 20 miles
an hour and the gasoline consumption 1 gallon for 25 miles."[546] The
car was steered with a tiller mounted on the side of the body and the
clutch "operating handle" was attached to this steering tiller column.[547]
Wire wheels with 28 x 2 1/2-inch tires were installed on an angle iron-
reinforced wooden frame with three-quarter elliptical springs and a
72-inch wheelbase.[548] In some respects, the "type C" descriptions from

the various automotive journal accounts of Chicago's Third Annual Automobile Exhibition specify a car that might have appeared, at first glance, similar to Carter's first friction-drive transmission vehicle built later, in the summer of that year, with a Brennan air-cooled motor under the hood. However, the 1903 air-cooled Jaxon gasoline automobile shown in Chicago is consistently described as having a planetary transmission, so clearly this vehicle did not possess Carter's friction-drive transmission arrangement; this Jaxon "type C" prototype would soon be modified and marketed as the Jaxon Light Runabout.[549]

The March 4, 1903 *Jackson Daily Citizen* provided a postscript to the Detroit and Chicago automobile shows:

> Byron Carter, who is manager for the Jackson Automobile Co., was seen today and asked about the venture they made in Chicago and Detroit. It will be remembered that they took a carload of their machines and exhibited them with others from every part of the country. [Carter said,] "That was a good move, and we sold a lot of machines; in fact we have all the orders we can fill for the season and shall be busy every day from now on. Not only are we using our own force of men in turning out machines at our own factory, but we are compelled to place orders for parts of the machines with foundries and machine shops in the city. One firm of well known machinists now have an order for 100 engines and that will keep them busy. We are having as much of our work done here as is possible and it means a great deal for the industries of Jackson." Asked how many machines they would be likely to turn out this coming summer he replied that they would have to finish and ship about 200 to keep their contracts with people who have ordered vehicles. "We are making about an equal number of steam and gasoline just now, but gasoline seemed to be preferred in the Chicago exhibition. We showed only the steam auto. in Detroit and got one of the best compliments given any company for machines. We have been back from Chicago about a week and went purely on a business speculation and we were successful beyond our expectations."[550]

The newspaper prophetically concluded this article: "As a business the automobile industry promises to become one of Jackson's staple ventures."[551]

Fig. 142. An engraving of the 1903 Jaxon Light Runabout gasoline car powered by an air-cooled five-horsepower two-cylinder Brennan engine mounted under the front hood; the first Jackson gasoline auto brochure (fig. 140) described the Jaxon Light Runabout as "especially designed for the business man, the doctor or professional man." An experimental prototype of this car, labeled a Jaxon "type C," was shown at Chicago's Third Annual Automobile Exhibition February 14–21, 1903. The February 26, 1903 *Motor Age* magazine described it as having a planetary transmission with shaft drive to the rear axle's bevel-gear differential assembly. The February 19, 1903 issue of *The Motor World* added that this air-cooled prototype was equipped with wire wheels and side-tiller steering (the same steering control as was installed on the Jaxon Steam Surrey and B. J. Carter's first friction-transmission car). The tiller was replaced by a tilting steering wheel, and the motor carriage's wheels were constructed with wood spokes (vs. wire spokes) once the Jaxon Light Runabout model was put into production. The 650-pound Jaxon Light Runabout appears to have been offered for a relatively short time in 1903 only and was priced at $650. *Author's collection*

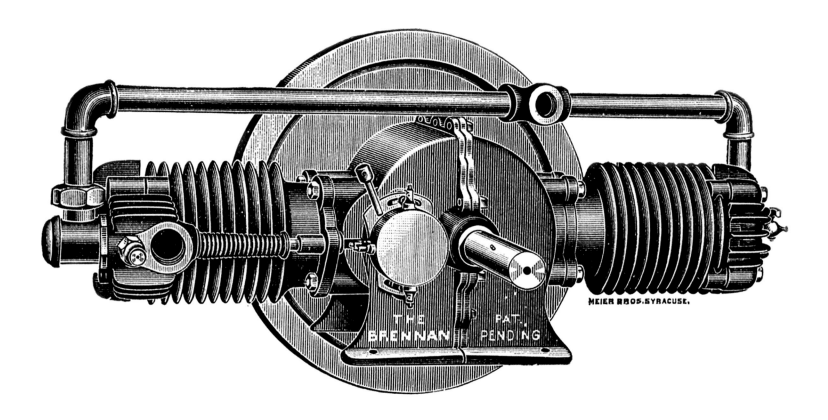

Fig. 143. An illustration of an air-cooled, horizontally opposed four- or five-horsepower two-cylinder gasoline engine built by the Brennan Manufacturing Co. of Syracuse, New York, like those used by the Jackson Automobile Company in the 1903 Jaxon Light Runabout with shaft drive. *Author's collection*

Fig. 144. The Jackson Automobile Company designated its water-cooled seven-horsepower (later rated at six horsepower) one-cylinder gasoline auto as the Jaxon Light Touring Car, shown in this illustration from Jackson's first gasoline-car sales brochure for 1903. The Jaxon Light Touring Car was equipped with a water-cooled one-cylinder gasoline engine of B. J. Carter's "own special design," built by the Jackson Automobile Company and mounted lengthwise amidships under the front seat. Power was delivered to the rear axle by chain drive. Interestingly, the car had a tilting steering wheel. The Jaxon Light Touring Car, at 1,050 pounds, weighed 400 pounds more than the Jaxon Light Runabout and was listed at $800 in the first 1903 brochure, but by March 1903 the price was reduced to $750. By April 1904 the price was further reduced to $650. The popular Jaxon Light Touring Car was continued into the 1905 model year, and by then it had been rebranded as the Jackson Runabout Model "A." Throughout its years of production, this model was painted maroon. *Author's collection*

At Long Last, Jaxon Gasoline Cars are Ready for Sale

Despite B. J. Carter's March 1903 statement that Jackson's gasoline car production was under way, and a *Cycle and Automobile Trade Journal* account that said the Jaxon gas car "was on the road in December 1902," it appears that Jackson struggled mightily to perfect its gasoline Jaxon models, and the final, standardized version of the Jaxon one-cylinder gasoline runabout, ultimately branded the Jaxon Light Touring Car, did not make its appearance in larger quantities until the summer of 1903.[552] As late as May 1903, this model had still simply been called the Jaxon Gasoline Car or gasoline runabout in national automotive journals.[553] A May 9, 1903 article in *Automobile Topics* noted, "The Jackson Automobile Company, Jackson, Mich., has within the past two weeks delivered three of their new and handsome gasolene runabouts, and expect to be able to produce from four to six finished machines per week for the balance of the season. While much attention is being paid to the gasolene cars by Manager Carter, he states that the steamers which the company has been building are coming through with their accustomed regularity, and that sales in that line are very good"[554] It is unclear whether the reporter was referring to the water-cooled one-cylinder gasoline Jaxon Light Touring Car or the air-cooled two-cylinder gasoline Jaxon Light Runabout; however, it seems likely it was the former, as the one-cylinder model became one of Jackson's popular staples for the next three years.[555] And the air-cooled Jaxon Light Runabout looks to have been a fairly short-lived, small-production offering. Why the Jackson Automobile Company gave these two distinctively different gasoline car models such confusingly similar names is now lost to history.

In June and July 1903, the Jackson Automobile Company was advertising the water-cooled one-cylinder Jaxon Light Touring Car both locally and nationally.[556] An ad in the July 1, 1903 *Jackson Daily Citizen* announced that the Jaxon gasoline touring car is "Now Ready for Delivery" and the price was $750.[557] The August 1, 1903 issue of the *Cycle and Automobile Trade Journal* reported, "Jackson Automobile Co., Jackson, Mich., are now actively on the market with their light gasoline touring car, on which they have been working for some time."[558] This magazine article further represented that "all parts are built in the company's own factory, and have been perfected after years of experience."[559] *The Automobile Review and Automobile News*, on August 15, 1903, added, "The Jackson Automobile Co. of Jackson, Mich., are turning out quite a number of Jaxons. It seems to stand the test of hard usage and cover[s] long distances with comparative ease. Their plant is well equipped for doing good work."[560]

The one-cylinder gasoline engine Carter had designed for the Jaxon Light Touring Car was re-rated at six horsepower, downgraded a bit from its earlier-advertised seven horsepower.[561] The price tag for the Jaxon Light Touring Car included standard equipment of lamps, fenders, tools, and one extra spark plug, and remained $750 until April 1904, when it was reduced to $650.[562] The Jaxon Light Touring Car was the only single-cylinder gasoline automobile the Jackson Automobile Company ever produced in quantity, and this popular machine would continue to be offered in the same form into the 1904 and 1905 model years.[563] (In 1905, it was rebranded the Jackson Runabout Model "A.")[564]

Fig. 145. The Jackson Automobile Company announced that the Jaxon Light Touring Car was "Now Ready for Delivery," with a $750 price tag, in this July 1, 1903 *Jackson Daily Citizen* advertisement. *Courtesy of the Jackson District Library*

Jaxon Cars Featured at the 1903 "Automobile Socials"

An extant photograph (fig. 146) establishes that Jaxon gasoline cars were indeed being manufactured in larger quantities by June or July 1903. This picture, which shows two Jaxon Light Touring Cars, two Jaxon Light Runabouts, and a Jaxon Steam Surrey Model "A" in the lineup, was likely taken during a June 9, 1903 "automobile social."[565] When early cars were a true novelty, they were often featured as part of town festivals or civic gatherings, and crowds would line up for a ride in the new horseless carriages. This June 9, 1903 automobile social was predicted to be "something new in the way of a social diversion, and promises to be a great success" and was "one of the most novel social events of the season."[566] The day before, the *Jackson Daily Citizen* wrote, "Every one will be given an opportunity to ride in an automobile for five cents at the automobile social on the [Mrs. W. D.] Ford lawn, tomorrow evening" at the corner of East Main Street and Seymour Avenue.[567] The reporter went on to say that "ice cream and cake will be served, for 10 cents extra" and that the Apollo Mandolin Club would provide "excellent music."[568] The event featured 11 automobiles and their owners. The machines were listed as the property of Jackson residents B. J. Carter (in an air-cooled two-cylinder Jaxon Light Runabout), George A. Matthews, Charles Lewis, Fred T. and Arthur L. Lockwood (both in one-cylinder curved-dash Oldsmobiles), L. H. Field, W. M. Thompson, F. W. Lipe, Carl Eberle, George W. Luke, and Fred Keiser, and Edward F. Lyon, Charles Lewis' son-in-law who was visiting from Detroit.[569] "The autos were kept busy all the evening, and proved a rare treat to many, there being 500 tickets sold for rides."[570] A close look at figures 146 and 147 reveals that some of the motorcars displayed posters for the then upcoming July 16, 1903 Jackson automobile races.

A second automobile social, called "one of the most popular out-of-doors functions," was conducted July 14, 1903, to promote the Jackson automobile races, with over 250 more paid rides.[571] Descriptions of this second automobile social list only eight automobiles, which does not match the lineup in figure 146.[572] B. J. Carter, George A. Matthews, Charles Lewis, Professor L. A. Harraden, and four other Jackson residents provided the motorcars for the second automobile social.[573]

Fig. 146. This photograph, which shows four Jaxon gasoline cars, a Jaxon Steam Surrey Model "A" (far right), and six Oldsmobiles, was likely taken during a June 9, 1903 "automobile social" held along East Main Street near its intersection with Seymour Avenue. Horseless carriages were often featured as part of town festivals or civic gatherings called socials, and crowds would line up (and pay) for rides in the new machines.

Fig. 146 (continued). These 11 machines were listed as the property of Jackson residents and one man from Detroit; among them were B. J. Carter (in a Jaxon Light Runabout), Charles Lewis, George A. Matthews, Fred T. and Arthur L. Lockwood (both in curved-dash Oldsmobiles), and L. H. Field. The June 10, 1903 *Jackson Daily Citizen* wrote, "The autos were kept busy all the evening, and proved a rare treat for many, there being 500 tickets sold for rides." A close look at the photograph reveals that some of the motorcars displayed posters for the upcoming July 16, 1903 Jackson automobile races. *Author's collection*

Fig. 147. A detail view of the four Jaxon gasoline cars shown at the automobile social; the two machines to the right are air-cooled Jaxon Light Runabouts, with B. J. Carter piloting the second car from the right. Why is it possible to glimpse the starting cranks under the seats even though the Light Runabout's motor was mounted under the front hood? It is because, according to the 1903 Jackson Automobile Company sales brochure, the Jaxon Light Runabout's front-mount air-cooled engine "is started from the seat," likely through some convoluted bevel-gear and chain-and-countershaft cranking mechanism. The two Jaxon gasoline machines to the left are water-cooled Jaxon Light Touring Cars with one-cylinder engines mounted under the bodies. Either Charles Lewis or L. H. Field is driving the Jaxon to the far left; this car has an unusual auxiliary passenger seat mounted directly to the hood, which, if occupied, could have made it difficult for the driver to see the road. *Author's collection*

Fig. 149. A close-up view of Fred T. Lockwood and an unidentified boy in a 1902 or early 1903 Oldsmobile during the same automobile social. *Author's collection*

Fig. 148. A close-up view of B. J. Carter, his daughter, Rachel, and a boy who appears to be Verne A. Trask in an air-cooled Jaxon Light Runabout during the automobile social. *Author's collection*

City of Jackson's July 16, 1903 Automobile Races

The *Jackson Daily Citizen*, in an article entitled "Thousands Witness It," proclaimed that an evening automobile parade on July 15, 1903, to draw attention to the next day's Jackson automobile races, had "attracted large crowds on the public streets and their display was accompanied by a brilliant exhibition of fireworks and colored lights, Roman candles were carried in the hands of riders . . . and for a time the city was ablaze. . . . A few scared horses were in evidence and a bicycle rider got in the way of an auto and suffered some damage to his machine, but that was all."[574] This article went on to report that at "about 8:30 [p.m.] a large number of autos assembled in front of the Elks' temple, and the great "Red Devil" and "999" [race cars built by Henry Ford] were the center of interest for some hundreds of people who crowded around them to study the wonder of which so much has been heard."[575] B. J. Carter, Charles Lewis, Professor L. A. Harraden, the Lockwood brothers, George W. Luke, Floyd Mitchell, and at least seven other motorists drove the numerous automobiles "of all sizes, shapes, and makes" that participated in the nighttime parade.[576]

Although Jackson had previously conducted automobile races in 1900 and 1902, the main 1903 race promised to be a much more spectacular event.[577] The enormous Red Devil race car was to be driven by Barney Oldfield, whom the *Jackson Daily Citizen* labeled, "the greatest automobile driver in the world," and the 999 was to be piloted by a well-known former bicycle racer Tom Cooper, whom the newspaper called, "the western champion" of auto racing.[578] Starting with Oliver E. Barthel's preliminary engineering and design work for Henry Ford's second larger race car, Ford collaborated with Cooper and a team of several assistants in 1902 to create these two distinct but similar racers.[579] The Red Devil and 999 race cars were heavily engineered, with then huge engines rated at 70 to 100 horsepower, having four cylinders, each with a bore and stroke of seven inches.[580] The 999, which had been completed in August 1902, was named for the New York Central's impressive locomotive, the 999.[581] On Jackson's race day, these two racing automobiles would run five-mile heats, and the racer who beat at least two of the three runs would win; the prize was a substantial $1,000. In addition, five "open" automobile contests for amateur racers would be part of the day's events.[582]

In the July 16, 1903 races at the Jackson Fair Grounds, Barney Oldfield, in the Red Devil auto, retained his title as "King of the Chauffeurs" and broke the then world record for speed by driving a mile in one minute, ten seconds (nearly a 60-mile-per-hour average over a five-mile run on a half-mile track).[583] A crowd of about 2,000 had cheered on "the nervy chauffeur," and Oldfield's and Cooper's faces were "covered with sand and oil" by the end of the heats.[584] The "open" amateur automobile races were won by Charles Lewis in a Jaxon Steam Surrey, Fred T. and Arthur L. Lockwood in Oldsmobiles, a Mr. Burgess in a "skeleton" Oldsmobile, and Carl Eberle. Winning speeds for all of these "open" races never exceeded 35 miles per hour.[585] Among the other competitors were B. J. Carter, Professor L. A. Harraden in a "2000 pound Winton machine," Floyd Mitchell, and W. M. Thompson.[586]

A dispute arose between B. J. Carter and Lockwood Brothers after the races had concluded. Carter, who had also competed in the "open" automobile races, in the 1,200-pound class, protested against participation by the Oldsmobile "skeleton" auto.[587] Carter claimed "it was a racer, not a road machine, and ineligible" to race, when only "standard machines" were supposed to have been entered.[588] In a card to the *Jackson Daily Citizen*, the Lockwoods somewhat apologetically responded, "We feel it but just to state that we were informed that only standard machines were to be entered. We had two cars of that type at the track ready to start, but noting that there was not a standard competing machine in our class on the grounds, we then entered a skeleton machine. We would not have done this had there been no other machine of that type ready to compete."[589]

The committee in charge of the Jackson automobile races "ascertained the skeleton was in reality a racer, but as the event was then over, could do nothing in the matter."[590] In the committee's *Jackson Daily Citizen* statement, it expressed "sorrow that the unpleasant incident occurred, realize they were imposed upon and justify Mr. Carter in making his protest."[591] This open exchange in the Jackson newspaper demonstrates just how competitive B. J. Carter must have been when it came to promoting his automobiles. Carter's reaction is not surprising, as winning automobile races, even local events, in the early 20th century was a proven approach motorcar manufacturers frequently used to establish that a manufacturer's cars delivered power, speed, and endurance.

Fig. 150. A 1902 or 1903 photograph of Henry Ford (right) and Barney Oldfield with the "999" Race Car; this 70- to 100-horsepower four-cylinder behemoth competed in the July 16, 1903 automobile races conducted at the Jackson Fair Grounds and was driven by former bicycle racer Tom Cooper. Starting with Oliver E. Barthel's preliminary engineering and design work for this second, larger race car, Ford had collaborated with Cooper and a team of several assistants in 1902 to build the machine. The other similar but distinct race car Ford constructed sometime later, called the "Red Devil," also competed and was the winning entrant in Jackson's 1903 race; it was driven by Barney Oldfield. *From the Collections of The Henry Ford, ID# THF23014*

Close of the Jackson Automobile Company's First Year in Business

In a January 1, 1905 *Cycle and Automobile Trade Journal* piece, the Jackson Automobile Company claimed that about 150 one-cylinder gasoline Jaxon Light Touring Cars had been built in the 1903 model year, which may be a bit inflated.[592] No reliable data has been found on total production numbers for the Jaxon Steam Surrey models either. (Although B. J. Carter in a March 4, 1903 *Jackson Daily Citizen* interview had said that about 200 automobile orders had been obtained at the February 1903 Detroit and Chicago automobile shows, with a preference for the gasoline runabouts at Chicago, where both Jaxon gasoline and steam machines were exhibited.)[593] Accordingly, it seems plausible that at least 50 Jaxon Steam Surreys were built and sold in 1903, and that the remaining 150 autos of the 200 purchase orders Carter referenced were Jaxon Light Touring Cars. This estimate is supported by the March 5, 1903 article in *The Iron Trade Review* that reported, "A number of manufacturers of steam carriages have adopted this new [Reliance low water] alarm as a part of their standard equipment, the company's last order being from the Jackson Automobile Co., Jackson, Mich., for 50 columns to equip the same number of steam carriages which that company is running through in one lot."[594] By comparison, Oldsmobile declared it had sold 4,000 of its own one-cylinder curved-dash gasoline runabouts in 1903, more cars than any other U.S. automaker's output that year.[595]

The Jackson Automobile Company's annual report for calendar year-end 1903 was filed with the Michigan Secretary of State on March 7, 1904.[596] This annual report indicated that the original $24,000 capitalization was still intact, that assets, in this case, personal property, had increased from $2,000 (at year-end 1902) to $15,000, and that the company was carrying $23,027 of liabilities in the form of debt (a significant increase from the $3,000 at year-end 1902).[597] As in the 1902 annual report, only a balance sheet was included and no revenue and expense information was shown. Additionally, several agencies had been established to sell Jackson automobiles, including the K. C. Machinery Co. in Minneapolis, Minnesota, and the Excelsior Carriage Co. in White River Junction, Vermont.[598]

By 1904 many viewed gasoline motors as far superior to steam engines and a more efficient and convenient mode of power for automobiles. Steam cars were typically equipped with finicky, sometimes dangerous gasoline or kerosene burners and required varying amounts of start-up time to heat the boiler and build enough steam pressure before the machine would actually begin moving. A well-tuned gasoline-powered auto of this time, while sometimes difficult to crank start, was generally not subject to these substantial firing delays. And so, even though a May 9, 1903 article in *Automobile Topics* reported, "Manager Carter . . . states that the [Jaxon] steamers which the company has been building are coming through with their accustomed regularity, and that sales in that line are very good," Jaxon Steam Surrey production would in actuality cease by the end of 1903 or early in 1904.[599] Because these Jaxon Steam Surrey models were nearly identical to B. J. Carter's design for his improved 1901 steam carriage with his patented three-cylinder engine, this transition may have caused Carter a tinge of sadness. Carter had worked tenaciously to design, finance, and manufacture the improved Carter steam carriage in 1901 and 1902.

An October 1, 1903 article in *The Motor World* reflected the sentiment many motorists held as 1904 approached: "Steam is out of date and will soon be dead" and any new steam carriages will be "overshadowed by the popular gasoline and electric cars."[600] There were a few hold-outs that continued to build steam cars after 1904, most notably the Stanley Motor Carriage Company and the White Sewing Machine Company; by 1931, however, the last remaining major U.S. steam-car manufacturer, Doble Steam Motors Company, had folded.[601] Interestingly, experiments to perfect steam-powered automobiles have continued to the present day.

The Jackson Automobile Company's complete departure from steam-car manufacturing is evidenced by an October 19, 1904 advertisement in *The Horseless Age* (fig. 151), in which Jackson offered for sale one remaining complete Jaxon Steam Surrey Model "A" and all Jaxon steam-carriage parts still in Jackson's inventory, including 12 Carter automatic oil pumps.[602]

WE have the following which we would like to sell, together or separately. We will put a price on this stock that will be very attractive.

One two-seated steam automobile; the front seat closes and makes a nice appearing front; has been run about 100 miles.

7 boilers (new), 17 and 19 inch, with copper flues.

12 boiler shells.

5 steam engines without jackets or pumps.

2 engines with jackets.

12 oil pumps, Carter automatic.

2,400 copper tubes, ½"x16½".

30 air tanks, copper, 7x30.

40 sets cylinder castings machines.

40 sets castings for differential.

224 steering knuckles.

3 brass differential sprockets.

8 4x4 steps pads.

9 air gauges, No. 100.

Jackson Automobile Co.
Jackson, Mich.

Fig. 151. The Jackson Automobile Company had ceased manufacturing Jaxon Steam Surreys by the end of the 1903 model year. Its complete exit from steam-car building is evidenced by this advertisement from the October 19, 1904 issue of *The Horseless Age*, in which the company offered for sale one remaining Jaxon Steam Surrey Model "A" and all Jaxon steam-carriage parts still in stock, including 12 Carter automatic cylinder oil pumps. *Courtesy of Todd and Faith Holton*

The Jackson Automobile Company's 1904 Model Year

It was summarily announced in the May 11, 1904 issue of the *Jackson Daily Citizen* that "Byron J. Carter has severed his connection with the Jackson Automobile Co. Mr. [Edwin O.] Abbott, late of the Cadillac Automobile Co., of Detroit, has been secured as superintendent of the local establishment."[603] It would appear that B. J. Carter's resignation from the Jackson Automobile Company was not sudden, as he and his soon-to-be former partners, Matthews and Lewis, had had an opportunity to develop a succession plan and, as noted, had already hired a new general plant superintendent when Carter departed. Two weeks later, the *Jackson Daily Citizen* reported that "Byron J. Carter, of this city, has . . . been granted a patent on a transmission gearing."[604] Ironically, a transmission with "gearing" was exactly what Carter was attempting to avoid with his newly patented friction-drive transmission configuration; he would soon pursue the manufacture of automobiles equipped with these friction-drive transmissions.

Now that Carter, the Jackson Automobile Company's primary founder and inventive engineer, was leaving, it was inevitable the company's operations would be affected significantly. Given the timing of Carter's departure, he undoubtedly would have participated in designing and testing the Jackson Automobile Company's first two-cylinder touring cars introduced for the 1904 model year. (Design and road tests of these machines had been under way for several months in 1903 before the 1904 model year cars were announced to the public). A January 1, 1905 *Cycle and Automobile Trade Journal* piece provided more detail and reported that development of a two-cylinder Jackson "was begun in July 1903, two identical cars being placed on the road for test driving before August first [1903]. . . . An extended period of road work, from July, 1903 to October 1, 1904, was occupied in" perfecting the two-cylinder touring car models.[605]

Apparently no two-cylinder Jackson touring cars were considered ready for public exhibition at the 1904 Chicago Automobile Show February 6–13, 1904, as Jackson only displayed its one-cylinder gasoline Jaxon Light Touring Car there.[606] The *Cycle and Automobile Trade Journal* emphasized that Jackson had no new 1904 models completed in time for the Chicago show: "The 1904 model of the Jaxon light gasoline touring car, made by the Jackson Automobile Co., of Jackson, Mich., and exhibited at Chicago, is the same as the 1903 model, which we have described."[607] The *Jackson Daily Citizen* reported that B. J. Carter, Charles Lewis, George A. Matthews, Fred T. and Arthur L. Lockwood, and several other Jackson motorists all attended the Chicago auto show.[608] Somewhat surprisingly, the Jackson Automobile Company did not exhibit any cars at the nearby February 15–20, 1904 Detroit Tri-State Automobile and Sportsmen's Show, which according to *The Motor World*, had opened to "zero weather, the sharp ping of rifle shots and the barking of dogs."[609]

Jackson's first 1904 two-cylinder automobile was initially called the "Jaxon Two Seated Surrey" and, for reasons lost to history, had been rebranded as the "Orlo" Family Touring Car by June or July 1904. As had been the case in 1903 with its Jaxon gasoline models, the Jackson Automobile Company was very slow in actually placing its new 1904 two-cylinder models on the market. An announcement and advertisements for the Jaxon Two Seated Surrey did not even appear until April 1904 and the engravings used to illustrate this new two-cylinder machine were oddly out of proportion.[610]

Fig. 152. A Jackson Automobile Company serial number dash tag with serial number 263, from 1904; this tag was separated from the original automobile long ago, so the specific Jackson model on which this dash tag was used is unknown. *Courtesy of Todd and Faith Holton*

Fig. 153. Jackson's first two-cylinder touring car, introduced by April 1904, was called the Jaxon Two Seated Surrey; the Jackson Automobile Company was one of the first U.S. motorcar builders to lengthen a car's wheelbase sufficiently to accommodate side-entrance doors to the back seat, which was a significant development in making automobiles more practical for family use. The Jaxon Two Seated Surrey had an 82-inch wheelbase and was powered by a 12-horsepower horizontally opposed two-cylinder water-cooled motor located amidships under the auto's front seat, with a planetary transmission and chain drive to the rear axle. It was priced at $1,100; two optional doors for the rear side entrances were offered for an extra $25. *Courtesy of Gregory R. Loftness*

The Jaxon Two Seated Surrey was powered by a 12-horsepower (4 1/2-inch bore x 5-inch stroke), opposed two-cylinder, water-cooled motor located amidships under the auto's front seat, with a planetary transmission and chain drive to the rear axle, and 30-inch clincher tires.[611] It weighed approximately 1,600 pounds.[612] Gasoline and water tanks, batteries, and the radiator were all located under the hood.[613] A float-feed Kingston carburetor and a mechanical oiler were standard equipment.[614] The Jaxon Two Seated Surrey was priced at $1,100, with two doors available for the side entrances as a $25 option.[615]

The illustrations of the Jaxon Two Seated Surrey show an automobile with a relatively long 82-inch wheelbase and side entrances for backseat passengers (and not the tiny single back door used on most rear-entrance tonneaus for autos of this era with shorter wheelbases).[616] The Jackson Automobile Company, which labeled these side entrances "a distinctively new feature" and "a convenient side entrance instead of an unhandy rear door" in advertisements, has sometimes been credited as the first U.S. motorcar builder to offer backseat side-entrance doors, which was a significant development in making automobiles more practical for family use.[617] Prior to this point, access to an automobile's rear seat, if it had one, was made through a small rear door in the detachable tonneau's back seat; early automobiles' wheelbases simply were not long enough to accommodate side entrances for the backseat passengers. Cleveland's mayor, Tom Johnson, had remarked, in late 1903, when he was trying to squeeze himself into a rear door of an automobile's tonneau "that he did not know of but two other vehicles with rear doors, one was a dump cart and the other a hearse, and he was not inclined to enter either just at present."[618]

Experimentation with and improvements to the Jaxon Two Seated Surrey were apparently ongoing until June or July 1904, when the Jackson Automobile Company announced the "Orlo" Family Touring Car (the "Jaxon" label had been permanently dropped for these new two-cylinder touring car models).[619] An *Automobile Review* reporter, in the July 30, 1904 issue, wrote that "in producing this [Orlo] car it has been the object of the designers, the Jackson Automobile Company, Jackson, Mich., to get something that is convenient for riders to get in and out of, and at the same time distribute the weight of the engine and passenger load that it might not be too heavy on either front or rear tires."[620] To further this comfort-driven design, semi-elliptical suspension springs were used all

Those Doll-Size Doors.

Fig. 154. A 1903 cartoon from *The Motor World*, which illustrates the potential difficulty of accessing an automobile's rear tonneau through its single small entrance door; Cleveland's mayor, Tom Johnson, quipped in late 1903, "that he did not know of but two other vehicles with rear doors, one was a dump cart and the other a hearse, and he was not inclined to enter either just at present." *Courtesy of Gregory R. Loftness*

Fig. 155. Arthur L. Lockwood driving a 1903 Ford Model "A" with a rear-entrance tonneau (there are no side doors for the backseat passengers) on West Cortland Street in front of the Jackson Corset Co. factory; this car is likely the same Ford purchased new by Arthur's brother, Fred, which was described in the August 19, 1903 *Jackson Daily Citizen. Author's Lockwood negative collection*

Fig. 156. By June or July 1904 the Jackson Automobile Company had introduced the "Orlo" Family Touring Car. The Orlo closely resembled the earlier Jaxon Two Seated Surrey but for the wheelbase, now lengthened four inches to a rather long, for its day, 86 inches. The power rating of the Orlo's two-cylinder engine had also been increased to 16–17 horsepower, which was "capable of carrying four or five persons 30 miles per hour over ordinary country roads" in the 1,675-pound car. The Orlo's price was $1,125, the same, coincidentally, as the Jaxon Two Seated Surrey, if a new owner had bought the Surrey with optional rear doors. *Author's collection*

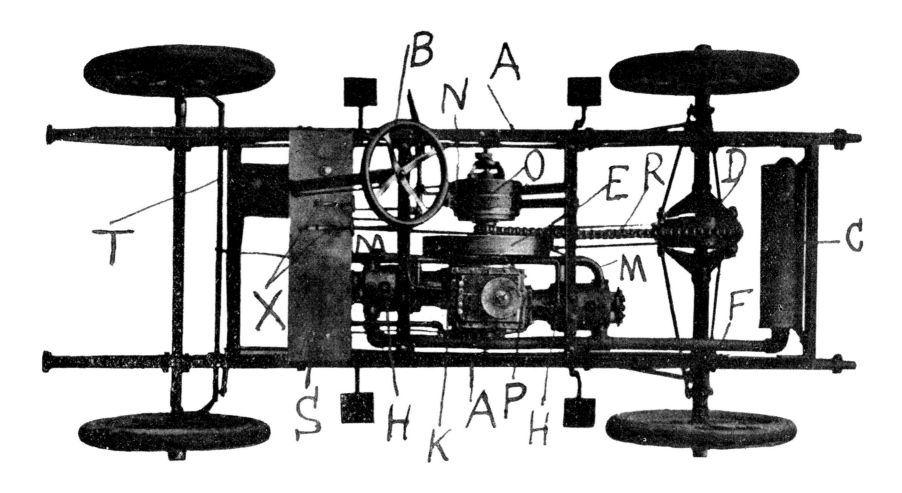

Fig. 157. Photograph of the Orlo Family Touring Car engine and running gear from the July 30, 1904 issue of *Automobile Review*; the intentional central placement of the engine to minimize motor vibration and to balance the car's weight from front to back is visible in this image. *Author's collection*

Fig. 158. The April 26, 1904 issue of the *Jackson Daily Citizen* reported, "A fine sample of automobile delivery wagon[s] was seen on the streets yesterday afternoon. They are the product of the Jackson Automobile Co." To build these light trucks, Jackson factory workers simply attached delivery bodies by four bolts to standard Jaxon Two Seated Surrey or Orlo two-cylinder touring-car chassis. *Author's collection, courtesy of the Jackson District Library*

Fig. 159. The main Jackson Automobile Company factory building at Park Avenue and Park Place, where finished automobiles were held for shipping; the lineup in this photograph is composed of a 1904 Orlo delivery car at the back and seven brand-new 1905 Jackson Model "C" two-cylinder touring cars. An unpainted wood touring-car body sits on sawhorses to the left, awaiting multiple coats of finishing varnish. *Author's collection, courtesy of Ernest F. Scheifler and Ronald G. Bean*

round. The Orlo Family Touring Car closely resembled the Jaxon Two Seated Surrey, although the wheelbase had been lengthened four inches to a rather long, for its day, 86 inches.[621] The power rating of the Orlo's opposed two-cylinder engine with a float-feed Kingston carburetor had also been increased to 16–17 horsepower (from the Two Seated Surrey's 12-horespower), which was "capable of carrying four or five persons 30 miles per hour over ordinary country roads" in the 1,675-pound car.[622] The motor was described as "manufactured especially" for the Jackson Automobile Company, with a double-geared pump for circulating cooling water.[623] Only one operating lever was needed, "making control very simple."[624]

Other mechanical features were generally similar to those of the Jaxon Two Seated Surrey. The Orlo's price was $1,125, which was the same cost as the Jaxon Two Seated Surrey if a new owner had bought the Surrey with optional rear doors.[625] It does not appear that the Orlo Family Touring Car could be purchased without rear doors.

Preliminary production of light delivery trucks was also under way in conjunction with building the Jaxon Two Seated Surrey and then, later, with the Orlo Family Touring Car. The April 26, 1904 issue of the *Jackson Daily Citizen* stated, "A fine sample of automobile delivery wagon[s] was seen on the streets yesterday afternoon. They are the product of the Jackson Automobile Co."[626] Very soon after, *The Horseless Age* announced in a May 4, 1904 article that the Jackson Automobile Company "has begun the manufacture of delivery vehicles."[627] To build these light trucks, delivery bodies were simply installed at first on the Jaxon Two Seated Surrey running gear (overall weight was 1,600 pounds) and then shortly after, when the Orlo Family Touring Car was announced, on an Orlo two-cylinder touring-car chassis (overall weight was 1,780 pounds).[628] A Jackson Automobile Company advertisement stated that "by the easy removal of four bolts [from the Orlo touring car body], a delivery body can be substituted without disturbing any of the operating mechanism."[629] The price for the Orlo chassis fitted as a delivery wagon was $1,225.[630]

The Jackson Automobile Company continued to include the one-cylinder Jaxon Light Touring Car as part of its 1904 lineup as well, built in all respects the same as the 1903 design (with the price reduced from $750 to $650 in April 1904).[631] In fact, the popular Jaxon Light Touring Car was still offered in Jackson's 1905 sales catalog, but by then it was called the Jackson Runabout Model "A."[632]

Total Jackson Automobile Company production for the 1904 model year was 234 motorcars, of which 100 were claimed to be the new two-cylinder models.[633] And several more agencies for the factory had been established: Chicago and southern Illinois; Boston; Cincinnati and Akron, Ohio; Terre Haute, Indiana; Minneapolis, Minnesota (somewhat ironically called the Motor Car Co.); White River Junction, Vermont; Trenton, New Jersey; Buffalo and Rochester, New York; and surprisingly, Buenos Aires, Argentina (where a number of Jacksons had been shipped in October 1904).[634] Within a year, it was stated that there would soon be 600 men in the Jackson Automobile Company's workforce.[635]

The Jackson Automobile Company's annual report for calendar year-end 1904 was filed with the Michigan Secretary of State on March 3, 1905. This annual report indicated that the original $24,000 capitalization was still intact (with capital now comprising $16,000 in the form of cash and $8,000 in the form of property). Byron J. Carter was no longer listed as a shareholder, and the shares of common stock had been revalued and were distributed 115 shares to Charles Lewis, as president, 115 shares to George A. Matthews, as secretary and treasurer, and 10 shares to the company's new sales manager, Fred L. Holmes. Assets made up of personal property and receivables had decreased slightly from $15,000 (at year-end 1903) to $14,109.48, and the company was carrying $25,500 of liabilities in the form of debt (an increase from $23,027 at year-end 1903).[636] As before, only a balance sheet was included and no revenue and expense information was shown in the 1904 annual report.

By the end of 1904, the Jackson Automobile Company had begun to use the first version of its famous motto: "No Sand Too Deep, No Hills Too Steep."[637] By 1906, this motto would be revised to "No Sand Too Deep, No Hill Too Steep," and in 1908, the phrasing was consistently changed to "No Hill Too Steep, No Sand Too Deep."[638] This motto would become one of the most noteworthy and well-known automotive slogans of the early 20th century.

Unfortunately, the Jackson Automobile Company would now need to strive for success without B. J. Carter's creative influence, ingenuity, automotive design and invention capabilities, many years of motorcar and mechanical experience, and his strong drive and ambition.

Fig. 160. The two original Jackson Automobile Company partners who remained after B. J. Carter's May 1904 resignation, George A. Matthews (front seat, right) and Charles Lewis (back seat, right), are shown testing a prototype of the 1905 Jackson Model "C" two-cylinder touring car. (The backseat passenger on the left is unidentified.) This prototype was built with 1904-style step plates and not the running boards that were standard equipment on the production model of the 1905 Model "C." The driver is Fred L. Holmes (born 1874), a Jackson Automobile Company traveling agent who was promoted to sales manager within a year of B. J. Carter's departure. Holmes became a Jackson Automobile Company shareholder and executive in late 1904 but resigned in June 1911 to accept the position of manager for the Clarke-Carter Automobile Company (no connection to B. J. Carter), which manufactured the Cutting car in Jackson. This photograph was taken during the winter of 1904 in front of the City of Jackson's imposing Romanesque stone post office on South Mechanic Street near the intersection with Washington Street; the Elks Temple, which still stands, is in the background. *Courtesy of the Ella Sharp Museum*

Fig. 161. Close-up view of the occupants of the Jackson car seen in fig. 160; their glum expressions may be due to the frigid weather or perhaps a realization that the Jackson Automobile Company's future would be more challenging without the benefit of B. J. Carter's inventive mind, motorcar- and engine-designing talents, and his drive to succeed. *Courtesy of the Ella Sharp Museum*

A New Direction: B. J. Carter Dedicates His Energies to the Friction-Drive Transmission

After leaving the Jackson Automobile Company in May 1904, Carter formed a new enterprise in Jackson, The Motorcar Co., to find a market for and to build more of his friction-drive transmission vehicles based on his newly issued U.S. patent (no. 761,146), which was filed September 21, 1903, and granted May 31, 1904 (only 20 days after Carter's resignation was made public).[639] Even though it appears Carter's resignation was not entirely abrupt (George A. Matthews and Charles Lewis had had time to find and hire Carter's replacement before Carter announced his resignation), one gets the impression that Carter's separation from the Jackson Automobile Company may have been a bit acrimonious, and, given the date his patent was granted, it is highly likely that Carter's interest in pursuing his friction-drive transmission is ultimately what precipitated his May 1904 resignation.

From the September 21, 1903 application date for his patent, it is clear that Carter was experimenting with a friction-drive transmission mechanism in 1903 while he was still a manager and factory superintendent for the Jackson Automobile Company, and his friction-drive-transmission design experiments and associated machining work were probably conducted in the Jackson factory under the gaze of his partners and other plant workers. (This would

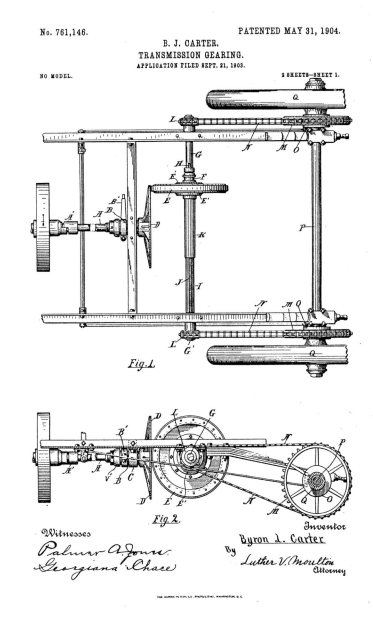

Fig. 162. Sheet 1 of the patent drawing for B. J. Carter's friction-drive transmission; this U. S. patent (no. 761,146) was granted May 31, 1904, 20 days after Carter disclosed his resignation from the Jackson Automobile Company. *Courtesy of Buzzy Carter Maurer*

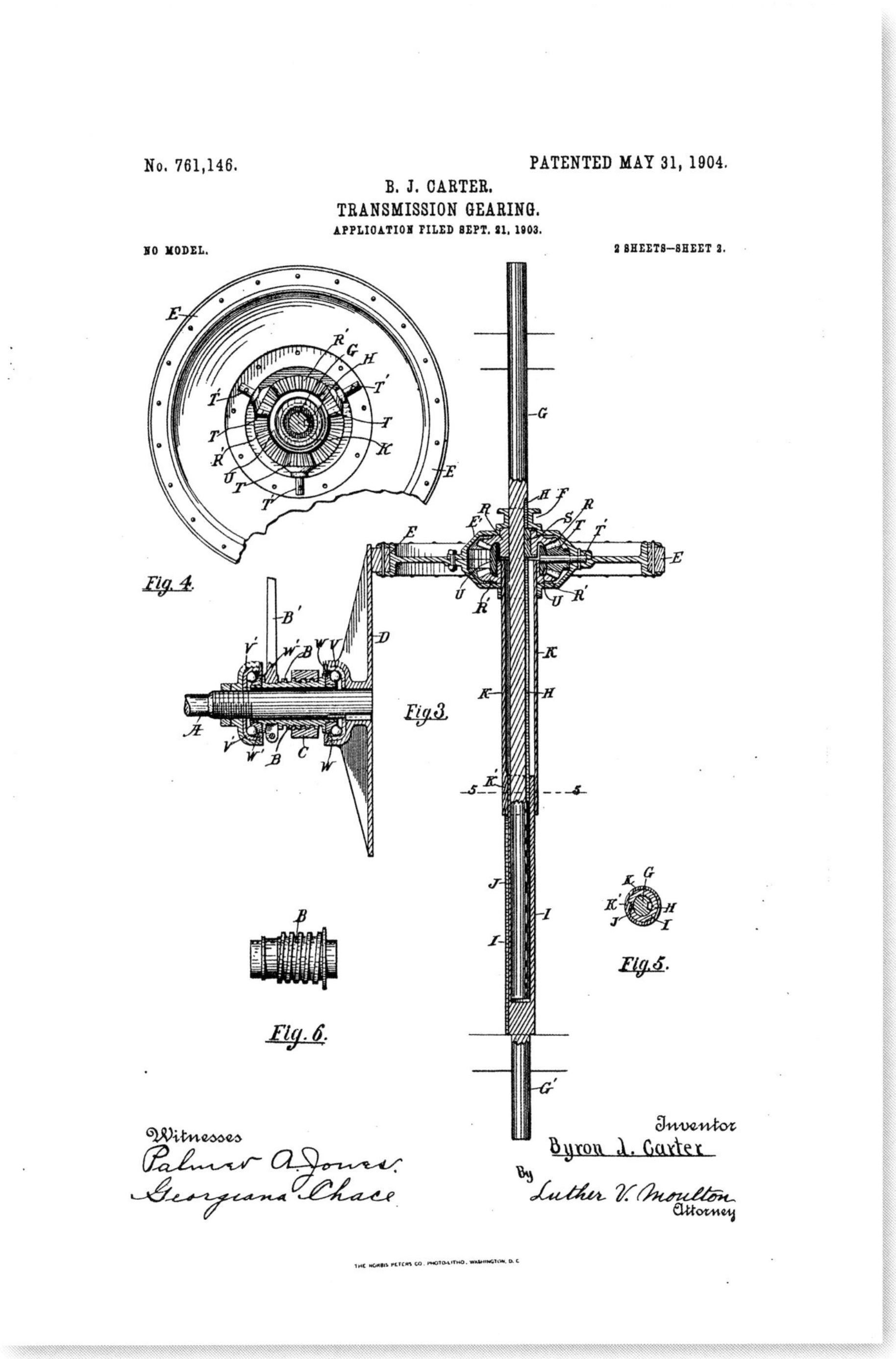

No. 761,146.

B. J. CARTER.
TRANSMISSION GEARING.
APPLICATION FILED SEPT. 21, 1903.

PATENTED MAY 31, 1904.

NO MODEL.

2 SHEETS—SHEET 2.

Fig. 4.

Fig. 3.

Fig. 5.

Fig. 6.

Witnesses
Palmer A. Jones.
Georgiana Chace

Inventor
Byron J. Carter
By
Luther V. Moulton
Attorney

THE NORRIS PETERS CO., PHOTO-LITHO., WASHINGTON, D. C.

have been a matter of expedience, since his former 204 West Cortland Street machine shop was now otherwise occupied by Lockwood Brothers.) Carter actually used several Jaxon car components in building his experimental friction-drive-transmission machine, which would not have gone unnoticed. If Matthews and Lewis had been aware of Carter's friction-drive transmission experimentation, then they may have questioned the sincerity of Carter's focus on maximizing 1903 Jaxon car production, which had experienced numerous delays with overly optimistic delivery dates. To add to this high-pressure situation, Carter also had the demanding role of lead designer for the two-cylinder motors to be installed in 1904 and 1905 Jackson models. (A January 1, 1905 *Cycle and Automobile Trade Journal* article indicated that design work for the 1904 Orlo Family Touring Car and the 1905 Jackson Model "C" had actually begun in July 1903.)[640]

It seems reasonable that Carter would have tried to persuade Matthews and Lewis that a Jackson automobile with a friction-drive transmission could be successfully built and sold. Given Carter's ultimate resignation, however, it is apparent that the three partners did not share the same views on Carter's future with the Jackson Automobile Company. And all three would undoubtedly have approached the question differently. Carter was the inventive, mechanical mind behind the operation, but the older Matthews and Lewis were seasoned industrialists

Fig. 163. Sheet 2 of the patent drawing for B. J. Carter's friction-drive transmission, filed September 21, 1903, and granted May 31, 1904; Carter later assigned this patent (no. 761,146) to the Motorcar Company when it was incorporated in Detroit on September 22, 1905. *Courtesy of Buzzy Carter Maurer*

with considerable manufacturing experience, and they held the purse strings. Launching the Jackson Automobile Company in 1902 and 1903 had proven to be incredibly difficult, and Jaxon vehicle production had commenced several months later than was originally anticipated and announced to the trade. The Jackson Automobile Company's tenuous early years were described in George A. Matthews' biography written in the *History of Michigan, Volume 3*, published in 1915: "The [Jackson] gasoline motor was in its infancy, and it was only after repeated trials and costly experiments that it was proven to be a suitable motive power. During the first two years, the outlook was dark, and there were times when the other stock-holders in the Company were ready to give up the undertaking."[641] By early 1904, however, the Jackson Automobile Company had begun to achieve some modicum of success, and it seems probable that the staid businessmen Matthews and Lewis would have had no appetite for a major Jackson automobile design revision or detour such as Carter's newly invented and untested friction-drive transmission. One of Carter's obituaries, only four years later, alluded to this when it stated that "the friction drive was first ridiculed," and another obituary added, "In order to carry out his [friction-drive] ideas with greater freedom, he resigned from the Jackson Automobile Co."[642] (Even if Matthews and Lewis had been interested in equipping some Jackson cars with friction-drive transmissions, perhaps Carter placed a much higher value on his soon-to-be-patented invention than they were willing to pay him.)

Another issue may have involved Carter's patent for his improved three-cylinder steam engine, which was the essential element of the Jaxon Steam Surrey and had made up a significant portion of the value of Carter's initial contribution to the new Jackson Automobile Company venture. By 1904 this steam-engine patent was essentially worthless, as Jaxon Steam Surrey production had ceased and steam cars were rapidly falling out of favor. In light of these developments, it is possible that Matthews and Lewis may have asked Carter for a financial investment or a more expansive engineering and factory production role to maintain his position within the Jackson Automobile Company.

The author may be stretching too much here, but the conceivably contentious ending of B. J. Carter's relationship with George A. Matthews and Charles Lewis may be illustrated by certain circumstances, which may have been more than mere coincidences. First, Carter's longtime associates since the early 1890s, Arthur L. Butcher, John H. Carpenter, and Charles A. Trask, who had followed Carter to work with the Jackson Automobile Company in various capacities, all severed their connections with the firm (or perhaps were fired) around the time of Carter's resignation in May 1904. Another illustration may be the guest list of those who attended Carter's April 8, 1908 funeral service at Squire and Martha Carter's home in Jackson.[643] Neither Matthews' nor Lewis' name was among the list of honored guests.[644] Conversely, 14 Motorcar Company directors, executives, and department heads, including Carter's longtime associate Charles A. Trask, traveled from Detroit to serve as active or honorary pallbearers.[645]

B. J. Carter's decision to resign from the growing Jackson Automobile Company in May 1904 would have been difficult and risky. It had taken him two years to raise stable financing to build his steam carriages on a larger scale. After a somewhat rocky start, the Jackson Automobile Company was, by early 1904, making significant sales progress with its one-cylinder gasoline Jaxon Light Touring Car, and two-cylinder five-passenger models had been successfully introduced in March or April 1904. The company was beginning to establish a good reputation in the ever-more-crowded field of automakers.

However, in 1903, Carter had developed a strong conviction that his friction-drive transmission was superior to and much simpler than multiple-gear, planetary, and other transmission designs. Since his likely proposal to install the as yet unproven friction-drive transmissions in Jackson cars had gone nowhere, Carter undoubtedly concluded that he would need to realize the successful production of his friction-drive transmission machines elsewhere—that he was left with no choice but to resign from the Jackson Automobile Company and seek new investors. He would not have made this decision lightly; finding investors for automotive ventures was becoming ever more difficult in 1904, as new auto inventions were rapidly entering the market by the hundreds. Other inventors would be competing to convince moneymen that their ideas were much better than the others, including B. J. Carter's newly minted friction-drive transmission.

Friction-Drive Transmission Experiments

A 1910 advertisement for B. J. Carter's friction-drive motorcar, by then called the Cartercar, made this bold statement: "The Cartercar has no clutch to slip – no gears to strip. . . . The friction transmission of the Cartercar provides any speed from zero up without noise. . . . The single lever control makes it easy to operate. The driver never becomes confused. Any inexperienced person can readily learn to drive the Cartercar without injury to its mechanism."[646]

A Cartercar sales catalog proclaimed: "A bright boy can learn to care for and drive a Cartercar in a few days' time."[647]

Another advertisement promised: "Any blacksmith in any town can repair it."[648]

These would be the primary selling points throughout the manufacturing life of Carter's wonderful machines with friction-drive transmissions.

Several different Cartercar sales catalogs included the same promotional account of Carter's efforts to develop a successful friction-drive transmission for automobiles. In summary, they represent that Carter had in 1901 realized the shortcomings of geared transmissions for automobiles. He then commenced transmission-design experimentation and was attracted to a friction-type system. Carter soon found that little reliable data had been published on the subject that could serve as a basis for his calculations of efficiency and capacity; he would have to determine on his own which materials, in combination, would deliver the highest coefficient of friction and would have excellent strength and wear qualities. Carter tested various alloys of aluminum once he had concluded that aluminum would be the best material for the friction disk. He also developed a replaceable compressed cotton-fiber pasteboard traversing-wheel surface lining to engage with the face of the aluminum friction disk. Incidentally, several other inventors had developed friction-drive transmissions during this same time; the Cartercar catalogs, in self-serving prose, pronounced that all others had failed in one way or another. B. J. Carter made a declaration in the July 26, 1906 issue of *The Motor Way*, which referenced Carter's extensive and "severe" friction-drive-transmission experiments: "There is no use going into the business unless you have a car that you can bank upon to give the service which is expected."

The first automobile with a Carter friction-drive transmission was built during the summer of 1903, likely in the Jackson Automobile Company factory, and was completed and "on the road" by September 1, 1903.[649] Carter promptly filed a patent application for the friction-drive transmission on September 21, 1903. In assembling the friction-drive prototype (fig. 164), Carter installed a 1903 Jaxon Light Runabout or Light Touring Car body, a Jaxon steam-car steering tiller on the side, and perhaps used some frame components and wheels from the Jaxon models. However, the friction-drive transmission assembly and side drive chains to the rear axle were entirely different from any Jaxon. This is speculative, however; by its appearance and reported specifications, Carter's first friction-drive machine may have simply been a substantially modified adaptation of a Jaxon Light Runabout with its air-cooled Brennan gasoline engine under the hood.

More specifically, Carter's first experimental runabout with a friction-drive transmission car had a 75-inch wheelbase, 28-inch tires, weighed about 650 pounds, and was powered by a 3 3/16 x 4-inch horizontally opposed two-cylinder air-cooled Brennan motor installed under the front hood; these specifications were nearly identical to those of the 1903 Jaxon Light Runabout.[650] The friction-drive apparatus was, however, completely different and was the essence of simplicity. The aluminum-alloy driving disk was 15 inches in diameter, flanged and ribbed so as to be practically rigid. The traversing, or friction, wheel was also 15 inches in diameter with a 1 1/2-inch "effective face" of "'millboard,' cotton [fiber] pasteboard, between metallic holding jaws."[651] Drive from the friction transmission was accomplished by two chains, one on each side of the automobile, to the divided rear axle. The machine's infinite choice of ratios between the engine and the rear wheels essentially allowed the engine to run at constant speed. The 1903 Carter friction-drive auto "would make about 25 miles [per hour] on a good road and handled perfectly, but did not attract much attention because the car was so light."[652]

B. J. Carter recounted in a Cartercar sales catalog's promotional story that he had driven this first friction-drive auto for about two years, and he had then sold it to Ralph H. Miller of Ann Arbor, Michigan, in 1905.[653] After the machine had been run for more than 25,000 miles without repairs, the Cartercar Company purchased it from Ralph H. Miller "to be preserved for exhibition purposes."[654]

Fig. 164. A factory-issued photograph of B. J. Carter's first experimental automobile with a friction-drive transmission and double side-chain drive, completed by September 1903; it was powered by an air-cooled horizontally opposed two-cylinder Brennan motor (see fig. 143) installed under the front hood. In assembling this friction-drive prototype, Carter used a Jaxon Light Runabout or Light Touring Car body, a Jaxon steam-car steering-tiller assembly, and perhaps employed some frame components and wheels from the Jaxon models as well. Carter indicated in a promotional story in later Cartercar sales catalogs that he had driven this first friction-drive auto for about two years and then sold it to Ralph H. Miller of Ann Arbor, Michigan, in 1905. It was claimed that Carter's first 1903 friction-drive motorcar ran for more than 25,000 miles without repairs, after which the Motorcar Company purchased it "to be preserved for exhibition purposes." *Author's collection*

The Motorcar Co.'s Automobile Production in Jackson

It appears that B. J. Carter's first friction-drive automobile venture, The Motorcar Co., of Jackson, was never formally incorporated, as no articles of association or 1904 or 1905 annual reports, required by the Michigan Secretary of State from registered corporations, were found in the Archives of Michigan collections. Likewise, the Motorcar Co. is not listed among the incorporated entities in the 1905 *Jackson City Directory's* corporations section either.[655] However, the company does appear elsewhere in the 1905 *Jackson City Directory*, under the heading "Automobile Manufacturer," with Byron J. Carter shown as its sole proprietor.[656] There is no reference to The Motorcar Co. in the 1904 *Jackson City Directory*, as it would have been printed prior to Carter's resignation from the Jackson Automobile Company. In general, information regarding The Motorcar Co. during its short tenure in Jackson is rather scarce, as the archive of Jackson's daily newspapers from July 1, 1904, through June 30, 1912, was either destroyed in a warehouse fire or was misplaced decades ago, depending on whom you ask.

The location of The Motorcar Co. is shown in the 1905 *Jackson City Directory* as 204 West Cortland Street, the address of Carter's former bicycle and first automobile-manufacturing operations.[657] Carter had retained ownership of this building during his time at the Jackson Automobile Company. (In fact, his estate was still listed as owning the property in 1916.)[658]

As already noted, Lockwood Brothers had leased the 204 West Cortland Street shop from B. J. Carter in September 1902. After his May 1904 resignation from the Jackson Automobile Company, it would appear that Carter asked Lockwood Brothers to move out in order that he could resume designing and manufacturing cars at this location. The *Jackson Daily Citizen* indicated that Lockwood Brothers was still operating a garage and electrical shop at 204 West Cortland Street in late June 1904.[659] However, the 1905 *Jackson City Directory* shows that Lockwood Brothers had by late 1904 (which probably means earlier, given the directory's printing schedule) vacated 204 West Cortland Street. Lockwood Brothers' new address was nearby at 210–212 West Cortland Street.[660]

It is unknown when The Motorcar Co. actually started building more friction-drive cars in Jackson beyond Carter's original 1903 prototype; a November 19, 1905 *Detroit Free Press* piece, however, reported that Carter had started production of friction-drive-transmission autos within four or five months after resigning from the Jackson Automobile Company. In this newspaper interview, Frank P. Caughey, president of Carter's automobile enterprise (after it was relocated to Detroit in late 1905), said that Carter's initial friction-drive-transmission cars were "manufactured on a small scale by Mr. Carter because he did not have capital to spread"; Caughey added that Carter's new cars had "been running for fourteen months [since August or September 1904]. The cars were made in Jackson."[661]

B. J. Carter had maintained strong ties with Charles A. Trask, and it seems plausible that Trask, who by then was operating The Trask-Field Gas Engine Co., might have provided some engineering, machining, and manufacturing work for Carter and The Motorcar Co. in 1904. In an April 26, 1964 *Jackson Citizen Patriot* article, Charles Trask's daughter, Marjorie I. Schley, said that her father had worked with B. J. Carter when Carter started building Carter friction-drive automobiles in Jackson, and then later in Detroit with the Cartercar enterprise.[662] The Trask-Field Gas Engine Co. manufacturing arrangement with The Motorcar Co., if any, would likely have been short. In 1904 Charles A. Trask either resigned from The Trask-Field Gas Engine Co. or was bought out by the Fields. Trask is not even listed in the 1905 *Jackson City Directory* because he had moved to Ypsilanti, where he worked as a machinist.[663] Within a year, he established Trask & Cornwell, an Ypsilanti automobile repair business, with William C. Cornwell.[664] Ypsilanti is located about 46 miles east of Jackson, so a consistent daily engineering and machining work arrangement between Carter and Trask on Carter's friction-drive cars in late 1904 or 1905 seems unlikely, but it is plausible that Trask may have done work for Carter on an as-needed contract basis. Once the Motorcar Company was incorporated and moved to Detroit, Trask soon followed Carter there in December 1906 to design and build the Cartercar. In a January 6, 1940 letter he sent Della Carter, Trask wrote, "It is 36 years ago now that I went to Ypsilanti and 33 years ago last month that I went to Detroit to work for Byron & Mr. Palmer."[665] (By 1907, Trask was listed in the *Detroit City Directory* as a draftsman with a residence in the city.)[666] According to the *Jackson*

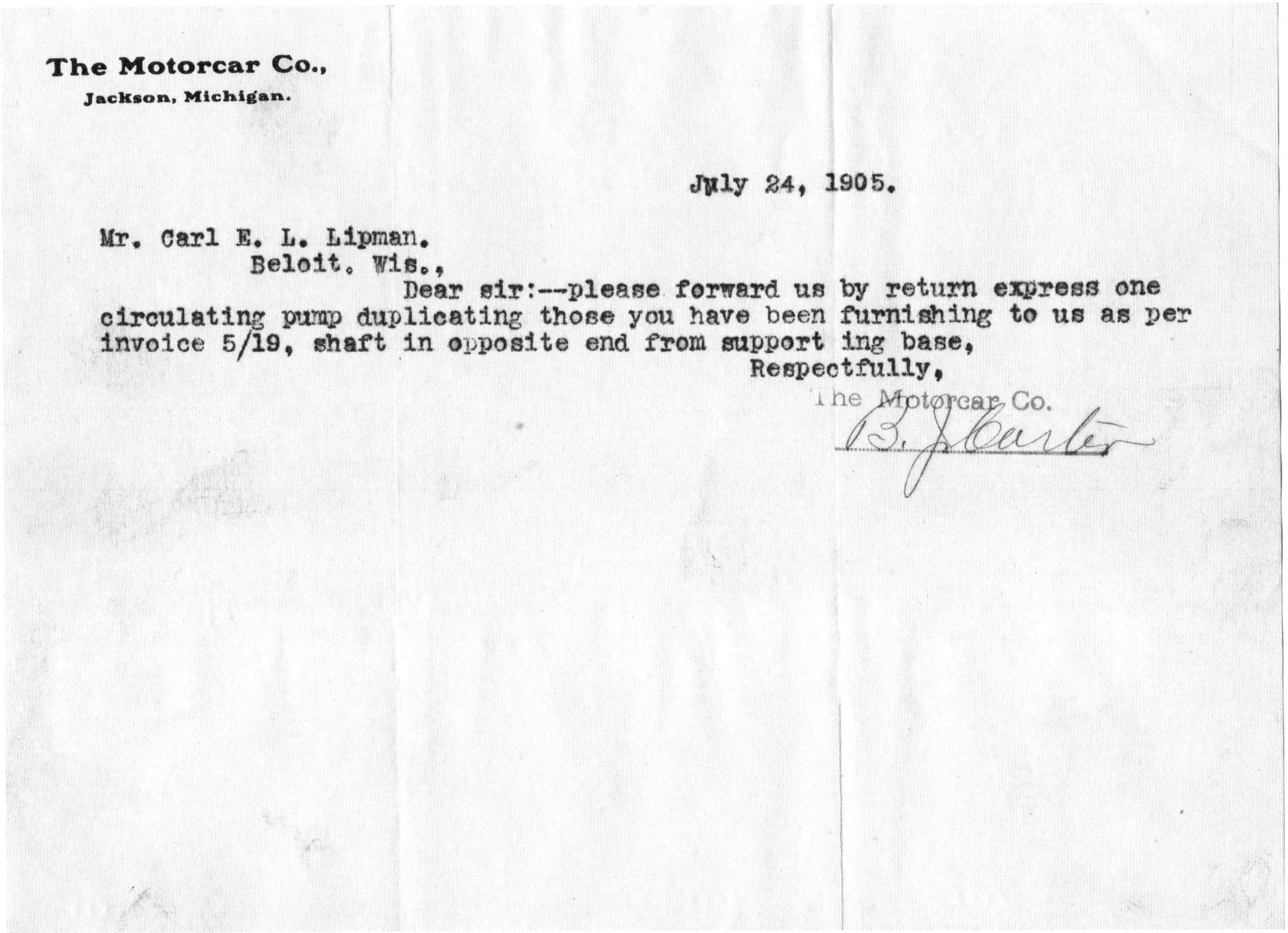

The Motorcar Co.,

Jackson, Michigan.

July 24, 1905.

Mr. Carl E. L. Lipman.
        Beloit, Wis.,
                Dear sir:---please forward us by return express one
circulating pump duplicating those you have been furnishing to us as per
invoice 5/19, shaft in opposite end from support ing base,
                                        Respectfully,
                                        The Motorcar Co.

Fig. 165. A July 24, 1905 letter signed by B. J. Carter on behalf of The Motorcar Co. of Jackson to Carl E. L. Lipman, a Beloit, Wisconsin, manufacturer of circulating oil and water pumps for automobiles; in this letter, Carter ordered one circulating pump and also referred to a May 19, 1905 invoice for multiple identical automobile pumps. This note clearly establishes that The Motorcar Co. had undertaken some modest production of automobiles with friction-drive transmissions by early 1905. *Author's collection*

Fig. 166. The Motorcar Co.'s 1905 Model "C" automobile, built in Jackson, with a friction-drive transmission and drive chains on both sides illustrated in the March 1, 1905 issue of *Cycle and Automobile Trade Journal*; the Model "C" was powered by a 10-horsepower vertical two-cylinder engine under the front hood; from the illustration, it appears the motor was water cooled with a tube-and-fin radiator in front. The car had not yet been upholstered. This friction-drive car was built on a wood-armored frame, had a 78-inch wheelbase and 30-inch tires, weighed 800 pounds, and was offered at $850. *Courtesy of Gregory R. Loftness*

Citizen account of Byron J. Carter's April 8, 1908 funeral, where Trask was a pallbearer, he had by then achieved the position of a Motorcar Company department head, undoubtedly in engineering.[667] He would ultimately serve as Cartercar's chief of the engineering department and factory production manager.[668] Trask and his family would relocate to Pontiac, Michigan, shortly after Cartercar moved there in late 1908.[669] Trask resigned from Cartercar in March 1912, and then relocated to Indianapolis.[670]

An extant piece of correspondence confirms that modest friction-drive-transmission car production by The Motorcar Co. in Jackson was definitely under way by May 1905 (fig. 165). In this July 24, 1905 note from B. J. Carter to Carl E. L. Lipman, a Beloit, Wisconsin, manufacturer of circulating oil and water pumps for automobiles, Carter ordered one circulating pump and referenced an earlier, May 19, 1905 invoice for multiple identical automobile-motor circulating pumps.

Descriptions of three different friction-drive Carter models built by The Motorcar Co. of Jackson, one illustrated in a somewhat unfinished state (fig. 166), were included in the March 1, 1905 issue of *Cycle and Automobile Trade Journal*.[671] The brand "Cartercar" is not mentioned anywhere in these auto descriptions, which may indicate that the Cartercar name was not in use until after the organization was greatly expanded in Detroit. The Carter machine illustrated in this article, the Model "C," had a price of $850 fully equipped with "storm apron," side lamps, and tools. The car developed 10 horsepower through a two-cylinder vertical engine with a bore and stroke of 4 1/2 x 4 inches under the front hood, which was equipped with a sight-feed oiler, likely manufactured by Carl E. L. Lipman.[672] The Model "C" was built on a wood-armored frame, had a 78-inch wheelbase and 30-inch tires, and it weighed 800 pounds. Of course, it was equipped with B. J. Carter's patented friction-drive transmission with side-chain drive. Figure 166 suggests that the Model "C" was water cooled, as the machine appears to have a tube-and-fin radiator in front.

The *Cycle and Automobile Trade Journal* piece reported that The Motorcar Co. also offered a Model "A" and a Model "B," which were "similar in exterior appearance to Model C."[673] The Model "A" had a 6 1/2 horsepower air-cooled engine with a bore and stroke of 3 1/2 x

4 inches; the car weighed 700 pounds and cost $650. The Model "B" had a 7 1/2 horsepower water-cooled engine with a bore and stroke of 3 1/2 x 4 inches; it weighed 750 pounds, and cost $700. The wheelbase of both was 75 inches, and the tire size was 2 1/2 x 28 inches. These Carter automobiles were equipped with side lamps and tools.[674]

The first 1906 model year catalog for the Cartercar, after B. J. Carter's operation was relocated to Detroit, offered prospective Cartercar buyers the opportunity to request testimonials from a list of owners who had previously bought one of Carter's friction-drive-transmission automobiles. Given the timing of the first Cartercar sales catalog's printing, these machines would all have certainly been produced by Carter's The Motorcar Co. in Jackson, sometime before November 1905. And the automobiles would not have yet likely been branded "Cartercar." The catalog names 11 owners of Carter's earliest friction-drive autos built in Jackson: Ralph H. Miller of Ann Arbor, who had bought the 1903 prototype runabout, six purchasers from Jackson, a second Ann Arbor owner, two purchasers from Concord, Michigan, and one from Clinton, Michigan. Some prominent citizens were among these first Carter friction-drive automobile buyers: George W. Luke, a former top and upholstery "trimmer" and foreman for the Fuller Buggy Company, who founded the American Buggy Top Co. in August 1903 (by 1912, it was a $350,000 automobile-top enterprise in Jackson); George A. McKeel, a Withington & Cooley Manufacturing Co. foreman, who was the titular head of a related sheet metal goods manufacturing firm called George A. McKeel & Co. Ltd. (incorporated March 2, 1903, with William Sparks and brothers Phillip H. and Winthrop Withington; by 1908, The Sparks-Withington Company Ltd. absorbed the McKeel firm); Elmer W. Grinnell, owner of Grinnell Brothers, a huge piano, phonograph, and "musical merchandise" retailer in Jackson and Detroit; Harry N. Hanchett, advertising manager for Grinnell Brothers; and an Ann Arbor physician.[675]

It is unknown whether B. J. Carter manufactured any additional friction-drive cars in Jackson beyond these 11 machines. Carter's efforts had attracted the attention of several distinguished Detroit businessmen and engineers who would soon motivate him to relocate to Detroit and commence major operations there to build a new automobile called the "Cartercar."

The Motorcar Company is Moved to Detroit to Build the Cartercar

The first 1906 Cartercar sales catalog and various periodical accounts of the day similarly state, "Learning indirectly of the success of Mr. Carter's Friction Drive Automobile, a party of Detroit gentlemen, including a number of mechanical engineers familiar with automobile construction, visited Jackson, and, after a most searching investigation, arranged to move Mr. Carter and his business to Detroit, where it might be most quickly expanded and developed. Exhaustive tests have been made, proving absolutely that the Carter system of Friction Transmission is not only the simplest, but the most efficient of all known devices for the purpose. These facts established, attention was directed to the designing of a line of automobiles embodying this most admirable feature," which the 1906 Cartercar sales catalog also labeled as "a radical departure from established practice in automobile construction."[676]

In a November 19, 1905 *Detroit Free Press* interview, Frank T. Caughey, the Motorcar Company's president, said, "We thought that Detroit was the center of the automobile business and we decided to have the factory here. . . . We are not going into this as an experiment to drop it again. It is the purpose of the company to develop the immense business the simple [friction-drive] mechanism makes possible."[677] The Motorcar Company of Detroit was incorporated September 22, 1905, with authorized capital stock of $150,000, of which $75,000 was initially subscribed (7,500 common shares of stock at a par value of $10 per share) and first held by only five shareholders.[678] The new company's articles of association stated that its purpose was "to manufacture and deal in automobiles and motor vehicles of every description, and their parts, and to acquire patents necessary to such business."[679] Although the original articles of association filed with the State of Michigan show the new entity's name as "The Motorcar Company," 1906 sales catalogs and advertisements omitted the upper case "The" from the start. The Motorcar Company would soon build new "friction drive automobiles from the designs of Byron J. Carter."[680] The October 15, 1905 *Detroit Free Press* reported that "the company will confine the manufacture to one style and size of light car, for five passengers, and to delivery wagons for the 1906 trade. It will not establish a large manufacturing plant, but will buy the parts, equip the engine with Mr. Carter's

ingenious device and assemble the car in its shops."[681] This new Carter-designed machine would be known as the "Cartercar" and was advertised with the new motto, "The Car Ahead."[682]

The Motorcar Company's early annual reports, certain automotive journals, and the *Detroit Free Press* listed B. J. Carter as second vice president along with the following prominent Detroit businessmen as the firm's other corporate officers and investors: president Frank T. Caughey, who was an owner of Caughey & Curran grain merchants and president of the machinery and engineers' supplies firm called Wray-Austin Machinery Company, Inc.; first vice president Fred Postal, who was president of Detroit's Hotel Griswold; secretary, and later general manager, Randall A. Palmer, who was secretary and treasurer of the Pittsburgh Shafting Company and owner the of the Detroit engineering firm Palmer-Bee Company; treasurer and director of sales Harry R. Radford, who was vice president and general manager of the Detroit Coin Wrapper Company; and director George A. Young, who was secretary and treasurer of Young Brothers. Other investors and stockholders were Benjamin Noble, George B. Palmer, Charles A. Young, Benjamin Middleditch, and James H. Cook, in addition to 17 others.[683] By the time the 1905 annual report was filed with the Michigan Secretary of State on March 5, 1906, the original roster of five stockholders had grown to 28 stockholders.[684] Like the Jackson Automobile Company, B. J. Carter's new venture had the substantial support and know-how of well-established men of business. Unlike the Jackson Automobile Company, the Motorcar Company would have the considerable benefit of a much larger, experienced group of these gentlemen investors, some of whom were engineers, working on its behalf.

B. J. Carter appears to have been well compensated for his friction-drive patent and other contributions to the Motorcar Company. Article VII of the firm's articles of association states that Carter received $75,000 as follows:

1. $35,000 for Carter's friction-drive transmission patent (United States Patent No. 761,146);

2. $25,000 for the goodwill of the business conducted by B. J. Carter, trading as The Motorcar Co. at Jackson, Michigan; and

3. $15,000 for patterns, drawings, and formulas.[685]

Fig. 167. The Motorcar Company, with several new investors and a substantial capital infusion, was reorganized and incorporated September 22, 1905, in Detroit to manufacture the new "Cartercar" automobile equipped with B. J. Carter's patented friction-drive transmission. Two of Carter's new partners in the Motorcar Company of Detroit were Randall A. Palmer (left), the firm's secretary and general manager, and Harry R. Radford (right), director of sales. *Author's collection*

The 2,500 shares of Motorcar Company common stock granted to B. J. Carter, as specified in the 1905 annual report, would have been worth $25,000, at a par value of $10 per share.[686] It seems probable that Carter received the remaining $50,000 (equivalent to $1.35 million in 2015) of his $75,000 remuneration in the form of cash.

In his November 19, 1905 *Detroit Free Press* interview, Frank T. Caughey, the Motorcar Company's president, said that "Mr. Carter will move here and give his attention to the manufacture of the machines."[687] Shortly after, Carter and his family did indeed relocate from their Jackson home to 512 Commonwealth Avenue in Detroit; by 1906, B. J. Carter was listed at this address in the *Detroit City Directory*.[688]

On a somewhat folksy note, the first 1906 Cartercar sales catalog included an October 6, 1905 letter written by Ralph H. Miller of Ann Arbor, the man who had purchased B. J. Carter's first experimental friction-drive car built in 1903: "Your favor of September 29th [1905] received. I have been using a light machine made by Mr. Carter, which

has a friction transmission, and it has proven very satisfactory. Wishing you success in the venture, I am yours truly, Ralph H. Miller."[689]

The Motorcar Company moved quickly to establish a manufacturing facility in Detroit. By October 1905 the enterprise had set up temporary quarters at 24 Atwater Street East, where "Byron J. Carter, the inventor of the device which distinguishes the auto from other makes, has built a sample car," which was already being tested.[690] The November 19, 1905 *Detroit Free Press* and the November 22, 1905 issue of *The Horseless Age* reported that the Motorcar Company had moved from these temporary offices to the former Stearns laboratory building on Twenty-First Street near Baker Street, where the Motorcar Company leased part of the facilities "and has started to manufacture the Carter motor car."[691] This plant had been vacated by Frederick Stearns & Co. manufacturing pharmacists in October 1899, when the firm relocated to a large complex at the corner of Jefferson and Bellevue avenues.[692] The full address for the new Motorcar Company factory shown in early Cartercar factory brochures and most advertisements was 220–230 Twenty-First Street; alternately, the factory's address was listed as 224–256 Twenty-First Street in Detroit city directories.[693] Frank T. Caughey, in his November 19, 1905 *Detroit Free Press* interview, said, "Work has already been started at the Stearns plant, as Mr. Carter brought what machinery he had from Jackson."[694] Additionally, articles in the November 30, 1905 issue of *The Automobile* and the December 14, 1905 issue of *Motor Age* reported that the Motorcar Company "is now putting in new machinery, preparatory to the manufacture of a friction drive car, to be listed at $1,250, after the design of B. J. Carter, who is superintendent of the new company" and that "the first model is nearly completed."[695] It appears that the Motorcar Company was moving rapidly to build momentum and commence manufacturing, and it would soon offer the new 1906 season friction-drive-transmission Cartercars for sale.

The Motorcar Company of Detroit's annual report for calendar year-end 1905 was filed with the Michigan Secretary of State on March 5, 1906. This 1905 annual report indicated that the original $150,000 capitalization was still intact, that assets, namely personal property, cash, and B. J. Carter's patents, drawings, patterns, and goodwill, were valued at $75,000, and that the company was not carrying any debt. As was typical of the annual reports filed with the Michigan Secretary of State at this time, it included only a balance sheet; no revenue and expense information was shown.[696]

Fig. 168. After a short occupancy in temporary quarters at 24 Atwater Street East, the newly incorporated Motorcar Company moved to a leased factory building at 220–230 Twenty-First Street (the address used in early Cartercar factory brochures and most advertisements; alternatively, the factory's address was listed as 224–256 Twenty-First Street in Detroit city directories). The factory building's exterior is shown in this photograph. *The Horseless Age* reported that the Motorcar Company had "commenced operations" in this factory by late November 1905. *Author's collection*

Carter Car friction drive - Detroit Mich 1906

Fig. 169. A group of Motorcar Company factory workmen in 1906, either before or after a baseball game (note the baseball glove and ball in the foreground); this photograph was taken near one of the Motorcar Company factory entrances. The Cartercar in the midst of this crowd appears to be a Cartercar Model "D" runabout introduced in the summer of 1906 for the 1907 season. *Courtesy of the Ella Sharp Museum*

Fig. 170. A 1906 Cartercar out for a drive with Randall A. Palmer, the Motorcar Company's corporate secretary and general manager, in the passenger seat, likely in Detroit; the driver is not identified but probably was affiliated with the new Motorcar Company as well. *Courtesy of the National Automotive History Collection, Detroit Public Library*

The Motorcar Company's Inaugural 1906 Season

The U.S. automobile market was becoming increasingly competitive by 1906, and thoughtful design and assembly standards were more important than ever. For the Motorcar Company's inaugural automobile season (the word "season" was typically used in Cartercar's advertising in place of the term "model year"), B. J. Carter and the other Motorcar Company engineers and managers adopted a keep-it-simple approach and offered the 1906 Cartercar with only one type of chassis onto which different styles of bodies could be bolted.[697] The first 1906 Cartercar sales catalog advertised that "the body of the 'Cartercar' may be removed or replaced in five minutes, as the tank, batteries, etc. are so located that no wires or pipes are disconnected in the operation."[698] This same one-chassis approach would work incredibly well for Henry Ford during the Ford Motor Company's production of its Model "T" from October 1, 1908, through May 26, 1927. (Ford built and sold 15 million Model "T" cars.)[699]

This simplified production methodology may also have resulted from B. J. Carter's experience at the Jackson Automobile Company, where a wider variety of cars (initially with either a steam or gasoline engine) had made consistent, reliable manufacturing harder to organize and launch. Interestingly, the Jackson Automobile Company continued to offer several different motor sizes, chassis assemblies, and body styles with various new models annually throughout its nearly 20 years of car manufacturing (and they consistently experienced production missteps and had difficulty filling orders for nearly all of these years).

The 1906 Cartercar running gear was powered by a 20-horsepower two-cylinder horizontally opposed engine under the hood and was "designed especially for this model and possessing several original and unique features," which when combined with the friction-drive transmission could achieve "any speeds, 1 to 40 miles per hour."[700] Of course, this machine was equipped with B. J. Carter's patented friction-drive transmission system.[701] Unlike the friction-drive-transmission machines Carter had built in Jackson, which had two side drive chains to transmit power from the friction-drive assembly to the rear axle, the 1906 Cartercar was equipped with an off-center single drive chain to the rear axle. The wheelbase was 94 inches long over a pressed-steel frame on 30-inch tires.

The Motorcar Company's initial offerings for 1906 were two touring cars: a Model "A" with a somewhat conventional five-passenger touring body and a Model "B" with a more elaborate Victoria-style body (sometimes called a "tulip" body). Both touring cars' bodies were constructed of wood with a pressed-steel dash and were painted "Brewster" green with a "Derby" red chassis.[702] Each weighed approximately 1,650 pounds.[703] Standard equipment for 1906

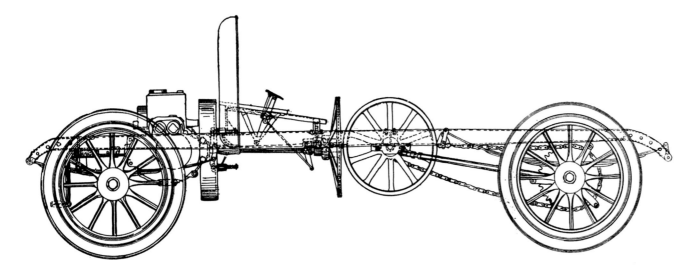

Fig. 171. An elevation drawing of the 1906 Cartercar chassis, which illustrates the simplicity of B. J. Carter's patented friction-drive transmission, at center, along with the engine and other running-gear assemblies; the wheelbase was 94 inches over a pressed-steel frame on 30-inch tires. *Author's collection*

Fig. 172. An overhead view of the Cartercar chassis from the first 1906 sales catalog, published by the Motorcar Company of Detroit in the fall of 1905; unlike the friction-drive-transmission machines Carter built in Jackson, which had two side drive chains from the friction-drive assembly to the rear axle, the 1906 Cartercar was equipped with an off-center single drive chain to the rear axle. Note the rubber running board matting, which is prominently embossed with the brand "Carter." *Author's collection*

Fig. 173. The water-cooled 20-horsepower two-cylinder horizontally opposed Cartercar engine for 1906, which was installed in front under the hood; in this photographic engraving, the radiator is not depicted in order to provide a better view of the engine. The 1906 sales catalog states that the motor was "designed especially for this model," possibly by B. J. Carter. *Author's collection*

Cartercars was three polished brass oil lamps (two for the dash and a tail lamp), a brass bulb horn, floor mats, and a set of tools.[704] The 1906 sales catalog did not mention whether any special equipment such as acetylene gas headlamps (which were shown in 1906 catalog engravings of models "A" and "B"), a rubberized canvas top, or any special colors could be ordered. The first 1906 Cartercar sales catalog had another more serious omission—prices were not shown. The November 30, 1905 issue of *The Automobile*, early Cartercar advertisements in national journals, and the Motorcar Company's supplementary Booklet "B," issued by June 1906, ultimately stated that the price for the 1906 Model "A" was $1,250.[705]

In a May 1, 1906 *Cycle and Automobile Trade Journal* article, the technical writer, Hugh Dolnar, reported that B. J. Carter had taken him on a 54-mile Cartercar test run from Sharpe's Chop House in

Detroit to Pontiac and back on April 1, 1906.[706] Carter was piloting a Cartercar "tester's rig," which the writer indicated was "one of the first lot of 'Cartercars.'"[707] On that day, the dirt roads around Detroit and Pontiac were "at the breaking up of winter, with ice and snow yet in the ditches, in horrible condition, deeply rutted by narrow tired farm wagon wheels, with several long mud holes in which the 'Cartercar' wheels sank more than the tire diameter, and where dry, the deep, narrow ruts held the pneumatics like a vice, and there was little indeed of this usually excellent road surface that was not a most trying succession of bumps and holes, so that the passenger sat forward and hung on with both hands and watched the road, and rode it as best he could, and out of it all get [*sic*] the worst shaking up of his motoring experience."[708] The *Cycle and Automobile Trade Journal* writer reported, "This run was made at the writer's urgent request and wholly against Carter's wishes. The motor had no hood, and there was no shield under the friction, and both motor and transmission, as well as the writer's eyeglasses, were liberally plastered in mud. The friction drive could not well have had a more severe test, and it performed to admiration throughout the entire bouncing of this hardest of all Pontiac runs."[709]

It appears that that the Model "B," with its Victoria-style body, was discontinued by May or June 1906, as it is no longer referenced in Cartercar advertising by then.[710] This elaborate design in automobile-body manufacturing, a carryover from carriage days, had essentially gone out of fashion during 1906. Cartercar's supplementary Booklet "B," issued by June 1906, which formally added the Model "C" delivery vehicle to the Cartercar line, did not show the Model "B" Victoria but did show the Model "A" touring car.[711]

The Model "C" delivery car had actually been introduced by February 1906 and was displayed, along with at least one other Cartercar, a Model "A," at Detroit's February 12–17, 1906 Tri-State Automobile and Sportsmen's Show in the Light Guard Armory.[712] Interestingly, the *Detroit Times* reported that the Motorcar Company, in its Detroit show display on opening night, had hitched a friction-drive-transmission assembly "to an electric motor which spun the big disks round at a lively clip, and the novel operation of the simple-looking device kept people around the car three or four deep all evening."[713] A *Cycle and*

Model "A"

Fig. 174. The 1906 Cartercar Model "A" touring car, as illustrated in the first 1906 sales catalog; the Model "A" was equipped with a handsome five-passenger wood touring body, which was varnished "Brewster" green with a "Derby" red running gear and wheels. The car weighed approximately 1,650 pounds and was priced at $1,250. *Author's collection*

Model "B"

Fig. 175. The 1906 Cartercar Model "B" touring car, as illustrated in the first 1906 sales catalog; the Model "B" possessed more elaborate "Victoria" wood coachwork (sometimes called a "tulip" body), which was varnished "Brewster" green with a "Derby" red running gear and wheels. The machine weighed approximately 1,650 pounds. Note the bold "Carter" name, which was embossed in the rubber running board matting. *Author's collection*

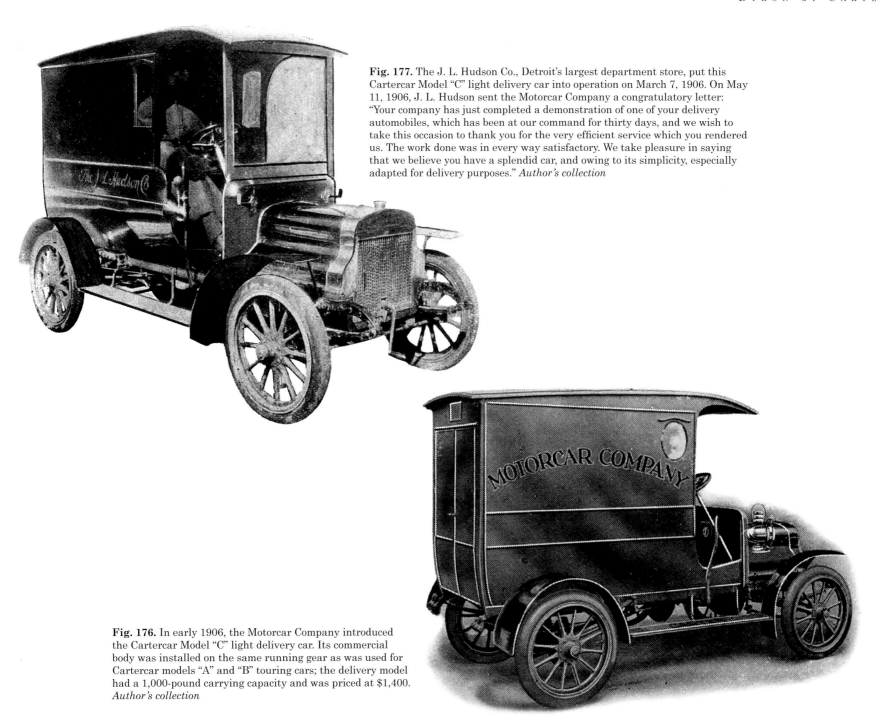

Fig. 177. The J. L. Hudson Co., Detroit's largest department store, put this Cartercar Model "C" light delivery car into operation on March 7, 1906. On May 11, 1906, J. L. Hudson sent the Motorcar Company a congratulatory letter: "Your company has just completed a demonstration of one of your delivery automobiles, which has been at our command for thirty days, and we wish to take this occasion to thank you for the very efficient service which you rendered us. The work done was in every way satisfactory. We take pleasure in saying that we believe you have a splendid car, and owing to its simplicity, especially adapted for delivery purposes." *Author's collection*

Fig. 176. In early 1906, the Motorcar Company introduced the Cartercar Model "C" light delivery car. Its commercial body was installed on the same running gear as was used for Cartercar models "A" and "B" touring cars; the delivery model had a 1,000-pound carrying capacity and was priced at $1,400. *Author's collection*

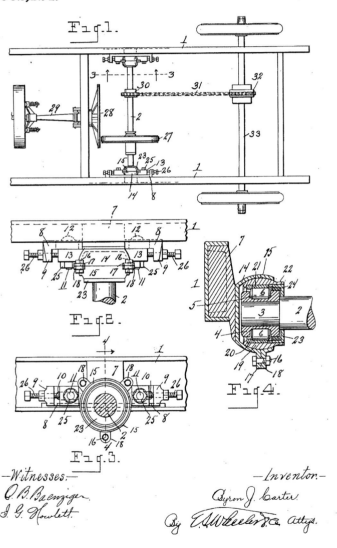

Fig. 178. Patent drawing for B. J. Carter's adjustable journal bearing, a component of the friction-drive transmission assembly (after the rear-axle chain drive mechanism was simplified from two side chains to one central chain); this U.S. patent (no. 962,124) was filed September 4, 1906, a year after the Motorcar Company had been incorporated in Detroit, and was not granted until June 21, 1910, nearly four years later. Carter likely would have assigned his right to this pending patent to the Motorcar Company when it was first filed. It is uncertain why Carter did not file for this patent earlier, in conjunction with designing the Cartercar chassis for the 1906 season. The four-year grant time for this Carter patent would indicate that the U.S. Patent and Trademark Office had become backed up, with slower turnaround times, thanks to the huge influx of automotive and other related patent applications after 1905. It is also possible that the Motorcar Company may have been challenged to prove to patent office officials that this adjustable journal bearing was a novel device that had not been previously claimed or patented by another inventor. *Courtesy of the United States Patent and Trademark Office*

Figs. 179 & 180 (opposite). A second patent that B. J. Carter filed September 4, 1906, the same day he filed the adjustable journal bearing patent in fig. 178; this U.S. patent (no. 983,349) was granted for the "frictional transmission mechanism" and covered the construction and arrangement of various structural elements required to provide simple, economical, and efficient "movement of the frictional transmitting disk to enable it to be applied with the requisite pressure against the friction wheel on the driven shaft." The September 4, 1906 patent application was not granted until February 7, 1911, nearly four and a half years later. B. J. Carter likely would have assigned his right to this pending patent to the Motorcar Company when it was first filed. This longer timing from application to grant is further evidence that the U.S. Patent and Trademark Office was becoming quite backed up. It is also possible the Motorcar Company may have been challenged by patent office officials to prove that this frictional transmission mechanism was sufficiently novel and distinct, so as not to have been previously claimed or patented by another inventor. *Courtesy of the United States Patent and Trademark Office*

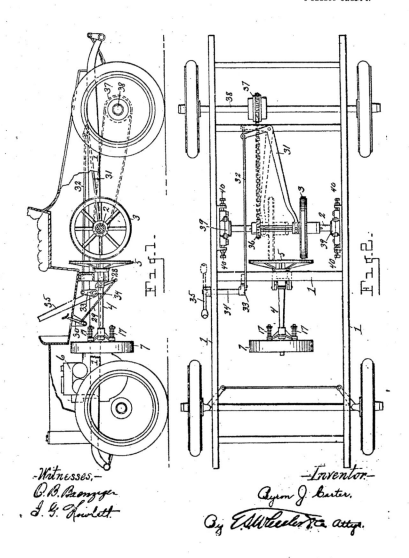

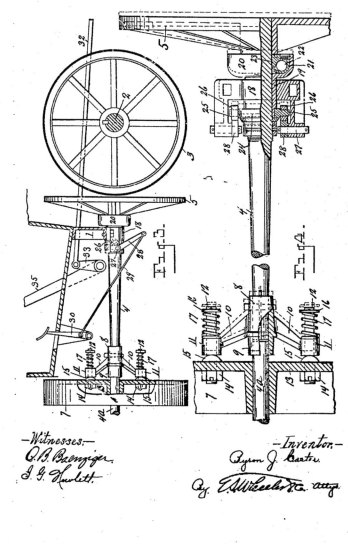

Fig. 181. Harry E. Legg's business card, when he was sales manager of Cartercar Wisconsin Co., state distributor for the Cartercar. *Author's collection, courtesy of Susan Dunek*

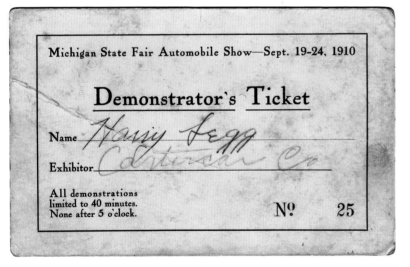

Fig. 182. Harry E. Legg's demonstrator's ticket for his Cartercar exhibition and hill-climbing ramp at the Michigan State Fair Automobile Show, September 19–24, 1910. Legg was only 20 years old at the time of this Cartercar exhibition. *Author's collection, courtesy of Susan Dunek*

Automobile Trade Journal reporter made a March 29, 1906 test run with a new Cartercar Model "C" light delivery car already in service for The J. L. Hudson Company, Detroit's largest department store (fig. 177).[714] His article reported that J. L. Hudson had put this vehicle into operation on March 7, 1906, with excellent efficiency and service results.[715] The Model "C" delivery body was fitted to the exact running gear as was used on Cartercar models "A" and "B." The Cartercar delivery car weighed about 1,800 pounds, had a 1,000-pound carrying capacity, and was offered at a price of $1,400.[716]

In light of persistent skepticism regarding Carter's friction-drive transmission, the Motorcar Company set about making highly visible public demonstrations of the Cartercar's power, agility, strength, and durability by running the cars up huge wooden test ramps, which Cartercar sales agents would temporarily erect at state fairs and other events attended by large crowds. One of the earliest documented hill-climbing events is illustrated in the September 27, 1906 issue of *The Automobile* magazine.[717] The short article described the Cartercar as "climbing a grade of 50 per cent at the state fair recently held at Detroit, Mich. The [wooden] incline was so steep that the wheels would not hold until the timbers were dressed with a friction-producing fluid."[718] These hill-climbing demonstrations soon became quite popular and set the Motorcar Company down a long path of conducting other unusual and wild, sometimes downright silly, well-publicized advertising stunts. In fact, a 1913 *Detroit Free Press* article reported that "putting on the show" was the approach Harry R. Radford, general manager, took and "that the methods used by the Cartercar company of Pontiac in preparing and handling their exhibits are worthy of the modern stage manager."[719]

Blueprints were soon made available from the factory in order that Cartercar sales agents could safely build their own hill-climbing demonstration ramps for local fairs and festivals.

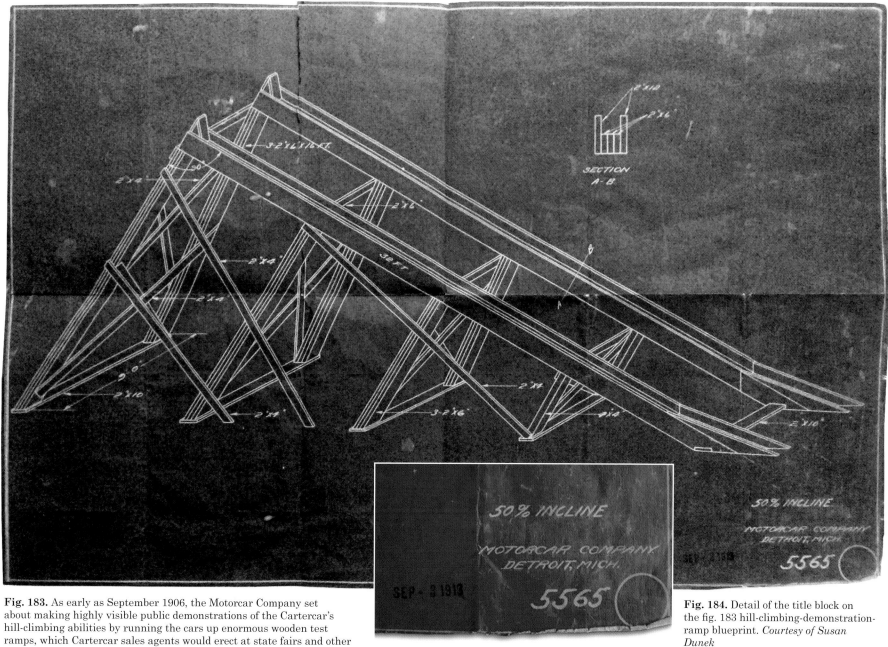

Fig. 183. As early as September 1906, the Motorcar Company set about making highly visible public demonstrations of the Cartercar's hill-climbing abilities by running the cars up enormous wooden test ramps, which Cartercar sales agents would erect at state fairs and other events with large attendance. To assist in building a relatively safe demonstration ramp, typically at a 50 percent incline, the Motorcar Company developed a set of standard blueprints. This example was sent by the Cartercar factory to Harry E. Legg, who by 1913 had been promoted to sales manager of Cartercar Wisconsin Co. *Courtesy of Susan Dunek*

Fig. 184. Detail of the title block on the fig. 183 hill-climbing-demonstration-ramp blueprint. *Courtesy of Susan Dunek*

Fig. 185. This photograph from Harry E. Legg's papers shows a driver, possibly Legg himself, demonstrating the hill-climbing prowess of a 1912 Cartercar Model "H" four-cylinder touring car on a Cartercar incline ramp at the Illinois State Fairgrounds in Springfield. The structure in the background is the Dome Building, which had originally been erected for horticultural exhibits at the 1893 World's Columbian Exposition in Chicago. Following the Chicago exposition, the Illinois State Fair purchased and dismantled the building, and then reassembled a portion of the structure in Springfield in 1895. *Courtesy of Susan Dunek*

Fig. 186. Another Cartercar hill-climbing-demonstration ramp on exhibition at the Iowa State Fair; the Cartercar driving up the ramp appears to be a 1908 Model "A," and the Cartercar adjacent to the ramp is a late 1908 or 1909 two-cylinder Gentleman's Roadster (later called a Gentlemen's Roadster). *Author's collection*

Fig. 187. Auto Ajax, pictured in this 1909 photograph, performed a trick of holding an automobile of "ordinary power" with ropes for at least 60 seconds, or until the car's motor stalled. A two-cylinder Cartercar piloted by Louis Engel Jr., Buffalo, New York, Cartercar sales agent, bested him at Luna Park in Buffalo, after which Auto Ajax proclaimed, "The only time in my career as a professional that I have ever met with defeat, was at Luna Park, pulling against a 24 H. P. Cartercar. This car gave me a tough pull." *Author's collection*

Fig. 188. Factory-issued photograph of Edwin D. Doan, a Cartercar distributor and tightrope walker from Saginaw, Michigan, who balanced above a moving Cartercar for over 10 miles during the July 10, 1909 Glidden Tour Parade in Detroit; the Cartercar appears to be a 1910 Model "L" four-cylinder touring car. *Author's collection*

In addition to launching a prominent, new automobile venture, B. J. Carter, and his wife, Della, welcomed a new son, Kenneth Gillette Carter, on May 1, 1906 (died September 30, 1976), making 1906 an important year in more ways than one. Kenneth's daughter Linda "Buzzy" Carter Maurer assisted the author in research for this book.

Cartercar's 1906 season had a promising finish, as it was reported that 101 automobiles had been produced.[720] The February 1, 1907 *Cycle and Automobile Trade Journal* stated that "the friction drive 'Cartercars,' had a very successful year in 1906, having always unfilled orders on their books . . . the Detroit factory was run over-time, and the output was fully up to expectation."[721] This article went on to say, "The friction speed-change and reverse is the simplest, the cheapest and the most easily handled of all motor-car gears, and the entire satisfactory performance of each and every one of the considerable number of 'Cartercars' made and sold in 1906, is proof of the strongest possible character that the much questioned friction-drive is an unqualified success when properly designed and built."[722]

By the end of 1906, Cartercar had also established an impressive list of sales agencies in 23 cities and towns: New York; Los Angeles; Chicago; Minneapolis; Denver; Philadelphia and Pittsburgh, Pennsylvania; Tacoma and Seattle, Washington; Akron, Cleveland, Cincinnati, and Rising Sun, Ohio; Bay City, Cassopolis, Detroit, and Port Huron, Michigan; Milwaukee, Wisconsin; San Antonio, Texas; Leesburg, Florida; Brattleboro, Vermont; Utica, New York; and Ord, Nebraska.[723]

The Motorcar Company's annual report for calendar year-end 1906 was filed with the Michigan Secretary of State on February 1, 1907. This 1906 annual report indicated that the original $150,000 capitalization was intact with $118,360 subscribed, that assets totaled $104,534.40 (up from $75,000 in 1905) composed of personal property, cash, accounts receivable, and B. J. Carter's patents, drawings and patterns, and goodwill, and that the company was carrying a relatively small $10,271.86 of debt. Twenty-four additional individuals had acquired stock in the Motorcar Company (beyond the original 28 shareholders listed in the 1905 annual report), and each had been added to the roster of investors. B. J. Carter was still listed as owning 2,500 shares. Like the 1905 annual report, it included only a balance sheet; no revenue and expense information was shown.[724]

Fig. 189. By the end of 1906, the Motorcar Company had established an impressive list of Cartercar sales agencies in 23 cities and villages. This late 1906 photograph shows the New York City Cartercar sales agency, called the Carter Car Co., managed by C. H. Galt and located at 1697 Broadway. *Courtesy of the National Automotive History Collection, Detroit Public Library*

Fig. 190. Charles A. Trask collaborated with B. J. Carter on various mechanical and engine projects in Jackson. In December 1906, he followed Carter to Detroit to work in designing and manufacturing the Cartercar and was soon promoted to chief engineer and factory production manager. He remained a friend of Della Carter and her family after B. J. Carter's death and gave her this photograph. Trask is shown driving a four-cylinder 1910 Cartercar Model "H" Roadster with Miniature Tonneau (or a 1911 Model "H" touring car) accompanied by his wife, Rose J. Trask, née McKenna, in the back seat with their daughter, Marjorie Iva Trask, and the family dog. Their son, Verne Alva Trask, sits in front with his father. *Courtesy of Sallie Sparks Kendall*

1907 Season for the Cartercar

In its 1907 sales catalog, the Motorcar Company stated, "It is our purpose to manufacture but one size and type of chassis of the 'Cartercar' for the season of 1907, believing that the concentration of our energies will result in greater perfection in our product and economies in manufacture."[725] The 1907 Cartercar chassis (or running gear) was equipped with a modestly larger two-cylinder motor, at 20 to 24 horsepower, than was installed in the 1906 Cartercar.[726] The 1909 Cartercar sales catalog no. 10 indicated that this larger 24-horsepower motor with an improved oiling system had been designed by B. J. Carter "late in the year 1906" and that the engine "embodies many special features of exceptional merit, the most important of which are protected by letters patent."[727] This uptick in power was primarily achieved by increasing the cylinder bore from 5 to 5 1/2 inches. Cartercar also represented in its 1907 sales catalog that the motor's "valve gear is a recent invention of Mr. Carter (patent pending). It eliminates wear and noise and has many advantages, particularly as regards the quick opening and easy seating of the valves."[728] The February 15, 1907 *Detroit Free Press* confirmed the Motorcar Company "is today building its own motors, where but six months ago the engines were built outside of Detroit."[729] No record of these particular B. J. Carter motor- or valve-assembly patents was found in the U. S. Patent and Trademark Office; perhaps they were patent applications that were submitted but ultimately not granted. (The U.S. Patent and Trademark Office generally does not retain early patent applications that were considered but never granted.)

The 1907 wheelbase was lengthened by two inches to 96 inches. And a sturdy cast-aluminum dash replaced the pressed-steel dash used on 1906 cars. All cars were now painted "Brewster" green with no contrasting red chassis; however, the Model "C" delivery car paint scheme was listed as "optional."[730] A Cartercar sales catalog described the process of painting (or, actually, the application of many coats of varnish, some colored), which required five to eight weeks for preparation,

repeated applications of varnish, sanding in between, and adequate varnish drying times.[731] Extra equipment could be purchased in the 1907 season at an additional cost: special colors, various top styles, acetylene gas headlamps and a requisite acetylene (carbide) generator, speedometers, clocks, and extra tires with covers and holders.[732] Other specifications for the 1907 models are shown in figure 196.

Cartercar announced the "latest" Cartercars in the October 1, 1906 *Cycle and Automobile Trade Journal* for the 1907 season: a Model "D" runabout and a Model "E" touring car; a 1907 Cartercar runabout had also been illustrated in *The Horseless Age* and *The Motor Way* two months earlier.[733] Incidentally, the *Cycle and Automobile Trade Journal* article mentioned that the new Model "D" runabout was similar to Cartercar's Model "B" runabout; however, no information about or illustrations of a 1906 or 1907 Model "B" runabout could be located.[734] Even though engravings of these earliest 1907 machines clearly show 1906-style radiators and hoods, the supplementary Cartercar sales brochure for the first Model "E" specifically indicated that it was a 1907 model.[735] The Model "E" was equipped with an Artz folding rear tonneau. This rear seat could be folded and collapsed into a trunk-like compartment, which then converted the Model "E" touring car to a sporty two-passenger runabout.[736]

Fig. 191. Rear view of the 1907 Cartercar Model "D" runabout (first style), which was introduced in July 1906 and still retained the 1906-style radiator, hood, and dash. *Courtesy of Gregory R. Loftness*

Model "E" Folding Tonneau "Cartercar"

Fig. 193. The first version of the 1907 Cartercar Model "E" with folding Artz tonneau open; this rear seat could be collapsed into a trunk-like compartment, which then converted the Model "E" touring car to a two-passenger runabout (see fig. 192). Even though this Model "E" still retained the 1906-style radiator and hood, a supplementary Cartercar sales brochure for the first Model "E" specifically indicated that it is a 1907 model. Price was $1,350 including floor mats, horn, tools, and three oil lamps. *Author's collection*

Model "E" Folding Tonneau "Cartercar"

Price, $1350.00 including mats, horn, tools
and three oil lamps.

Fig. 192. First version of the 1907 Cartercar Model "E" with folding Artz tonneau closed, converting it to a sporty two-passenger runabout. *Author's collection*

Fig. 195. An overhead view of the Cartercar chassis from the 1907 Motorcar Company sales catalog; the friction transmission's aluminum-alloy driving disk is clearly illustrated. *Author's collection*

Fig. 194. The 1907 season water-cooled 20- to 24-horsepower two-cylinder horizontally opposed Cartercar engine and friction-drive transmission assembly; Cartercar's 1909 sales catalog stated that B. J. Carter designed this two-cylinder engine in late 1906; it was built in the Cartercar factory and installed in all Cartercars virtually unchanged from 1907 through the 1909 season. A 1907 Cartercar sales catalog indicated that the valve gear for this motor was "a recent invention of Mr. Carter (patent pending). It eliminates wear and noise and has many advantages, particularly as regards the quick opening and easy seating of the valves." The adjustable journal bearings covered by U.S. patent no. 962,124 (fig. 178) are labeled "H" in this engraving from the 1907 Motorcar Company sales catalog. *Author's collection*

1907
SPECIFICATIONS

	Model "A"	Model "C"	Model "D"	Model "E"	Model "F"
TYPE	Fixed Tonneau	Delivery	Runabout	Artz Folding Tonneau	Detachable Tonneau
CAPACITY	5 Passenger	1000 lbs.	2 Passenger	2 and 4 Passenger	2 and 5 Passenger
MOTOR	2-Cyl. Opposed	2-Cyl. Opposed	2-Cyl. Opposed	2-Cyl. Opposed	2-Cyl. Opposed
HORSE POWER	20-24	20-24	20-24	20-24	20-24
WHEEL BASE	96 inches	96 inches	96 inches	96 inches	96 inches
SIZE OF TIRES	30 x 3½	30 x 3½	30 x 3½	30 x 3½	30 x 3½
GASOLINE CAPACITY	15 gals.	15 gals.	15 gals.	15 gals.	15 gals.
COLOR	Brewster Green	Optional	Brewster Green	Brewster Green	Brewster Green

Equipment; 3 oil lamps, tube horn, mats, tire repair kit dry cell batteries, battery box of pressed steel with tray for small tools on running board. All bodies are ironed for tops. Special colors or equipment extra. Only standard American tires are used.

Fig. 196. A chart of Cartercar's 1907 season specifications organized by model; standard equipment and extras are set forth in the bottom paragraph.

MODEL "A" Fixed Tonneau 5-Passenger Car
Price, $1,350.00 F. O. B. Detroit

MODEL "C" DELIVERY VEHICLE
1,000 Pounds Capacity
Price, $1,400.00 F. O. B. Detroit

Figs. 197–202. Engravings of the various 1907 Cartercar models from the 1907 Motorcar Company sales catalog. *Author's collection*

MODEL "D" RUNABOUT
Price, $1,250.00, F. O. B. Detroit

MODEL "E" ARTZ FOLDING TONNEAU (Closed)
Price, $1,350, F. O. B. Detroit

MODEL "E"   Artz Folding Tonneau (Open)
Price, $1,350.00 F. O. B. Detroit

MODEL "F" DETACHABLE TONNEAU
Price, $1,400.00, Including Tonneau, F. O. B. Detroit

Fig. 203. Seven Cartercar two-passenger runabouts or roadsters in service for the Detroit Fire Department in front of the department's headquarters at the intersection of Wayne and Larned streets; Detroit's fire department was a loyal Cartercar customer, starting with two early purchases when the Motorcar Company was still quite new: a 1907 Cartercar Model "D" two-cylinder runabout (first style), second from the right in this image, used by the superintendent of Detroit's fire alarm system, and a 1907 Model "D" two-cylinder runabout (second style), at the far right, used by the fire department's "master mechanic." The *Detroit Free Press* reported that the Detroit Fire Department's five other Cartercar runabouts were 1911 Model "H" four-cylinder roadsters. *Author's collection*

Fig. 204. A close-up view of the three different styles of Cartercars purchased by the Detroit Fire Department (right to left): a 1907 Model "D" runabout (second style); a 1907 Cartercar Model "D" runabout (first style); and a 1911 Model "H" roadster. *Author's collection*

By the spring of 1907, the original Cartercar slogan, "The Car Ahead," was sometimes being replaced by or paired with the more catchy motto "No Gears to Strip—No Clutch to Slip," which was suspiciously similar in structure to Jackson's slogan, "No Hill Too Steep, No Sand Too Deep."[737] Cartercars were catching on, and, by the end of 1907, the friction-drive transmission was no longer considered to be a risky, unproven novelty. Customer loyalty had grown rapidly as well, with some great publicity along the way. For example, the Detroit Fire Department, which had purchased a 1907 Cartercar runabout in late 1906 for its superintendent, came back to Cartercar and bought another runabout, a Model "D," in June 1907.[738] This Cartercar was to be used by the fire department's master mechanic.[739]

The Motorcar Company entered into a manufacturing licensing agreement in mid-1907 with a separate Detroit automobile enterprise called the Carter Runabout Company. The June 11, 1907 *Detroit Free Press* announced that the Carter Runabout Company had been incorporated on June 10 and was capitalized at $250,000; the article reported "a contract [had been] entered into by Elmer L. Allor, one of the stockholders with the Motorcar Co., of Detroit, whereby the new concern acquires the right to manufacture a certain make of automobile."[740] The newspaper article was inaccurate regarding Elmer L. Allor's Motorcar Company stockholder status, as his name is not shown on any of the stockholder rosters included in the Motorcar Company's annual reports. The *Detroit Free Press* piece further indicated that Motorcar Company shareholders Frank T. Caughey, George W. Miller, Randall A. Palmer, and George A. Young were also stockholders in the Carter Runabout Company, each holding 10 shares of common stock valued at $100 per share.[741] Six days earlier, *The Horseless Age* had written, "We understand that a number of the stockholders of the Motorcar Company of Detroit, Mich., are forming a company to manufacture runabouts equipped with four cylinder motors and sliding gear transmissions."[742] The Motorcar Company quickly dispelled the offensive concept of a Carter vehicle built with anything other than a friction-drive transmission: *The Horseless Age* on June 19, 1907, indicated that the Motorcar Company "denies that it or any of its stockholders are interested in a company to manufacture runabouts equipped with four cylinder motors and sliding gear transmissions, as reported in our issue of June 5, 1907, and informs us that the Carter Runabout Company has been incorporated to manufacture two cylinder runabouts with the Carter friction transmission under license from the Motor Car [*sic*] Company."[743] The true purpose of this venture is a mystery today, as the Motorcar Company had announced its own 1907 Cartercar runabout models at least 11 months earlier and had already been producing runabouts for some time.[744] More information is needed to confirm whether the Carter Runabout Company ever manufactured any automobiles and, if it did, the brand that was used for these machines.

Even though B. J. Carter occupied a privileged position at Cartercar, he remained on the front lines and was active in promoting the machine he had invented. *The Automobile* reported that Carter had driven one of the two Cartercars entered in the Cleveland Automobile Club's September 10–12, 1907 sealed bonnet (hood) competition, which was a grueling

446-mile run in drenching rain over three days.[745] In addition to the Cartercars, six other automobiles participated in the run including two Jacksons, one piloted by the soon-to-be famous race car driver, Robert R. Burman. While the Cartercars did not finish in first place, one finished second, and they successfully maneuvered the muddy, slippery route and beat both Jackson cars.[746] This solid outcome was achieved even though the Cartercars received substantial penalty points because both had broken gasoline pipelines that needed to be fixed and, in one case, the hood seal was broken during the repair. Ultimately, the other Cartercar's hood seal had to be broken as well, to replace a faulty spark plug. One of the cars also had a bent front axle that resulted in a challenging replacement job on the road.[747] *The Horseless Age* wrote, "The friction drive Cartercars were examined after the contest and the friction facings found in good shape. The performance of these cars was closely followed by those interested in this type of transmission, and it is reported to have more than met expectations."[748] Carter's willingness to endure this punishing competition would certainly have emphasized his unwavering commitment to the Cartercar enterprise.

The Motorcar Company had produced a respectable 264 Cartercars for the 1907 season.[749] In examining Cartercar's 1907 season, the December 1, 1907 *Cycle and Automobile Trade Journal* wrote, "The Cartercar factory capacity has been doubled in 1907. The management expects to produce about 600 Cartercars during the season of 1908, all on one chassis with different bodies, passenger and delivery . . . this single chassis production enables the Cartercar to offer a considerable variety of low-cost cars, meeting the requirements of middle class purchasers."[750] They were proud of their manufacturing operations, and the *Detroit Free Press* reported, "The Motorcar Company invites anyone to visit the factory and see just how they build a Carter car, and the materials used."[751]

The Motorcar Company's annual report for calendar year-end 1907 was filed with the Michigan Secretary of State on March 30, 1908. This 1907 annual report indicated that the original $150,000 capitalization was intact, with $127,060 subscribed, that assets totaled $163,105.75 (up from $104,534.40 in 1906) comprising personal property, cash, accounts receivable, and B. J. Carter's patents, drawings and patterns, and goodwill, and that the Motorcar Company was carrying $47,310.20 in debt (up from $10,271.86 in 1906). Three additional people had

acquired stock in the Motorcar Company (beyond the 52 shareholders at the end of 1906), and each had been added to the roster of investors. B. J. Carter's stock holdings had increased by 75 shares to 2,575 shares, perhaps from a bonus or some form of executive compensation. As in earlier annual reports, only a balance sheet was included and no revenue and expense information was shown.[752]

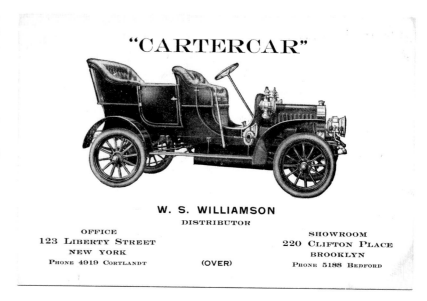

Fig. 205. As evidenced by this 1907 business card, Cartercar had either moved its New York City sales agency from the 1906 Midtown Manhattan location at 1697 Broadway (fig. 189) to 123 Liberty Street in Lower Manhattan, or perhaps it had opened a second New York City agency. This card indicates that a Brooklyn Cartercar showroom was established in 1907 as well. *Author's collection*

Figs. 206–216. A series of professional interior photographs of the Motorcar Company factory building at 220–230 Twenty-First Street in Detroit; descriptions of the various manufacturing phases and functions of the respective factory areas shown are inscribed in white text on each of the photographs. Based on the serial numbers scrawled in chalk on the Cartercars' dashes in the picture labeled "Chassis Assembling Dep't." (fig. 210), which range from numbers 672 to 696, these pictures were taken very late in the 1908 season and shortly before Cartercar's relocation to the larger manufacturing plant it acquired in Pontiac, Michigan. These high-quality photographs were contained in a leatherette album with laced binding, which Cartercar made available to its sales agents and dealers as a promotional piece. *Author's collection*

GENERAL MACHINE DEP'T.

MOTOR TESTING DEP'T.

FRAME ASSEMBLING DEP'T.

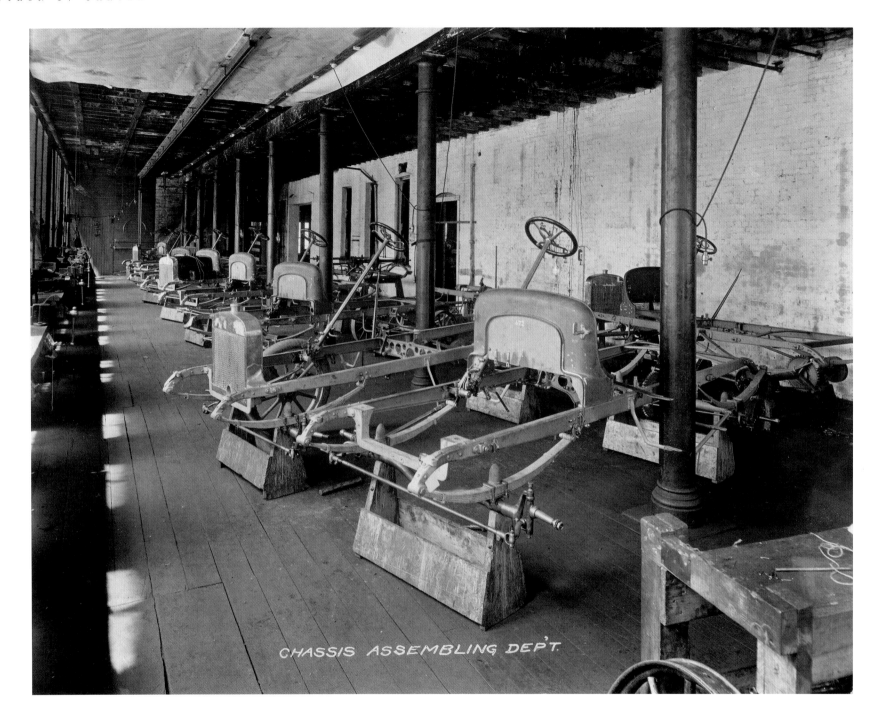

CHASSIS ASSEMBLING DEP'T.

TESTING ROOM

PAINTING AND TRIMING DEP'T.

ONE OF THE VARNISH ROOMS.

CHASSIS PAINTING DEP'T.

FINAL ASSEMBLING DEPT.

1908 Season for the Cartercar

Cartercar's sales catalog for the 1908 season stated, "We shall continue our policy of adhering steadfastly to a limited number of models, which will be refined and improved as the opportunity presents."[753] The October 6, 1907 *Detroit Free Press* reporter sounded a bit surprised in writing, "One concern, the Motorcar Co., who make the friction driven Cartercar, has even announced that there is really no change at all in their car for the next season . . . and they will therefore continue the same models with but a few trivial changes."[754] Accordingly, the various 1907 Cartercar models were continued essentially unchanged for the 1908 season at the same prices and with a single type of chassis for all models.[755] The 1908 sales catalog illustrations were nearly identical to those used for the various models in 1907, except that a metal toolbox was now pictured on the driver's-side running board, and the 1908 Model "C" delivery car featured a panel-side body that appeared more robust than the slightly more antique-looking delivery body installed in 1907.[756]

Two additional (or improved) models were added during the course of the 1908 season. The sporty, updated Model "D" runabout, called the Model "G" Gentleman's Roadster later in 1908, was offered with "French Gray" paint and a rumble, also called a mother-in-law, seat at $1,250; this model had been introduced by March 1908, when it appeared in *Cycle and Automobile Trade Journal*.[757] A light open delivery car was also added as a special-order vehicle later in 1908 (this offering may have technically been considered a 1909 Model "C" Open Delivery Car).[758]

Demand for Cartercars had clearly grown rapidly, as production for the 1908 season was 325 automobiles; this, however, was substantially fewer than the 600 cars the Motorcar Company had predicted for the 1908 season at the close of the 1907 calendar year.[759] It was reported in August 1908 that about 75 men were employed in the Motorcar Company factory in Detroit, which seems low in light of the significant production output.[760]

Fig. 218. An overhead view of the Cartercar chassis from the 1908 Motorcar Company sales catalog; this engraving illustrates that virtually no changes or updates had been made to the 1907 chassis for the 1908 season. *Author's collection*

Fig. 217. A cutaway view of the water-cooled 20- to 24-horsepower two-cylinder horizontally opposed Cartercar engine for the 1908 season, which was designed by B. J. Carter and manufactured in the Motorcar Company factory; the motor's cylinders were 5 1/2 inches in diameter with a 4 1/2-inch stroke. *Author's collection*

Fig. 219. The 1908 Cartercar sales catalog was the first to illustrate the Cartercar with an "extra equipment" folding top "of any style and materials. Prices and samples will be furnished upon request." The Model "A" touring car is shown in this illustration with a high-quality extension top with locking landau irons and equipped with a front roll-down windscreen that had a thin transparent sheet of mica (often called isinglass) for viewing the road ahead. *Author's collection*

1908
SPECIFICATIONS

	Model "A"	Model "C"	Model "D"	Model "E"	Model "F"
TYPE	Fixed Tonneau	Delivery	Runabout	Artz Folding Tonneau	Detachable Tonneau
CAPACITY	5 Passenger	1000 lbs.	2 Passenger	2 and 4 Passenger	2 and 5 Passenger
MOTOR	2-Cyl. Opposed	2-Cyl. Opposed	2-Cyl. Opposed	2-Cyl. Opposed	2-Cyl. Opposed
HORSE POWER	20-24	20-24	20-24	20-24	20-24
WHEEL BASE	96 inches	96 inches	96 inches	96 inches	96 inches
SIZE OF TIRES	30 x 3½	30 x 3½	30 x 3½	30 x 3½	30 x 3½
GASOLINE CAPACITY	15 gals.	15 gals.	15 gals.	15 gals.	15 gals.
COLOR	Brewster Green	Optional	Brewster Green	Brewster Green	Brewster Green

Equipment: 3 oil lamps, tube horn, mats, tire repair kit, dry cell batteries, battery box of pressed steel with tray for small tools on running board. All bodies are ironed for tops. Special colors or equipment extra. Only standard American tires are used.

Model "A"
Fixed Tonneau 5-Passenger Car
Price, $1,350.00 F. O. B. Detroit

Model "C" Delivery Vehicle
1,000 Pounds Capacity
Price, $1,400.00 F. O. B. Detroit

Fig. 220. A chart of Cartercar's 1908 season specifications organized by model; standard equipment and extras are set forth in the bottom paragraph.

Figs. 221–226. Engravings of the various 1908 Cartercar models from the 1908 Motorcar Company sales catalog. *Author's collection*

Model "D"   Runabout
Price, $1,250.00. F. O. B. Detroit

Model "E"
Artz Folding Tonneau (Closed)
Price, $1,350.00 F. O. B. Detroit

Model "E"
Artz Folding Tonneau (Open)
Price, $1,350.00 F. O. B. Detroit
Specifications on Page 22

Model F   Detachable Tonneau
Price, $1,400.00, Including Tonneau,
Beetle Back Locker Extra.

Fig. 227. Cartercar's 1908 two-cylinder Gentleman's Roadster with a rumble seat for a third passenger; this model was first announced in March 1908 as a restyled Model "D" runabout at $1,250, but, by the end of 1908, it was designated the Model "G" Gentleman's Roadster with an increased price of $1,300. This model continued with little change into the 1909 season. *Courtesy of Gregory R. Loftness*

Fig. 228. Cartercar Model "C" two-cylinder Open Delivery Car from late 1908; this machine technically may have been considered a model for the 1909 season. The Open Delivery Car shown here appears to have been a special order for the firm of J. W. Young. *Author's collection*

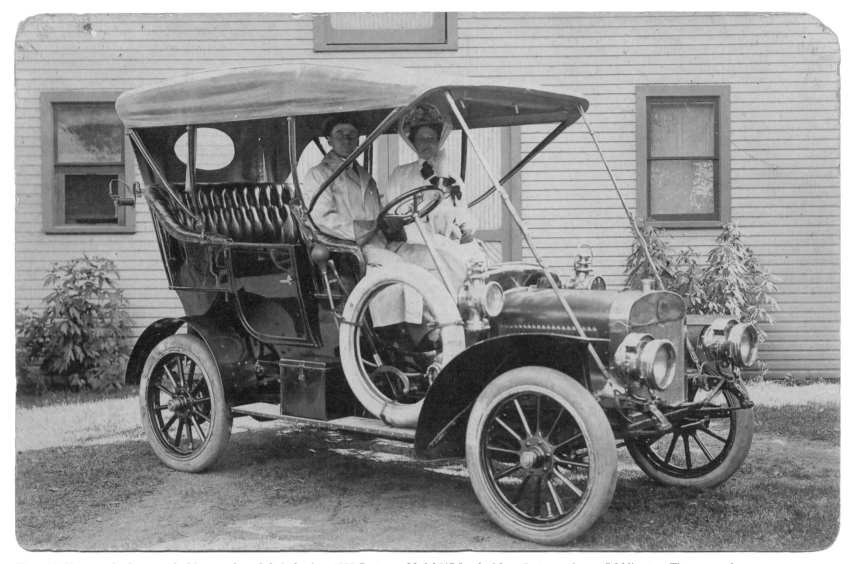

Fig. 229. Photograph of a smart-looking couple and their dog in a 1908 Cartercar Model "A" fitted with an "extra equipment" folding top. The man and woman wear motoring apparel typical of the time, including linen dusters, caps/hats, and gloves; this car had no windshield, so they would have likely worn goggles once they started their road trip. *Author's collection*

Fig. 230. A stylish 1908 Cartercar Model "A" painted in what the factory brochure called a "special color" (not the standard "Brewster" green). This paint job, the accessory windshield, special brass brackets for holding the spare tire with a rubberized canvas cover, and the "extra equipment" folding top would have increased this car's price substantially. *Author's collection*

Byron J. Carter's Untimely Death

B. J. Carter's highly productive and promising automotive career came to a shocking, tragic end when he was only 44 years old. Carter died on Monday, April 6, 1908, of an advanced case of pneumonia, which he had been battling for a week. The public outpouring of sorrow for this important citizen was immense: lengthy Carter obituaries appeared in at least six major national automotive journals of the day, and April 1908 Jackson and Detroit newspapers, among many other papers, included several detailed accounts of B. J. Carter's life and achievements.[761] A 1909 *Cycle and Automobile Journal* article said that Carter, ever the tenacious inventor, had, at the time of his death, been diligently working to create an enclosed, dirt-proof, and oil-tight case for the Cartercar's main drive chain: "Mr. Carter died suddenly in 1908, and the work of designing the Cartercar chain casing was taken up by Mr. R. A. Palmer, general manager of the Cartercar Company," who ultimately received a patent for the invention (no. 954,400), which was filed November 14, 1908, granted April 5, 1910, and assigned to the Cartercar Company.[762]

The circumstances surrounding B. J. Carter's passing have long been a point of speculation, and a dramatic tale has emerged about Carter's death being the impetus for the development of the first practical electric starter for automobile engines. This story, however, cannot be substantiated and appears to be without any merit. Carter's granddaughters Sallie Sparks Kendall and Buzzy Carter Maurer both knew their grandmother Della Carter very well. Della Carter moved back to Jackson in mid-1908 shortly after B. J. Carter's death. She initially resided with Squire and Martha Carter and remained a Jackson resident for the rest of her life.[763] Della Carter almost never spoke of her husband's death; in those rare instances when she did, however, she consistently said he had died from pneumonia. Mrs. Carter never alluded to any of the other extreme events recounted in certain narratives written many years after B. J. Carter's death. Further, none of the over 20 obituaries the author has read give the slightest hint that Carter's death occurred from anything other than a severe case of pneumonia.[764] Lastly, Byron J. Carter's death certificate shows Carter's cause of death as "(double) lobar pneumonia" with a contributory cause being "consolidated lung lower lobe left side" for a duration of "years." No other contributory causes of death, such as a

broken jaw or arm, are listed. This certificate records that B. J. Carter died in his home at 10:00 a.m. on April 6, 1908, after being under a doctor's care from April 1 through April 6, 1908.

In essence, the erroneous accounts of B. J. Carter's death state that Carter died in 1910 (not 1908, as was actually the case). They also have it that Carter had gallantly stopped to assist a women in crank starting her stalled car, which could be a very challenging and frustrating chore. The stalled auto's ignition was not set properly and the engine backfired, which caused the crank to "kick back" and hit Carter in his jaw (and arm, in one account), breaking it. These apocryphal stories then surmise that this jaw fracture led to complications, including pneumonia, which resulted in Carter's death. Upon hearing of the incident, Cadillac Motor Car Company founder and friend of B. J. Carter, Henry M. Leland, supposedly remarked in distress that he thought an electric self-starter for cars needed to be developed to eliminate the danger of hand cranking automobiles.[765]

Two of these accounts come from seemingly credible biographies written many years after Carter's death about prominent automobile men: Henry M. Leland, founder of Cadillac and the Lincoln Motor Company, and Charles F. Kettering, who developed the first practical electric starter for motorcars in 1911.[766] Upon reading relevant excerpts from these biographies about Byron J. Carter's death, it is easy to find blatant factual errors. First, as mentioned above, both incorrectly cite 1910 as the year of Carter's death but disagree on the month. Second, they both mention that Carter's jaw was broken, and Leland's biography states that Carter's arm was broken as well. Leland's biography also mentions that Carter's injuries did not seem serious at first, but that Carter nonetheless died of pneumonia a few weeks later. Kettering's biography states that "Carter was not a young man, and complications arising out of the accident caused his death."[767] Even though lifespans were certainly shorter 100 years ago, it is hard to imagine that Carter would have been considered an older man at the age of 44.

Another earlier account from a 1934 book about General Motors' history similarly refers to the deceased person who cranked the woman's car as an "elderly friend" of Henry M. Leland. Byron J. Carter is not identified by name in this piece.[768]

Fig. 231. This photograph, entitled *Designer Byron Carter in the Cartercar*, was published in the February 20, 1908 issue of *The Automobile*, less than two months before Carter's untimely death. This same image was featured in several later Cartercar promotional sales materials to honor B. J. Carter. *Author's collection*

One could continue to debate these various bits of information; the fact remains, however, that none of these dramatic events are described in any of B. J. Carter's obituaries. The early 1900s was a time of highly sensational journalism, and a story as shocking as the hand-cranking incident and resulting injury and death would have certainly been reported somewhere in a newspaper or obituary. And lastly, it seems entirely reasonable that Della Carter might have mentioned these tragic events, if they had been true, to her granddaughters.

In B. J. Carter's honor and memory, several of his descendants carefully preserved photographs and other historical materials including actual Cartercar autos. B.J.'s son, Kenneth, who was just under two years old when his father died, purchased a secondhand 1915 Cartercar touring car (serial no. 12014) in 1932. Kenneth's daughter and B. J. Carter's granddaughter Buzzy Carter Maurer and her husband, Dennis, own a 1909 Cartercar transitional Model "H" *two-cylinder* roadster with a rumble seat. And another of B. J. Carter's granddaughters, Sallie Sparks Kendall, and her husband, Bob, display an original brass Cartercar radiator insignia in their home.

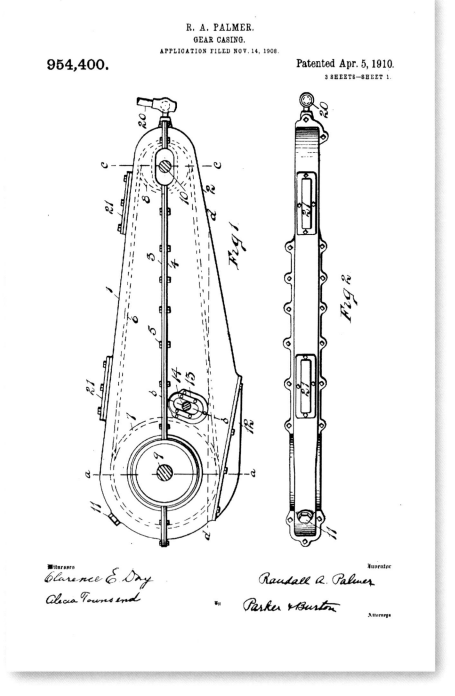

Figs. 232–234. Patent drawings for Cartercar's chain gear casing, which was an enclosed, dust-proof, and oil-tight case for the Cartercar's main drive chain. This U. S. patent (no. 954,400) was filed November 14, 1908, and was granted April 5, 1910. A June 1, 1909 *Cycle and Automobile Journal* article reported that B. J. Carter had diligently been working to create an enclosed case to protect the chain from road grit and to minimize wear: "Mr. Carter died suddenly in 1908, and the work of designing the Cartercar chain casing was taken up by Mr. R. A. Palmer, general manager of the Cartercar Company," who ultimately received a patent for the invention. Palmer assigned his patent to the Cartercar Company. *Courtesy of the United States Patent and Trademark Office*

R. A. PALMER.
GEAR CASING.
APPLICATION FILED NOV. 14, 1908.
954,400.
Patented Apr. 5, 1910.
3 SHEETS—SHEET 2.
21
1
8
18
18
10
Fig 3.
2
16
15
14
Fig. 4.
17
Witnesses
Clarence E. Day
Alecia Townsend
Inventor
Randall A. Palmer
By
Parker & Burton
Attorneys

R. A. PALMER.
GEAR CASING.
APPLICATION FILED NOV. 14, 1908.
954,400.
Patented Apr. 5, 1910.
3 SHEETS—SHEET 3.
7
1
9
9
Fig 5.
14
2
12
12a
12
1
12a
Fig 6.
Witnesses
Clarence E. Day
Alecia Townsend
Inventor
Randall A. Palmer
Parker & Burton
Attorneys

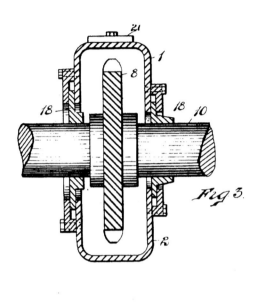

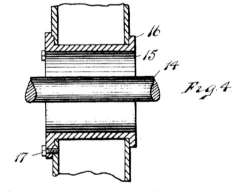

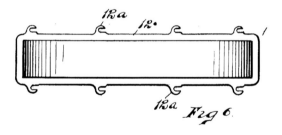

A Newly Reorganized Cartercar Company at the Close of the 1908 Season

The Motorcar Company jumped the gun a bit on August 26, 1908, when it indicated that an "inducement" had been offered by the City of Toledo, Ohio, to move Cartercar operations there.[769] However, major Motorcar Company news regarding a corporate restructuring and a company relocation to another city, Pontiac, would indeed be announced a little over a month later.

In an October 11, 1908 press release, five months after B. J. Carter's death, the Motorcar Company announced that the enterprise had changed its name to the Cartercar Company, perhaps to honor its late founder.[770] By this time, the "Cartercar" trade name had become well known and would have been a valuable commodity; Carter's patented friction-drive transmission had proven itself and had established a reputation for simplicity, flexibility, and durability. A new, more elaborate logo was developed about this time as well and was featured in 1909 Cartercar factory-issued sales materials and certain magazine advertisements (fig. 235).

The newly reorganized Cartercar Company was reincorporated October 8, 1908 (as termed in Cartercar's 1908 annual report), by merging the Motorcar Company and the Pontiac Spring & Wagon Works, which had been manufacturing high-wheeled motor buggies under the name The Pontiac Motor Vehicle Co. since 1907.[771] As part of this merger, the Cartercar Company would move to Pontiac, where it had acquired a more substantial five-story brick-and-concrete factory composed of four connected buildings covering two acres.[772] The April 24, 1909 *New England Automobile Journal* estimated that the new factory complex had over five acres of floor space in its four buildings.[773] Residents of Detroit expressed disappointment with Cartercar's decision to relocate to nearby Pontiac. Only one year earlier, the *Detroit Free Press*, in a piece about the Motorcar Company, had written, "It is putting it mildly to say that they contribute more than their share toward making Detroit famous as the automobile manufacturing center of the world."[774]

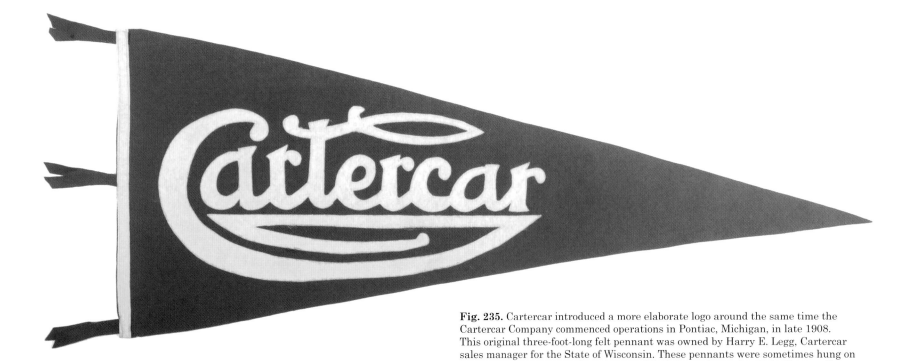

Fig. 235. Cartercar introduced a more elaborate logo around the same time the Cartercar Company commenced operations in Pontiac, Michigan, in late 1908. This original three-foot-long felt pennant was owned by Harry E. Legg, Cartercar sales manager for the State of Wisconsin. These pennants were sometimes hung on Cartercar autos in sales showrooms, exhibitions, and parades. A similar, smaller cutout metal version of this logo was used as an emblem (typically called a radiator script) on the fronts of Cartercar radiator cores during many of the remaining years of Cartercar production. *Author's collection, courtesy of Susan Dunek*

Fig. 236. The new two-acre Cartercar Company factory complex (four connected buildings with a dedicated water tower) in Pontiac, circa late 1908; this photograph was taken before Cartercar's signage and name had actually been applied to the building's exterior and water tower (not merely crudely scratched or marked on the negative by the photographer, as in this image). Prior to Cartercar's occupancy, this plant was home to the Pontiac Spring & Wagon Works; this company name is partially visible on certain exterior walls of the building in this image, despite the photographer's attempts to obscure. *Author's collection*

When Cartercar announced its move to Pontiac, Detroit had already experienced two painful automobile company departures: Oldsmobile had relocated to Lansing, and the Reliance Motor Truck Co. to Owosso, Michigan (this enterprise later formed part of the foundation for GMC trucks).[775] As a result of the Cartercar Company move, the *Detroit Free Press* wrote, "It is likely that many families will leave Detroit, as the present employees of the Detroit company will be given preference after the reorganization. The Pontiac plant will be in shape so that in all probability work will commence in the new location within 30 days. It is expected fully 400 men will be employed in the spring."[776] President Frank P. Caughey was pressed by a newspaper reporter to explain why the Motorcar Company was moving, and he replied, "It was like this. We needed more capital and more factory room. The opening in Pontiac presented itself. The buggy business had not been doing as well as formerly, and the stockholders wanted to engage in the automobile business, so the amalgamation [with the Pontiac Spring & Wagon Works] was arranged. We have had very nice treatment in Detroit. Of course, the capitalist has the privilege of putting his money where he wants it. That was not the reason for our company's leaving the city, however, nor were we influenced by labor conditions in Detroit, which have been very satisfactory to us."[777] Fortunately for the City of Detroit, another substantial automobile enterprise, the Paige-Detroit Motor Car Company, signed a lease for the Motorcar Company's former Detroit factory building within one year of Cartercar's departure.[778]

The Automobile, in its October 15, 1908 issue, reported, "The work of transferring the machinery and stock now in the old Motorcar company's factory, at Twenty-first and Baker streets, Detroit, will be undertaken at once, and it is expected that the new plant will be working full blast on the 1909 product within 30 days."[779] And the June 1, 1909 issue of *Cycle and Automobile Trade Journal* recounted that Cartercar had "removed from its Detroit factory to much larger premises in Pontiac . . . in November, 1908, with the intention of producing 1000 cars in 1909."[780] Further, the 1909 Cartercar sales catalog no. 10, which may have been issued in late 1908, stated, "We are now in our immense new factory at Pontiac, and with our greatly increased resources and equipment, shall be able to more quickly meet the demand for Cartercars."[781] It was also reported in mid-1909 that "R. A. Palmer, the secretary, with his associates, have laid out an ideal factory for accurate and rapid production . . . there will be a big advance in the production next year [1910 season starting in mid-1909]

that should make the Cartercar agents contented in mind as well as in purse."[782]

This plant had previously been occupied by Cartercar's newly merged partner, the Pontiac Spring & Wagon Works (aka The Pontiac Motor Vehicle Co.); it was where they had built horse-drawn vehicles and manufactured a relatively small number of the company's high-wheeled Pontiac motor buggies. Initial Cartercar Company announcements had indicated that Cartercar would continue production of the Pontiac motor buggy priced at $675; yet no evidence was found to prove that any manufacturing of these Pontiac cars actually occurred after the 1908 Cartercar takeover.[783] President Caughey in his October 12, 1908 *Detroit Free Press* interview also mentioned that the Cartercar Company would be "closely allied with the Rapid Motor Car company, manufacturers of commercial vehicles. . . . Some of the same men are interested in both companies, and we will work together."[784] Like the Reliance Motor Truck Co., Rapid would soon be acquired by General Motors Company to establish GMC trucks.[785]

Cartercar's new Pontiac facility was better situated for shipping and receiving than its former Twenty-First Street plant in Detroit, since it sat "at the junction of the Detroit, Grand Haven & Milwaukee and the Michigan Air Line Railroads."[786] The new Cartercar factory's address was shown as 18 Linfere Street in the 1910 Cartercar Company annual report; addresses on Franklin Road, which extends directly from Linfere Street, were sometimes used as well.[787]

According to the 1908 annual report of the Cartercar Company filed with the Michigan Secretary of State on February 20, 1909, the Cartercar Company valued its authorized capital stock at $350,000, divided into $50,000 of preferred stock and $300,000 of common stock, the par value of each share being $10; all $50,000 of preferred stock and $272,720 of the common stock were outstanding and held by 80 shareholders.[788] Poignantly, Bryon J. Carter's 2,575 shares were now listed under "B. J. Carter Estate."[789] Incidentally, this annual report for calendar year-end 1908 also showed that assets totaled $292,635.75 (up from $163,105.75 in 1907) and that Cartercar was now carrying a very modest $6,149.75 in debt (significantly down from $47,310.20 in 1907).[790]

General Motors' Acquisition and Cartercar's Ultimate Demise

On October 26, 1909, the board of directors of the General Motors Company approved the purchase of all 25,772 (or as many as might be obtainable) outstanding shares of Cartercar Company common stock; this board resolution valued the Cartercar shares at no more than $5.56 per share.[791] General Motors acted promptly, as the *Detroit Free Press* reported, "The General Motors company has absorbed the Cartercar company, of Pontiac, the deal being closed yesterday [November 1, 1909]. The Cartercar capitalization was $350,000, and it is announced that the transaction is very satisfactory to the stockholders, payment being made in cash and stock."[792]

The Cartercar Company purchase would be one of over 20 automobile-industry acquisitions made by General Motors' founder William "Billy" Crapo Durant. Durant had started this rapid series of acquisitions almost immediately after General Motors was created on September 16, 1908.[793] General Motors made quick work of buying up as many Cartercar Company common shares as it could: by March 1910, all but 23 of the 80 Cartercar shareholders listed in the 1908 annual report had sold out, and, by March 1911, the count of those who had held on to their Cartercar stock was down to 19 of the pre-acquisition shareholders.[794] The March 1, 1911 list of shareholders included in the 1910 Cartercar Company annual report filed with the Michigan Secretary of State shows that General Motors had converted the Cartercar Company shares of common stock still held by individual Cartercar shareholders (who were not affiliated with General Motors, as executives or bankers) to 500 shares of General Motors Company common stock (for two shareholders) and 5,000 shares of General Motors preferred stock for the other 17.[795] General Motors executives and its investment bank held the remaining 55,272 shares of General Motors common stock from the Cartercar transaction.[796]

Della Carter was among the Cartercar Company shareholders who sold off all Cartercar Company and associated General Motors Company stock within five months of General Motors' announced acquisition of Cartercar. (According to family history, considerable pressure was exerted on Mrs. Carter by General Motors representatives and her investment advisers to dispose of her Cartercar Company and new General Motors stock promptly; General Motors was then less than two years old and was portrayed to her as an overly risky investment.) During this period, the 2,575 common shares of Cartercar Company stock held by the B. J. Carter Estate were surrendered and converted to an unknown quantity of General Motors Company stock, for the benefit of Mrs. Della Carter, Rachel L. Carter, and Kenneth G. Carter, with Mrs. Carter as the children's guardian. A February 17, 1910 letter from General Motors to Della Carter's agent, Lacerne A. Patch (Jackson County's deputy treasurer and a Crum family relative of Martha J. Carter's), indicates that the B. J. Carter Estate held 70 preferred shares of General Motors stock at that time; however, 70 shares at General Motors' then current market price of $90 per share ($6,300) would not have equaled the approximate $14,317 value of Della Carter's original Cartercar stock holdings, using General Motors' purchase price cap of $5.56 per share multiplied by the B. J. Carter Estate's 2,575 shares.[797] Cartercar's 1909 annual report was not filed with the Secretary of State until March 26, 1910; this report provides no guidance on the number of General Motors shares B. J. Carter's heirs had received because all stock originally from the B. J. Carter Estate had apparently already been sold by the March 26, 1910 annual report filing date.[798]

Correspondence preserved by Buzzy Carter Maurer indicates that some of the B. J. Carter Estate preferred shares of General Motors Company stock were sold by Della Carter through her agent, Lacerne A. Patch, in several increments.[799] Della Carter disposed of 22 General Motors preferred shares on February 11, 1910, at $90 per share and another 48 preferred shares on February 28, 1910, at $90 per share.[800] On April 1, 1910, General Motors mistakenly paid Mrs. Carter a $45.50 dividend covering 13 of the 48 shares she had previously sold in February 1910; seven days later, General Motors sent her a note summarily asking her to repay this dividend amount.[801] It appears that all General Motors stock from the B. J. Carter Estate (for the benefit of his widow, Della, and Rachel L. and Kenneth G. Carter) had been disposed of by March 26, 1910, when the 1909 Cartercar Company annual report was filed with the Michigan Secretary of State; however, handwritten margin notes dated April 13, 1910, on one letter indicate that Rachel and Kenneth Carter may have still owned some converted General Motors stock after the Carters' February 1910 sale transactions.[802] Somewhat confusingly, the 1909 annual report included a list of all Cartercar Company (most by then converted to General Motors Company) shareholders, and the B. J. Carter Estate and the

Fig. 237. Rachel L. Carter, circa 1913. *Courtesy of Sallie Sparks Kendall*

Fig. 238. Kenneth G. Carter in 1925, when he was a senior at Howe Military Academy, Howe, Indiana. *Courtesy of Buzzy Carter Maurer. Reproduced with permission of Howe Military Academy*

240

names of Della, Rachel L., and Kenneth G. Carter are not shown on this shareholder list in the March 26, 1910 state filing.[803]

Within one week of its acquisition of the Cartercar Company, General Motors conspicuously flexed its muscle and commenced a patent infringement lawsuit, in early November 1909, against both the manufacturer of and the Detroit regional sales agent for the well-known Lambert friction-drive-transmission automobile.[804] The codefendants were the Buckeye Manufacturing Company of Anderson, Indiana, builder of the Lambert car, and J. B. McIntosh d/b/a McIntosh Automobile Co., general sales agent for the Lambert in Detroit and surrounding region.[805] The complaint was filed in the U.S. Circuit Court of Detroit; plaintiffs General Motors and the Cartercar Company claimed that B. J. Carter's original May 31, 1904 U.S. patent (no.761,146) for a friction transmission was a "basic one" and alleged that the means of power transmission by friction discs installed on Lambert automobiles infringed on the Carter patent because Buckeye was making use of Cartercar's patented "method of friction wheel engagement and operation."[806] The complaint further alleged that the Lambert parties had been and were actively building and distributing friction-drive-transmission motor vehicles, which infringed on the May 31, 1904 Carter patent.[807] For legal representation, General Motors retained the high-powered Detroit patent law firm of Parker & Burton.[808] (Parker & Burton represented Henry Ford and his interests in the famous Selden automotive patent and licensing lawsuit, which was being battled ferociously in the federal courts at this time.)[809]

An article from the April 4, 1912 issue of *Motor Age* seems to indicate that the Lambert parties may have turned the tables on the Cartercar Company and General Motors: "It is stated that the patent held by the Buckeye company and that of the Cartercar Co. were not . . . on the same inventions, inasmuch as J. [John] W. Lambert's patent covered the friction-drive feature and not a component part . . . at the present time the Lambert people have a case pending against the Cartercar Co. which is active in the courts."[810] In its counter suit, the Buckeye Manufacturing Company alleged that Cartercar had infringed on Lambert's "patent relating to the aluminum face plates in the friction drive."[811] There is little to indicate that the pending General Motors lawsuit had any impact on the design of the Lambert automobile's transmission. *The Motor World*, in a November 28, 1912 article titled "Friction Drive Lambert Practically Unchanged," proclaimed, "The Lambert friction drive mechanism remains exactly

as heretofore."[812] The *Detroit Free Press* reported that the federal judge hearing the protracted Cartercar/Lambert patent dispute had finally ended all litigation, when he "dismissed two bills representing counter complaints between the Cartercar company, of Pontiac, and the Buckeye Vehicle company" on May 28, 1914.[813] The question of which company, Cartercar or Buckeye, owned first rights to the friction-drive-transmission invention would soon be moot, as Cartercar Company operations were suspended in early 1915. In any event, the Buckeye Manufacturing Company and its successors continued to openly build and market Lambert friction-drive-transmission automobiles until 1917, so General Motors' high-handed patent infringement lawsuit was clearly unsuccessful in actually shutting Lambert down or even persuading it to discontinue use of the friction-drive transmission.[814]

The resolute Cartercar Company survived into 1915. While Cartercar's production volumes had never set any quantity records by auto-industry standards, Cartercar had consistently demonstrated sales-volume increases every year starting in 1906.[815] It was optimistically announced in February 1915 that the Cartercar Company would "put into operation a new manufacturing policy to provide for a larger quantity production. It was thought best to confine the line to one chassis with two body models" known as the Model "9," which the *Detroit Free Press* labeled "a masterpiece."[816] Nonetheless, the General Motors Company abruptly communicated three months later that the Cartercar plant would be closed and Cartercar production would terminate, with the closing date set for May 22, 1915.[817] In the process of winding down the Cartercar Company's operations, the General Motors' board of directors ratified the sale of the Cartercar replacement-parts business for $44,000.[818] A December 8, 1915 press release identified the purchaser as the Puritan Machine Company of Detroit, which would supply replacement and repair parts to the many remaining loyal Cartercar owners.[819] The coup de grâce for B. J. Carter's friction-drive marvel, the Cartercar, occurred in 1916, when the General Motors board of directors voted to formally dissolve the Cartercar Company (dissolution papers filed with the Michigan Secretary of State on January 3, 1917); General Motors had already shuttered Cartercar's factory over 19 months before this filing date.[820] Soon after, in February 1917, the enormous Cartercar Company four-building factory complex in Pontiac was sold to the Olympian Motors Co. for a mere $35,000, a small fraction of the amount originally paid by the General Motors Company.[821]

The Jackson Automobile Company Also Runs Out of Steam

The Jackson Automobile Company, which B. J. Carter had founded in July 1902, fared somewhat better than the Cartercar enterprise. The Jackson car was offered for 20 years, until December 1922, which was seven and a half years after the end of the once-popular Cartercar. Starting in 1906, George A. Matthews gradually brought his three sons into the family's automobile business and began distributing stock to them in 1908.[822] First, his youngest, 22-year-old Harry Eugene Matthews (December 12, 1883–March 28, 1956), initially worked as a Jackson Automobile Company clerk (starting in 1906), added purchasing agent duties (1907), and later served as corporate secretary (1910) and then treasurer (1917) as well.[823] After George A. Matthews acquired the Jackson Automobile Company interests of Charles Lewis and Fred L. Holmes in June 1910, he created senior Jackson corporate positions for his two older sons in tandem with their existing management duties at the Fuller Buggy Company: Frederick Charles Matthews (October 20, 1877–November 1, 1961), who started as Jackson's vice president (1910), then served as president for almost two years (1917); and Howard Adelman Matthews (October 11, 1881–May 3, 1949), who started as Jackson's treasurer (1910), assumed sales manager responsibilities (1912), was promoted to vice president and general manager (1917), and ultimately became Jackson's president (1919) until the Jackson Motors Corporation folded in December 1922.[824]

The Jackson Automobile Company's notable achievements included the Jaxon Steam Surrey with B. J. Carter's clever patented three-cylinder steam engine, touring cars with trendsetting side-entrance tonneaus introduced by 1904, a 50-horsepower engine with an overhead camshaft and valves and hemispherical cylinder heads designed in 1907, and an impressive list of racetrack wins at Indianapolis and elsewhere. As a result, the Jackson autos, like Cartercar, had a very loyal following of early goggle-wearing motorists. The Jackson also had an established reputation of success among the throngs of early auto-racing and hill-climbing enthusiasts.

Fig. 239. The Jackson Automobile Company introduced this logo in 1905, and it was in continuous use, with multiple variations, through 1922. A cutout metal version was used as an emblem (typically called a radiator script) on the front of Jackson automobile radiator cores throughout many years of Jackson production. This particular brass radiator script is an original from a 1909 Jackson touring car. In addition, diamond-shaped "Jackson" emblems were first soldered to the fronts of Jacksons' upper radiator tanks in 1910 and remained through 1922; they were initially constructed entirely of brass, and by 1911 distinctive cloisonné had been added. *Author's collection*

Fig. 240. The brass Jackson radiator script is prominent on this massive 1906 Jackson Model "G" touring car. The Model "G," developed in 1905, was Jackson's first four-cylinder motorcar. Its engine was rated 40–45 horsepower, and the $2,500 price tag was hefty (especially when compared to 1905 Jackson model prices: $650 for the one-cylinder Jackson Runabout Model "A" and $1,250 for the two-cylinder Model "C" touring car). *Courtesy of Charlie Beesley*

Fig. 241. Side view of the impressive 1906 Jackson Model "G"; the 2,400-pound touring car was equipped with elegant, curvaceous "King of the Belgians" wood coachwork for five passengers on a 108-inch wheelbase. Standard equipment included two acetylene headlamps and an acetylene gas generator, two side oil lamps, one oil tail lamp, tools, a tire repair kit, and tire pump; a folding rubberized canvas top was optional special equipment at an additional charge. This photograph shows the New York City Jackson sales agency, called the Gotham Automobile Company, located at 1655 Broadway. The Gotham Automobile Company shared this store space with Hatch & Company, sales agent for the Compound motorcar, which possessed a sophisticated three-cylinder gasoline engine: one cylinder was thrust by the force produced by exhaust gases expelled by the two explosive cylinders. As a result, the Compound auto's exhaust was much cooler and quieter, and the machine economized power. *Courtesy of the National Automotive History Collection, Detroit Public Library*

Fig. 242. Harry E. Matthews in July 1915.
Courtesy of Scott and Joyce Matthews

Fig. 243. Frederick C. Matthews in 1904.
Courtesy of Kenneth F. Soderbeck

Fig. 244. Howard A. Matthews in 1904.
Courtesy of Kenneth F. Soderbeck

Fig. 245. Howard A. Matthews in 1920.
Author's Collection

Fig. 246. George A. Matthews' three sons, Harry (left), Howard (center), and Fred (right), photographed inside the Newton Club House at "Camp Newton" during a July 4–10, 1915 Jackson Automobile Company dealers convention and distributors tour (referenced in the July 3, 1915 *Jackson Citizen Press*). The Matthews brothers and several Jackson dealers and distributors piloted six new 1915/1916 Jackson autos from Jackson north across rugged Michigan and ferried over Lake Michigan to "Camp Newton," which was a hunting compound in Alger County in the Upper Peninsula owned by Senator Frank T. Newton. Newton had served as a Michigan state senator 1909–1912, and then worked as the Jackson Automobile Company's assistant sales manager for several years starting in 1912. *Courtesy of Scott and Joyce Matthews*

Figs. 247 & 248. Two views of the second and final Jackson Automobile Company (and later, Jackson Motors Corporation) factory, which Jackson acquired on November 30, 1907. This expansive manufacturing facility at the southeast corner of the intersection of East Main and Horton streets, which still stands today, was built in 1895 by The Collins Manufacturing Company, a carriage firm that went bankrupt in late 1896. Another carriage and sleigh builder, the Jackson Vehicle Company, purchased the property on January 25, 1897, and sold it to the Jackson Automobile Company 10 years later. The first Lockwood-Ash Motor Company factory is visible in the background of the fig. 248 photograph These photographic postcards were made by Louis James Pesha, a noted photographer of early 20th-century Michigan landmarks, who operated the Pesha Art Co. in Marine City, Michigan. Pesha died accidentally in 1912 while driving his White steam-powered motorcar. *Author's collection*

Like many other car manufacturers of the day, however, the Jackson Automobile Company began to see a sharp decline in success in the mid-teens. Outdated factory manufacturing and assembly processes, World War I car-production restrictions, and the retooling of the entire factory to manufacture wartime munitions for a few short months before the November 11, 1918 Armistice nearly bankrupted the company. To regain lost ground, the business was reorganized and incorporated on April 18, 1919, as the Jackson Motors Corporation, and nearly $5 million was raised through stock sales, which breathed life back into the enterprise.[825]

Nonetheless, external negative forces would strike Jackson very hard in the ensuing two years. In a November 8, 1920 letter to Jackson Motors Corporation stockholders, Carl L. V. Exselsen, its corporate secretary-treasurer, wrote:

> July 1st of this year found the company in a highly prosperous condition and in excellent credit standing with its banks and trade sources of supply. Bona fide orders on the books were far in excess of factory capacity. Everything pointed to a phenomenal Summer and Fall business. During the early part of August, however, the company began to feel the first rumblings of the terrific [post-war] panic which a few weeks later broke with the suddenness of a storm and shook the entire automotive, wool, leather and other industries to their very roots. Almost over night every branch of the automotive industry found itself face to face with a money crisis. The dealers found their customary sources of money shut off and as a result were unable to pay drafts drawn on them for cars in transit which they had previously ordered. As a result, thousands of freight cars, filled with automobiles of all makes, congested the freight yards of every large city and many of these cars have not been unloaded to this day. This condition resulted in a wholesale cancellation of orders and one by one the great automobile factories of the country were either forced to shut down completely or run at a loss, on a greatly reduced production schedule. The factories in turn were forced to cancel orders with their sources of supply and a general stagnation in the industry quickly set it in.[826]

The Jackson Motors Corporation had gone into receivership by mid-1921 and, in a last-ditch effort to survive, its stockholders authorized that the company be taken over by Associated Motor Industries, Inc., on November 1, 1921.[827]Associated Motor Industries was ultimately a tenuous merger of the Jackson Motors Corporation, Jackson's several largest creditors, and two other financially distressed motorcar companies, National Motor Car & Vehicle Corporation and the Kentucky Wagon Manufacturing Co. (maker of the Dixie Flyer automobile).[828] Despite announcements for new 1923 Jackson car models in a November 8, 1922 press release, the prominent Jackson brand name was summarily discontinued two months later when the highly leveraged Associated Motor Industries was renamed National Motors Corporation through a stockholder vote on December 29, 1922.[829] The National Motors Corporation announced it would assemble 7,000 National six-cylinder Model Six-Fifty-One phaetons in the Jackson Motors Corporation plant, but the National business failed as well and was adjudged as bankrupt on February 26, 1924.[830] The author intends to someday write a comprehensive history of the Jackson Automobile Company and the Jackson Motors Corporation, which will span all the years these important automotive enterprises existed.

Byron J. Carter's Legacy

Unfortunately, B. J. Carter's vision of widespread use of his durable mechanical friction-drive "gearless" transmission, with its infinite range of speeds and simplicity in operation, was a fatality of the extremely competitive mid-1910s automobile market. By this time hundreds of other automakers had flooded buyers with improved geared- and planetary-transmission cars that were much easier to control than earlier versions of these transmissions, shifted more smoothly, and were less prone to damage by unskilled motorists. Auto engines, too, had become significantly more responsive, less finicky, and were easier to regulate than those manufactured before 1910, which made a highly variable transmission less important. By 1915, the friction transmission's flexibility and ease of operation did not distinguish the Cartercar from most other makes, as it had once done.

B. J. Carter ultimately got the last word on the transmission matter, however, as most of us today drive automobiles with some version of an automatic hydraulic transmission. While these automatic transmissions do not conform to the Cartercar's mechanical friction-wheel structure, they do meet our modern expectations, shared by B. J. Carter, that a car's transmission should be very easy to operate and highly responsive. And some of today's hybrid vehicles, most notably those of the Ford Motor Company, Toyota, and Lexus, have electronically controlled continuously variable transmissions, which approximate the flexibility and fluidity that Carter was striving to achieve when he filed a patent for his mechanical "gearless" friction-wheel transmission.[831]

The City of Jackson also has Byron J. Carter to thank for kicking off its long prominence in the automobile and automotive-parts manufacturing industries. Even though no complete automobiles are manufactured in Jackson today, Jackson continues to make an important, ongoing contribution to the United States and worldwide automobile industries through mass production of automotive parts, accessories, and components, prototype and specialty engineering and machining, and metal casting and forging.

Fig. 249. B. J. Carter, circa 1883. *Courtesy of Buzzy Carter Maurer*

Fig. 250. B. J. Carter, circa 1905. *Author's collection*

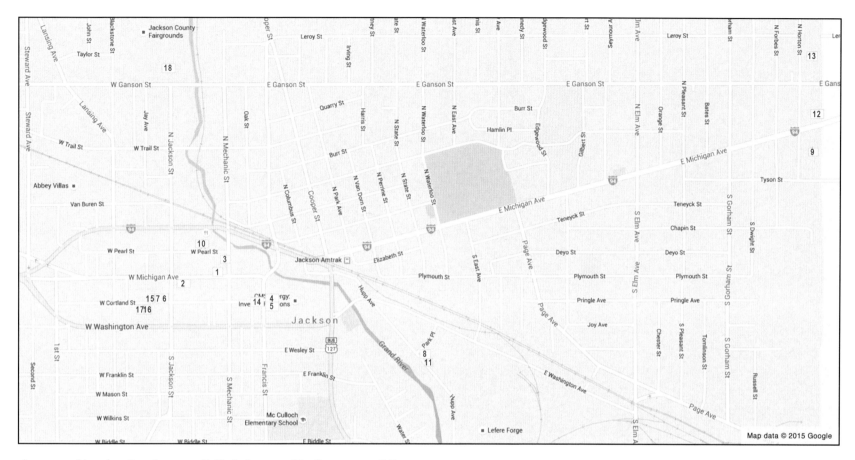

Appendix A: Jackson, Michigan, Reference Map

1. B. J. Carter's first steam job printing and rubber stamp manufacturing business (1884–1887) – 112 West Main Street (now West Michigan Avenue).

2. Second location of Carter's first steam job printing and rubber stamp manufacturing business (1887) – 167 West Main Street, the Bronson Block building.

3. Carter & Co. (B. J. Carter's second steam job printing and rubber stamp manufacturing business opened in 1887 or 1888) – 132 North Mechanic Street.

4. Jackson Rubber Stamp and Printing Co. (Carter's third and last steam job printing and rubber stamp business started in 1890) – 113 Francis Street.

5. Squire B. Carter's grocery store (opened in 1885 or 1886) – 217 Francis Street.

6. Squire B. Carter's first bicycle shop and home to various other business ventures (opened in 1889) – 122 South Jackson Street.

7. The Carters' brick bicycle store and repair facility, machine shop, and factory for The Motorcar Co. (building constructed in 1896) – 204 West Cortland Street.

8. Jackson Automobile Company (first factory 1902–1907) – northeast corner of Park Place and Park Avenue (now Hupp Avenue).

9. Jackson Automobile Company, later Jackson Motors Corporation (second factory 1907–1922) – southeast corner of East Main Street (now East Michigan Avenue) and Horton Street.

10. Charles A. Trask's Machine Shop – 136–138 West Pearl Street.

11. The Trask-Field Gas Engine Co. – 367–371 South Park Avenue (now Hupp Avenue).

12. Fuller Buggy Company – north of East Main Street at Ann Street and the City of Jackson's eastern city limits.

13. Lewis Spring and Axle Co. and E. C. Clark Motor Company – south of Leroy Street between North Horton Street and the Michigan Central Railroad tracks.

14. Lockwood Brothers (first location in 1901) – 131 East Cortland Street.

15. Lockwood Brothers (third location in 1904) – 210–212 West Cortland Street.

16. Jackson Corset Co. – 225 West Cortland Street.

17. Jackson Fire Station No. 1.

18. Jackson Fair Grounds (now Jackson County Fairgrounds).

Appendix B: Biographies of Charles Lewis and George A. Matthews from the *History of Michigan, Volume 3* by Charles Moore (Published in 1915)

Charles Lewis

It has been truly said that the Lewis Spring & Axle Company is the monument of the late Charles Lewis, as well as being Jackson's largest single industry, and in writing of those men who have contributed in small or greater measure to the fortunes of the city, it would be wholly out of keeping with the spirit and purpose of this work to omit mention of him whose name initiates this sketch, and whose destinies were coincident with the destinies of Jackson for a score of years. It would scarcely be possible, in the brief space that is available here to touch more than lightly upon the salient points in the career and activities of Mr. Lewis, but an effort will be made to outline in some degree his life and works, so as to present a concise and comprehensive record of his achievements, with some facts as to his early life.

Charles Lewis was a native of Winscombe, a town in the steel manufacturing district of England near Leeds. He was born on April 10, 1853, and he came to America as a boy of fourteen years [in 1867]. [He received his education in the public schools of his native country and at Auburn. He became a machinist's apprentice, and at an early age was appointed superintendent of a carriage-spring manufacturing plant at Amsterdam.] For some years he lived in Auburn, New York, and later he went to Amsterdam, New York, where he became the superintendent of a spring manufacturing plant.

In the early nineties the late Samuel D. Collins, of Jackson, Michigan, was engaged in the manufacture of vehicles, under the firm name of the Collins Manufacturing Company. Mr. Collins visited the Amsterdam factory, and there he met Charles Lewis.

Mr. Collins was at that time associated with certain other progressive Jackson men in the promotion of the Jackson Land and Improvement

Company. It was planned to buy some extensive tracts of outlying land, sell lots to members of the company at a profit, and use the gains in building factories, the stockholders to be reimbursed by the increase in value of the lots, due to the establishments of the factories. In pursuance of that plan, Mr. Collins, of the Jackson Land and Improvement Company, entered into an arrangement with Mr. Lewis whereby the Aspinwall Manufacturing Company of Three Rivers [Michigan] and a bridge manufacturing company were to establish themselves in Jackson, on condition that the land company furnish a site and build factories. The Aspinwall company and the bridge company were established south of the city, and the spring factory was established on the site of the present location of the Lewis Spring and Axle Company, at the eastern city limits.

Some $5,000 were expended in the building of the spring factory, it is recalled, and Charles Lewis, the practical mechanic in charge of the Amsterdam plant, came to the city and began the manufacture of carriage springs, under the firm name of Lewis & Allen [Spring Company, incorporated in 1891], the second member [Thomas E. Allen] being an accountant who came from the eastern plant with Mr. Lewis, and who had charge of the office end of the business of the new and struggling concern.

It would be a failure in veracity to say that the firm was prosperous from the start. It had its full measure of lean years, for the cash capital which the partners brought into the newly organized business did not exceed $3,000. That fact spelled hard sledding for the affairs of the business. After two or three years Mr. Lewis purchased his partner's interest. He was a far-sighted business man, and he knew how to make a good steel spring. The result was that after a season of ups and downs, the business began to grow. The year 1893 saw it planted firmly on a substantial basis, after the plant had been shut down because of a lack of cash capital to meet the running expenses, and from then to the present time the plant has made a yearly increase in its business.

In 1897 they added an axle department [and incorporated the Lewis Spring and Axle Company on September 24, 1897], and in 1898 Mr. Lewis allowed himself to become interested in the automobile business, the upshot of it being that he organized the Jackson Automobile Company in that same year [in fact, it was 1902]. In that venture they experienced a pleasing measure of success, and for ten years or more he continued in the business, though he finally decided to withdraw and devote all his time to the spring and axle end of his enterprise. In the autumn of 1911 he consolidated his several factories for the making of automobile axles in one splendid new factory on Horton street, and at the time of his death he was planning the construction of another factory which would have exceeded in size any of the former plants.

At the time of his death the Lewis Spring & Axle Company, engaged in the manufacture of automobile springs, front and rear axles, brake lever assemblies, transmissions and forgings, in its factory, occupied a floor space of 320,000 square feet. It employed, and still does, a force of seven hundred men, and it is a safe statement that "Lewis Quality'" in trade is a term that stands for excellence in workmanship and construction wherever automobiles are made and sold.

Mr. Lewis was always active in city affairs, and his activity took the form of promoting the best interest of the community at all times. As a member of the board of public works he gave much valuable time to the matter of improving the county roads and the public utilities of the city. He expended generous sums in providing equipment for the better building of roads, and was a pioneer in Jackson in that phase of its education. It was his aim and ambition to get the city to that place where it would employ business methods and progressive ideas in its administration, and he gave of his time and of his money to that end. It is safe to say that none ever realized, unless it might have been other members of the board of public works, the full value of the services he contributed to the city as a member of that body. [His political affiliation was with the Republican party.]

Mr. Lewis also served as a member of the Fire Commission for some time, and as a member of the State Board of Corrections and Charities, he gave much time to the improvement of conditions in the prisons and other correctional institutions of the state. Any institution for the relief and maintenance of the indigent old people of the community found a stanch supporter in him. The Odd Fellows' Home, in Cooley Park, made a strong appeal to his benevolent instincts, and he did all in his power to aid in securing the grounds for that purpose. It is a further tribute to his business acumen that he succeeded, despite the fact that the grounds were wanted by an opposing faction for a public park.

He was also a liberal contributor to the Jackson Friendly Home, an institution for aged women exclusively, and he personally solicited a good share of the funds which made the home a possibility.

Mr. Lewis, though a man temperate in all things, was not in favor of local option. He favored regulation of the saloon business, but he did not believe that the saloon should be abolished. The local optionists. however, won their fight, and the saloons went out of Jackson. One season was sufficient to convince the man that his position had been wrong, and he came out openly in favor of the temperance faction. Only a few weeks prior to his passing his name was found heading a subscription list for the carrying forward of anti-saloon work. Thus he was ever found to be. Did he cherish a conviction, he held it firmly. But he was always ready to be shown that he was in error in his opinion if facts could be produced to support the refutation of his ideas. It has been said that "A wise man changes his mind; but a fool, never." And Charles Lewis was one who knew how to change his mind when he found himself basing his arguments on a wrong idea.

Mr. Lewis was long a member of the Haven Methodist Episcopal church and served on its board of trustees for some years. He was a [32nd degree] Mason, with Knight Templar affiliations, and also was a Shriner and was a member of the Jackson lodge of Elks.

Mr. Lewis was married in Auburn, New York, on December 31, 1874, to Elizabeth A. Hollier, who survives her husband and has her residence in a fine old colonial home at 1609 East Main street, built by Mr. Lewis not more than five years prior to his death, which occurred on February 24, 1912 [at the age of 59 from heart disease exacerbated by asthma, with which he had long suffered].

Mrs. Lewis was born at Skaneateles, near Auburn, New York, on January 12, 1853, being a daughter of William J. Hollier and his wife, Mary Ann (Lewis) Hollier. Both were natives of England, where they were married in 1845. The Hollier family had its origin in Wales.

The five children of Mr. and Mrs. Lewis are: Minnie Belle, now the wife of E. [Edward] F. Lyon, of Detroit; Fred H., now managing head of the large manufacturing plants in Jackson founded by his father, and a prominent citizen of this city; Jessie May, who married Fred Bowman, of Buffalo, New York; Mary Frances, the wife of George Tygh,

of Jackson, and Miss Alice Winifred Lewis, who is now a senior in the Jackson high school [later married Raymond A. McQuillan of Jackson].

Among the many articles that have been published in local journals with reference to the life and work of Mr. Lewis, one is quoted here, from the pages of The Jacksonian, a journal published by the Chamber of Commerce of Jackson. It follows: "Charles Lewis was an admirer of young men and he always believed in giving the young man a chance. He felt that the future greatness of Jackson depended upon the younger generation; and he helped them with his money, with his advice and with valuable words of encouragement. His optimistic spirit was one of his greatest assets. His absolute and fearless honesty was another. There was no side of his great nature that did not breathe wholesouled geniality and inspire absolute confidence and trust. A growing community cannot be blessed with too many men of Charles Lewis' type. We wish there were more of them in Jackson.

"Charles Lewis was one of the incorporators of the Chamber of Commerce. From the date of its organization he served on its important committees and as one of the trustees of the Guaranty Association. The high regard in which he was held by every member is perhaps best attested by the following resolution adopted by the directors and later ratified by the entire membership at the annual banquet, by a rising vote taken in silence: 'But yesterday the Jackson Chamber of Commerce was proud to claim among its active working members a man of whom today, in the midst of his labors, has laid down the working tools of life.

"'We as an organization and to a man, individually, shall deeply and sincerely mourn the loss of Charles Lewis. We shall long feel the want of his enthusiasm, his ready moral and financial support and his wise council in all that pertained to the general welfare.

"'But while we shall miss the cheery smile, the happy greeting and the frank and friendly converse with him, we must still realize that all these were but the mere outward attributes of a life so lived among us as to long leave their firm impress for good upon this community.

"'Be it resolved, therefore, that this slight tribute to his memory be made a part of the records, and together with our heartfelt sympathy, be communicated to his family.'"

The mayor of the city, on the day following the death of Mr. Lewis, issued the following proclamation: "A sudden death has taken from us the Hon. Charles Lewis. In his vigorous personality was embodied the highest type of our citizenship. A life like his is an example, and Jackson had no nobler son. His wide sphere of beneficent activity is adorned at every point by the grateful remembrance of all our people of the good he did. In the business life of the city he was a sturdy pillar that stood square to every storm. In private life he was a devoted husband and father, and a faithful friend. In public life his zealous, disinterested and untiring service accompanied at all times by personal kindness, endeared him to all and inspired the confidence and affection of his associates. It is the lot of few men to be loved as he was.

"As a mark of respect to his memory, it is ordered that on Tuesday afternoon the public offices in this city be closed so that the city officers may attend the funeral in a body. All city officials will meet at one o'clock P. M. at the recorder's office for that purpose." "D. C. Sauer, Mayor of Jackson."

The Union Bank of Jackson, of which Mr. Lewis was long a director, also closed during the hour of the funeral, and other local establishments showed similar courtesy to the family and respect to the memory of a man who was much beloved in his own community.[832]

George A. Matthews

A leading figure in the industrial development of Jackson, a pioneer of the automobile industry, and a staunch supporter of the religious and educational affairs of his community – the late George A. Matthews was a man who richly merited the high esteem in which he was held by his fellow-citizens and business associates.

George Adelman Matthews was born in Thompson, a small village in Geauga county, Ohio, November 23rd, 1852. His father, Charles Matthews was a farmer, and his mother's maiden name was Ellen Daniels. The early years of Mr. Matthews' life were spent in the village school and in helping with the farm work at home. In his boyhood he developed the ambition and tireless energy which was a potent factor in his successful business career. He was known among his acquaintances as a boy who could pitch the most hay and harness a team in the shortest time, and his enterprise and initiative made him leader among his associates. After finishing the course of study which was provided, he taught for two years, working on the farm outside of school hours and during the summer vacation. By continuous application he was able to put aside enough money to take a course in a commercial college in Cleveland, where he laid the foundation of his business knowledge. At the completion of his commercial course, he entered the employ of a large coal company, in Cleveland, where he had valuable experience in the details of business, and was able to learn the principles of successful management.

On December 15th, 1875, Mr. Matthews married Esther Charlotte Hulbert, whom he had known since childhood and who was still a resident of Thompson. Mrs. Matthews was born December 21st, 1850 and was a daughter of Frederick and Charlotte Cibelia (Talcott) Hulbert. After his marriage, he returned to Thompson and purchased a farm, but his business instincts did not permit him to limit his efforts to farming, and he built up a thriving business in the wholesale marketing of eggs and dairy products. Seeking a larger field for his activities, he entered the employ of a carriage wheel manufacturing plant, at Madison, Ohio. He continued to live on the farm and have it worked under his supervision, driving each day five miles to his work in Madison and five miles home each night. His employers soon recognized his ability and integrity, and in a short time he was sent out to buy the material for their plant. This work he pursued with marked success, making trips on horse-back through the timber districts of West Virginia and the surrounding states in search of stock which could be used to the best advantage in the manufacture of carriage wheels. Eventually, this work brought him into contact with the officials of the American Wheel Company, and, appreciating his ability, they took him into their organization and sent him to Shortsville, N.Y., to take charge of a carriage wheel factory, at that place. He was next moved to Galion, Ohio, where he spent three and one-half years as general manager of a larger plant.

At this stage of his career, Mr. Matthews, having proven his ability as a successful director of manufacturing enterprises, determined to strike out for himself. He borrowed money and added to it what he had been able to save from his salary, and with this capital, in 1891, bought stock in the Fuller Buggy Company, of Jackson, Michigan [which had been incorporated on August 1, 1889]. A year later, at the death of Mr. [William B.] Fuller, who had been the chief stockholder, Mr. Matthews took over the entire business. The fact that the financial backers of the Fuller Company were willing to advance the money to finance the transfer of the stock, speaks volumes for the reputation of Mr. Matthews as a competent and thoroughly dependable executive. Their confidence was abundantly justified, and during the next ten years, the Fuller Buggy Company was transformed from a small plant of moderate promise into a nationally known factory for the production of carriages and vehicles. This company built up a large and thriving business which extended throughout the United States.

It was at about this time that Mr. Matthews, foreseeing the change which was destined to come into the field of transportation, began to direct his attention toward the production of motor cars. It was a natural step from the production of horse-drawn vehicles to the development of the automobile, and the rise of the industry has been due, in a considerable measure, to his efforts, for his unfailing faith in the future and untiring energy directed the development of one experiment after another until success was achieved. Mr. Matthews first started the Jackson Automobile Company in 1902 and devoted a generous share of his time and ability to its fortunes. In the beginning, the steam engine seemed to be the logical equipment for the automobile, and the first cars produced by the Jackson Company

were of this type. The gasoline motor was in its infancy, and it was only after repeated trials and costly experiments that it was proven to be a suitable motive power. During the first two years, the outlook was dark, and there were times when the other stock-holders in the Company were ready to give up the undertaking. With his wonderful energy and unfailing patience, Mr. Matthews brought the Company through the experimental period, and in 1903, produced a gasoline car which would give practical service in the hands of the average owner. In 1904, the Jackson Company produced a touring car, and in 1905, the output of the Company was largely increased. Cars were shipped to all parts of the United States, and their success built the foundation of an industry which has grown to national and international prominence. In 1907, the Jackson Automobile Company purchased property at the corner of East Main and Horton Streets, which more than doubled their capacity. It seemed at the time like a big move, but the faith which Mr. Matthews had in the Jackson car and the future of the automobile industry guided him in the right direction, and the business of the company in 1908 and 1909 made it necessary to erect new buildings, which again doubled the floor space of the factory. In 1910, Mr. Matthews acquired all of the stock in the Jackson Company, and the success of the business since that time has been a matter of common knowledge, not only in Jackson, but throughout the United States and abroad. At his death [which occurred suddenly while he was in his office on May 13, 1914 at the age of 61], the business was left to his family, Mrs. George A. Matthews and four children, Charles Frederick Matthews, Howard Adelman Matthews, Harry Eugene Matthews and Miss Mary Elizabeth Matthews. All three of the sons are officials and stockholders in the company, and all of them have given their active attention to its affairs for several years past. In financial circles Mr. Matthews was known as a "dependable man." His business associates and backers felt that his word was as good as his bond; that he spoke with a full knowledge of the details involved in the execution of his plans, and that he possessed a broad knowledge and indomitable will to carry through his projects. He was for many years a director of the Jackson City Bank, and was associated in several other industries in different parts of the country.

Mr. Matthews was a man of broad interests – a good citizen – who recognized a duty, not only to himself and family, but to the community in which he lived. He gave generously of his energy and ability to the institutions which make life easier and better for the world at large. In his support of the Haven Methodist Episcopal Church, he not only rendered financial assistance in every emergency, but gave generously of his time and strength for the furtherance of Church work. For a number of years he taught the Bible Class in his Church, and has always been faithful in its support. At the time when the school system of Jackson was in the process of development, Mr. Matthews took an active part in the work and served for many years as President of the School Board. He gave much of his time to the advancement of education in his community. He was prominent in the fraternal orders and was for many years a Mason, being both a Knight Templar and a Shriner. He was also a member of the Elks. In every department of the life of the community in which he lived, he took his part, and among all of his associates and acquaintances he was respected and loved.

Mr. Matthews was an unassuming man, whose generosity, though not ostentatious, was, nevertheless, ready and sympathetic. In his dealings with those who needed help, he was always ready to extend not only material aid, but to give his time and his attention to the solution of their troubles. It is rare indeed to find a man whose character has been so broadly and evenly developed – a leader in education, a staunch supporter of religious work, and of national prominence in commercial life. His many friends feel that to have been associated with such a pioneer for right, a man of such untiring energy and unselfish principles was both a privilege and inspiration, and his passing has left a great void.[833]

Citations and Notes

Preface

[1] George S. May, *A Most Unique Machine: The Michigan Origins of the American Automobile Industry* (Grand Rapids: William B. Eerdmans Publishing Co., 1975), p. 208.

[2] Ronald G. Bean, *Cartercar and Jaxon, 1900–1923: A Story of the 'Jackson' and 'Cartercar' Automobile Companies* (Saginaw: Ronald G. Bean, Publisher, 1975 / Ronald G. Bean, "The Jaxon," *The Bulb Horn*, July–August 1970: p. 6 / Ronald G. Bean, "Jackson: Part II," *The Bulb Horn* September–October 1970: p. 8 / Ronald G. Bean, "Cartercar: Part III of Jackson–Cartercar," *The Bulb Horn* November–December 1970: p. 24 / Ronald G. Bean, "Cartercar: Conclusion," *The Bulb Horn* January–February 1971: p. 12.

Byron J. Carter's Early Life

[3] *Jackson Daily Citizen* March 8, 1875: p. 5 / *Jackson Daily Citizen* May 11, 1880: p. 1 / *Jackson Daily Citizen* January 3, 1882: p. 7 / *Jackson Daily Citizen* November 29, 1884: p. 5 / *Jackson Daily Citizen* May 19, 1885: p. 5 / *Jackson Daily Citizen* January 29, 1886: p. 4 / *Jackson Daily Citizen* May 28, 1887: p. 4 / *Jackson Daily Citizen* June 4, 1887: p. 5 / *R. L. Polk & Co.'s 1884 Jackson City Directory*: p. 96.

[4] *R. L. Polk & Co.'s 1884 Jackson City Directory*: p. 96.

[5] *Detroit Times* April 6, 1908: p. 1.

First Business Ventures of B. J. Carter and Squire B. Carter

[6] *R. L. Polk & Co.'s 1885/1886 Jackson City Directory*: pp. 91, 334 / *R. L. Polk & Co.'s 1887 Jackson City Directory*: pp. 80, 92, 339 / *Detroit Free Press* April 1, 1887: p. 4.

[7] *Detroit Free Press* April 1, 1887: p. 4.

[8] Ibid.

[9] http://museumofprinting.org / http://www.hrc.utexas.edu/educator/modules/gutenberg/books/printing. Retrieved May 15, 2015.

[10] *R. L. Polk & Co.'s 1885/1886 Jackson City Directory*: p. 91.

[11] *R. L. Polk & Co.'s 1885/1886 Jackson City Directory*: p. 91 / *R. L. Polk & Co.'s 1887 Jackson City Directory*: pp. 92, 322.

[12] *R. L. Polk & Co.'s 1888 Jackson City Directory*: p. 354.

[13] *Detroit Free Press* April 1, 1887: p. 4 / *Jackson Daily Citizen* August 4, 1887: p. 4.

[14] *Jackson Daily Citizen* August 4, 1887: p. 4.

[15] *Detroit Free Press* April 1, 1887: p. 4.

[16] Ibid.

[17] *Jackson Daily Citizen* August 4, 1887: p. 4.

[18] Ibid.

[19] *Jackson Daily Citizen* August 5, 1887: p. 4 / *Note:* The term "forms" was not defined anywhere in the various applicable *Jackson Daily Citizen* articles and no on-point references to "forms" were found in any online sources about 19th-century job printing.

[20] *Jackson Daily Citizen* August 5, 1887: p. 4.

[21] *Jackson Daily Citizen* August 10, 1887: p. 5.

[22] *Jackson Daily Citizen* November 4, 1887: p. 7.

[23] *Jackson Daily Citizen* March 13, 1888: p. 5.

[24] *Jackson Daily Citizen* July 17, 1888: p. 5.

[25] *R. L. Polk & Co.'s 1887 Jackson City Directory*: p. 92 / *R. L. Polk & Co.'s 1888 Jackson City Directory*: p. 98.

[26] *Jackson Daily Citizen* March 2, 1888: p. 7 / *Jackson Citizen Press* February 25, 1913: p. 3 / State of Michigan Certificate of Live Birth for George R. Carter, state file no. 121-1-144-84.

[27] *R. L. Polk & Co.'s 1888 Jackson City Directory*: pp. 373, 375.

[28] *R. L. Polk & Co.'s 1888 Jackson City Directory*: p. 245.

[29] *R. L. Polk & Co.'s 1883 Jackson City Directory*: p. 207.

[30] *Jackson Daily Citizen* March 21, 1889: p. 6.

[31] *R. L. Polk & Co.'s 1887 Jackson City Directory*: p. 115 / *Jackson Citizen Patriot* April 9, 1922: p. 36.

[32] *Jackson Daily Citizen* May 27, 1889: p. 7.

[33] *R. L. Polk & Co.'s 1888 Jackson City Directory*: p. 245 / *R. L. Polk & Co.'s 1890 Jackson City Directory*: pp. 7, 198, 267, 411.

[34] *Jackson Citizen* April 7, 1908 / *R. L. Polk & Co.'s 1890 Jackson City Directory*: p. 224 / *R. L. Polk & Co.'s 1891/1892 Jackson City Directory*: p. 226.

[35] *R. L. Polk & Co.'s 1891 Jackson City Directory*: p. 269.

Earliest Bicycle Pursuits

36 *Jackson Daily Citizen* August 10, 1885: p. 4.

37 *Automobile Dealer and Repairer* April 1908: p. 37 / *Automobile Topics* April 18, 1908: p. 125 / *Motor Field* May 1908: p. 64.

38 *Jackson Daily Citizen* August 10, 1885: p. 4.

39 Ibid.

40 *Jackson Daily Citizen* July 20, 1886: p. 4.

41 *Catalogue of Star Bicycles Manufactured by the H.B. Smith Machine Co.* March 1886 / *Catalogue of 1887 Star Bicycles Manufactured by H.B. Smith Machine Co.*

42 David V. Herlihy, *Bicycle: The History* (New Haven and London: Yale University Press, 2004), p. 219.

43 Ibid.

44 David V. Herlihy, *Bicycle: The History* (New Haven and London: Yale University Press, 2004), p. 219 / "American Star bicycle, 1885 – 1890" Powerhouse Museum, Sydney, Australia (www.powerhousemuseum.com/collection/database/?irn=242363#ixzz3cist8kDX), http://from.ph/242363 |title=American Star bicycle, 1885-1890. Retrieved June 11, 2015.

45 G. W. Pressey. Velocipede. U.S . Patent 233,640, filed May 1, 1880, and issued October 26, 1880.

46 W. X. Stevens. Bicycle Brace. U.S . Patent 293,284, filed January 2, 1884, and issued February 12, 1884 / F. Jannus. Bicycle. U.S . Patent 331,199, filed April 6, 1885, and issued November 24, 1885 / David V. Herlihy, *Bicycle: The History* (New Haven and London: Yale University Press, 2004), p. 220.

47 *Catalogue of Star Bicycles Manufactured by the H.B. Smith Machine Co.* March 1886 / *Catalogue of 1887 Star Bicycles Manufactured by H.B. Smith Machine Co.*

48 *Jackson Daily Citizen* June 2, 1886: p. 4.

49 *Jackson Daily Citizen* August 3, 1887: p. 5.

50 *Jackson Daily Citizen* August 21, 1889: p. 7.

51 *Detroit Times* April 6, 1908: p. 1.

52 Ibid.

B. J. Carter Temporarily Relocates to Sheffield, Alabama

53 *Jackson Daily Citizen* April 26, 1890: p. 6.

54 Ibid.

55 Courtesy of Buzzy Carter Maurer: Original July 11, 1892 contract between Byron J. Carter and the Standard Machine Works.

56 *R. L. Polk & Co.'s 1894/1895 Jackson City Directory*: p. 104.

Business Operations in the Northwest Corner of Cortland and Jackson Streets

57 *Jackson Daily Citizen* March 21, 1889: p. 6 / *R. L. Polk & Co.'s 1890 Jackson City Directory*: p. 104.

58 *Jackson Daily Citizen* October 9, 1891: p. 5 / *R. L. Polk & Co.'s 1891/1892 Jackson City Directory*: pp. 102, 392 / *R. L. Polk & Co.'s 1893/1894 Jackson City Directory*: pp. 109, 431.

59 *Jackson Daily Citizen* March 22, 1892: p. 6.

60 *R. L. Polk & Co.'s 1894/1895 Jackson City Directory*: pp. 59, 105, 388.

The Carter Bicycle Enterprise and Other Business Expansions during the 1890s

61 *R. L. Polk & Co.'s 1894/1895 Jackson City Directory*: pp. 59, 165, 388.

62 *R. L. Polk & Co.'s 1898/1899 Jackson City Directory*: p. 505.

63 *Jackson Daily Citizen* March 29, 1894: p. 4.

64 *Jackson Daily Citizen* March 29, 1894: p. 4 / *Jackson Daily Citizen* March 1, 1895: p. 1 / *Jackson Daily Citizen* March 6, 1895: p. 1 / *Jackson Daily Citizen* March 28, 1899: p. 7 / *Jackson Daily Citizen* March 29, 1899: p. 8.

65 *Jackson Daily Citizen* July 31, 1894: p. 6.

66 *Jackson Daily Citizen* August 15, 1894: p. 6.

67 *Jackson Daily Citizen* September 29, 1894: p. 6.

68 *Jackson Daily Citizen* April 9, 1895: p. 1 / *R. L. Polk & Co.'s 1896 Jackson City Directory*: pp. 123, 539.

69 *Jackson Daily Citizen* April 9, 1895: p. 1.

70 *R. L. Polk & Co.'s 1897 Jackson City Directory*: p. 422.

71 *R. L. Polk & Co.'s 1896 Jackson City Directory*: p. 500.

72 *R. L. Polk & Co.'s 1897 Jackson City Directory*: p. 387.

Bicycle Operations Grow in an Impressive New Facility

[73] *Jackson Daily Citizen* January 30, 1896: p. 7.

[74] *Jackson Daily Citizen* March 6, 1895: p. 1 / *Jackson Daily Citizen* January 30, 1896: p. 7 / *Jackson Daily Citizen* February 8, 1896: p. 1.

[75] *R. L. Polk & Co.'s 1897 Jackson City Directory*: pp. 118, 536 / *R. L. Polk & Co.'s 1898/1899 Jackson City Directory*: pp. 130, 505.

Fred T. Lockwood: Photographer, Carter Employee, and a Boat-Motor Pioneer

[76] *R. L. Polk & Co.'s 1896 Jackson City Directory*: p. 280 / *R. L. Polk & Co.'s 1897 Jackson City Directory*: p. 271.

[77] *Jackson Citizen Patriot* September 14, 1919: p. 5.

[78] *Jackson Daily Citizen* November 29, 1898: p. 7.

[79] *Jackson Daily Citizen* March 9, 1901: p. 7.

[80] Ibid.

[81] *Jackson Daily Citizen* April 20, 1901: p. 7 / *Jackson Daily Citizen* May 4, 1901: p. 11.

[82] *Jackson Daily Citizen* June 9, 1902: p. 8.

[83] *Jackson Daily Citizen* September 20, 1902: p. 7 / *Jackson Daily Citizen* January 13, 1903: p. 4.

[84] *Jackson Daily Citizen* September 20, 1902: p. 7 / *R. L. Polk & Co.'s 1905 Jackson City Directory*: p. 376.

[85] *R. L. Polk & Co.'s 1905 Jackson City Directory*: p. 376.

[86] *R. L. Polk & Co.'s 1908 Jackson City Directory*: p. 67.

[87] Warranty Deed from Jackson Vehicle Company to George A. Matthews and Charles Lewis; November 30, 1907. Jackson County Register of Deeds, Jackson, Michigan, Liber 188, p. 90, Abstract Entry No. 34 / *R. L. Polk & Co.'s 1909 Jackson City Directory*: p. 397.

[88] "Feature Company: Lockwood-Ash" Antique Outboard Motor Club – Yankee Chapter, New England, http://yankeeaomci.org/feature_outboard.htm. Retrieved June 21, 2015.

[89] Jeffrey L. Rodengen, *Evinrude Johnson and the Legend of OMC* (Fort Lauderdale: Write Stuff Syndicate, Inc., 1993), pp. 26, 27 / "History of the Evinrude Outboard Company" Antique Small Engine Collectors Club, http://www.asecc.com/data/engines/evinrude.html. Retrieved June 21, 2015 / "The Origins of Evinrude" Crowley Marine, Denver, http://www.crowleymarine.com/history-of-evinrude/the-origins-of-evinrude.html. Retrieved June 21, 2015.

[90] Jeffrey L. Rodengen, *Evinrude Johnson and the Legend of OMC* (Fort Lauderdale: Write Stuff Syndicate, Inc., 1993), p. 21 / "History of the Evinrude Outboard Company" Antique Small Engine Collectors Club, http://www.asecc.com/data/engines/evinrude.html. Retrieved June 21, 2015 / "Feature Company: Lockwood-Ash" Antique Outboard Motor Club – Yankee Chapter, New England, http://yankeeaomci.org/feature_outboard.htm. Retrieved June 21, 2015 / "The Origins of Evinrude" Crowley Marine, Denver, http://www.crowleymarine.com/history-of-evinrude/the-origins-of-evinrude.html. Retrieved June 21, 2015.

[91] *Automobile Topics* July 3, 1939: p. 301.

[92] *Automobile Topics* March 13, 1939: p. 208.

[93] *Jackson Citizen Patriot* February 5, 1920: p. 3 / *R. L. Polk & Co.'s 1935 Jackson City Directory*: p. 270 / *R. L. Polk & Co.'s 1938 Jackson City Directory*: p. 248 / *R. L. Polk & Co.'s 1940 Jackson City Directory*: p. 234.

The 1890s Bicycle Craze in Jackson

[94] *Jackson Daily Citizen* August 2, 1895: p. 6.

[95] *Jackson Daily Citizen* July 31, 1895: p. 6.

[96] *Jackson Daily Citizen* August 2, 1895: p. 6 / *Jackson Daily Citizen* July 31, 1895: p. 6.

[97] *Jackson Daily Citizen* August 31, 1895: p. 7.

[98] *Jackson Daily Citizen* September 14, 1895: p. 6.

[99] Ibid.

[100] *Jackson Daily Citizen* September 21, 1895: p. 7.

[101] *Jackson Daily Citizen* June 13, 1896: p. 11.

[102] *Jackson Daily Citizen* June 12, 1896: p. 7 / *Jackson Daily Citizen* June 13, 1896: p. 11.

[103] *Jackson Daily Citizen* January 6, 1896: p. 6.

[104] *Jackson Daily Citizen* January 11, 1896: p. 6.

[105] *Jackson Daily Citizen* January 31, 1896: p. 6.

[106] *Jackson Daily Citizen* January 29, 1896: p. 6 / *Jackson Daily Citizen* January 31, 1896: p. 6.

[107] *Jackson Daily Citizen* March 28, 1896: p. 6.

108 *Jackson Daily Citizen* April 18, 1896: p. 10 / *Jackson Daily Citizen* April 21, 1896: pp 5 / *Jackson Daily Citizen* May 16, 1896: p. 6.

The Fowler Sextet

109 *Jackson Daily Citizen* March 11, 1896: p. 1 / *Jackson Daily Citizen* March 13, 1896: pp. 6, 8 / *Jackson Daily Citizen* March 19, 1896: p. 7.

110 *Jackson Daily Citizen* March 13, 1896: pp. 6, 8.

111 Ibid.

112 Ibid.

Dorothy Adell "Della" Carter

113 State of Michigan Marriage Certificate for Byron J. Carter and Dorothy A. Gillette, state file no. 2-339-1896, record 229 / *Jackson Daily Citizen* July 3, 1896: p. 4 / *Jackson Citizen Patriot* May 21, 1958: pp. 1, 5 & May 22, 1958: p. 5 .

114 Courtesy of Sallie Sparks Kendall: 1945 Christmas note from Charles A. Trask to Della Carter.

115 *Jackson Daily Citizen* July 3, 1896: p. 4.

116 *Jackson Citizen Patriot* November 30, 1960: p. 1.

A Prospecting Venture for Oil, Gas, and Minerals

117 *Jackson Daily Citizen* March 27, 1897: p. 11.

118 Ibid.

119 Brad Flory. "Oil boom in Jackson County: Who imagined it could be this big?" *Jackson Citizen Patriot* (MLive.com) February 24, 2013, http://blog.mlive.com/bradosphere/2013/02/oil_boom_in_jackson_county_who.html. Retrieved March 16, 2015.

B. J. Carter, the Employer and Mentor

JOHN H. CARPENTER

120 *R. L. Polk & Co.'s 1894/1895 Jackson City Directory*: p. 103 / *Jackson Daily Citizen* February 26, 1895: p. 7.

121 *Jackson Daily Citizen* February 26, 1895: p. 7.

122 *Jackson Daily Citizen* August 2, 1895: p. 6.

123 *R. L. Polk & Co.'s 1888 Jackson City Directory*: p. 286 / *R. L. Polk & Co.'s 1890 Jackson City Directory*: p. 102.

124 *R. L. Polk & Co.'s 1891/1892 Jackson City Directory*: p. 101.

125 *Jackson Daily Citizen* October 13, 1891: p. 7 / *R. L. Polk & Co.'s 1894/1895 Jackson City Directory*: p. 103 / *Jackson Daily Citizen* February 26, 1895: p. 7.

126 *R. L. Polk & Co.'s 1897 Jackson City Directory*: p. 116 / *Jackson Daily Citizen* September 4, 1900: p. 6.

127 *Jackson Daily Citizen* August 1, 1902: p. 4 / *R. L. Polk & Co.'s 1903 Jackson City Directory*: p. 153.

128 *R. L. Polk & Co.'s 1905 Jackson City Directory*: p. 164.

129 *Jackson Citizen Press* January 26, 1914: p. 7 / *Jackson Citizen Press* June 21, 1916: p. 8.

FRED T. LOCKWOOD

130 *R. L. Polk & Co.'s 1896 Jackson City Directory*: p. 280 / *R. L. Polk & Co.'s 1897 Jackson City Directory*: p. 271.

131 *Jackson Citizen Patriot* September 14, 1919: p. 5.

132 *Jackson Daily Citizen* March 9, 1901: p. 7.

FRANK N. BRADLEY

133 *R. L. Polk & Co.'s 1897 Jackson City Directory*: p. 99 / *R. L. Polk & Co.'s 1898/1899 Jackson City Directory*: p. 109.

134 *Jackson Daily Citizen* November 11, 1898: p. 7 / *R. L. Polk & Co.'s 1898/1899 Jackson City Directory*: p. 296.

135 *Jackson Citizen Patriot* September 14, 1919: p. 5.

136 *R. L. Polk & Co.'s 1901 Jackson City Directory*: p. 114.

137 *R. L. Polk & Co.'s 1907 Battle Creek City Directory*: p. 119.

ARTHUR L. BUTCHER

138 *R. L. Polk & Co.'s 1888 Jackson City Directory*: p. 93.

139 *R. L. Polk & Co.'s 1890 Jackson City Directory*: p. 98 / *R. L. Polk & Co.'s 1891/1892 Jackson City Directory*: p. 96.

140 *R. L. Polk & Co.'s 1893/1894 Jackson City Directory*: p. 103 / *R. L. Polk & Co.'s 1894/1895 Jackson City Directory*: p. 99 / *R. L. Polk & Co.'s 1896 Jackson City Directory*: p. 116.

141 Courtesy of Sallie Sparks Kendall: January 6, 1940 letter from Charles A. Trask to Della Carter.

142 *R. L. Polk & Co.'s 1897 Jackson City Directory*: p. 111.

143 *Jackson Citizen Patriot* September 14, 1919: p. 5 / *Jackson Daily Citizen* March 14, 1898: p. 6.

144 *Jackson Daily Citizen* March 14, 1898: p. 6.

145 *The Motor Vehicle Review* September 13, 1900: p. 33.

146 *R. L. Polk & Co.'s 1902 Jackson City Directory*: p. 130.

147 *R. L. Polk & Co.'s 1903 Jackson City Directory*: p. 146.

148 *R. L. Polk & Co.'s 1904 Jackson City Directory*: p. 148.

149 *R. L. Polk & Co.'s 1896 Jackson City Directory*: p. 195 / *R. L. Polk & Co.'s 1897 Jackson City Directory*: p. 187 / *R. L. Polk & Co.'s 1905 Jackson City Directory*: p. 157.

150 *R. L. Polk & Co.'s 1905 Jackson City Directory*: p. 157 / *R. L. Polk & Co.'s 1907 Jackson City Directory*: p. 154 / *R. L. Polk & Co.'s 1910 Jackson City Directory*: p. 160 / *Jackson Citizen Press* January 16, 1915: p. 9.

151 *Jackson Patriot* October 29, 1916: pp. 17, 18.

152 Ibid.

153 *Jackson Patriot* October 20, 1916: p. 3 / *Jackson Patriot* October 29, 1916: pp. 17, 18.

154 *Jackson Citizen Press* December 31, 1917: p. 1.

FRED P. HINCKLEY

155 *R. L. Polk & Co.'s 1898/1899 Jackson City Directory*: p. 241.

156 *Jackson Daily Citizen* May 3, 1890: p. 3 / *R. L. Polk & Co.'s 1890 Jackson City Directory*: p. 183.

157 *Michigan, Marriage Records, 1867–1952*. Michigan Department of Community Health, Division for Vital Records and Health Statistics / *R. L. Polk & Co.'s 1890 Jackson City Directory*: p. 183.

158 *R. L. Polk & Co.'s 1898/1899 Jackson City Directory*: p. 241.

159 *Jackson Daily Citizen* March 27, 1897: p. 11.

160 *R. L. Polk & Co.'s 1901 Jackson City Directory*: p. 258.

161 *R. L. Polk & Co.'s 1902 Jackson City Directory*: pp. 80, 262, 341.

162 *R. L. Polk & Co.'s 1904 Jackson City Directory*: p. 661.

LEWIS N. TUSSING

163 *R. L. Polk & Co.'s 1898/1899 Jackson City Directory*: p. 456.

164 *Jackson Daily Citizen* January 12, 1891: p. 7.

165 *R. L. Polk & Co.'s 1897 Jackson City Directory*: pp. 330, 420.

166 *Jackson Citizen Patriot* September 14, 1919: p. 5.

167 *R. L. Polk & Co.'s 1902 Jackson City Directory*: p. 503.

168 *R. L. Polk & Co.'s 1903 Jackson City Directory*: p. 543 / *R. L. Polk & Co.'s 1904 Jackson City Directory*: p. 553.

169 *R. L. Polk & Co.'s 1909 Jackson City Directory*: p. 539.

170 *R. L. Polk & Co.'s 1943 Jackson City Directory*: p. 366.

OTHER CARTER EMPLOYEES

171 *R. L. Polk & Co.'s 1897 Jackson City Directory*: p. 387.

172 Courtesy of Sallie Sparks Kendall: 1945 Christmas note from Charles A. Trask to Della Carter.

173 *R. L. Polk & Co.'s 1901 Jackson City Directory*: p. 358 / *R. L. Polk & Co.'s 1902 Jackson City Directory*: p. 366 / *R. L. Polk & Co.'s 1903 Jackson City Directory*: p. 405.

174 *R. L. Polk & Co.'s 1897 Jackson City Directory*: p. 155 / *R. L. Polk & Co.'s 1898/1899 Jackson City Directory*: p. 169 / *R. L. Polk & Co.'s 1900/1901 Jackson City Directory*: p. 180 / *R. L. Polk & Co.'s 1902 Jackson City Directory*: p. 183 / *R. L. Polk & Co.'s 1903 Jackson City Directory*: p. 208 / *R. L. Polk & Co.'s 1904 Jackson City Directory*: p. 209 / *R. L. Polk & Co.'s 1908 Jackson City Directory*: p. 230.

175 *R. L. Polk & Co.'s 1901 Jackson City Directory*: p. 183 / *R. L. Polk & Co.'s 1902 Jackson City Directory*: p. 186 / *R. L. Polk & Co.'s 1903 Jackson City Directory*: p. 212 / *R. L. Polk & Co.'s 1909 Jackson City Directory*: p. 236 / *R. L. Polk & Co.'s 1910 Jackson City Directory*: p. 232 / *R. L. Polk & Co.'s 1912 Jackson City Directory*: p. 226 / U.S., World War I Draft Registration Cards, 1917-1918 for Edward Joseph Doody.

176 *R. L. Polk & Co.'s 1896 Jackson City Directory*: p. 205 / *R. L. Polk & Co.'s 1897 Jackson City Directory*: p. 155 / *R. L. Polk & Co.'s 1898/1899 Jackson City Directory*: p. 215 / *R. L. Polk & Co.'s 1900/1901 Jackson City Directory*: pp. 229, 291 / *R. L. Polk & Co.'s 1902 Jackson City Directory*: p. 232.

Charles A. Trask: Master Machinist in Jackson and Chief Engineer for the Cartercar

177 *Jackson Daily Citizen* January 4, 1899: p. 3.

[178] *R. L. Polk & Co.'s 1885/1886 Jackson City Directory*: p. 273 / *R. L. Polk & Co.'s 1887 Jackson City Directory*: p. 278 / *R. L. Polk & Co.'s 1888 Jackson City Directory*: p. 306 / *R. L. Polk & Co.'s 1890 Jackson City Directory*: p. 334.

[179] *Jackson Daily Citizen* May 3, 1890: p. 3.

[180] *Jackson Daily Citizen* May 3, 1890: p. 3.

[181] *R. L. Polk & Co.'s 1891/1892 Jackson City Directory*: p. 339 / *Jackson Daily Citizen* February 9, 1891: p. 1.

[182] *R. L. Polk & Co.'s 1893/1894 Jackson City Directory*: p. 414.

[183] *R. L. Polk & Co.'s 1894/1895 Jackson City Directory*: p. 388.

[184] *Jackson Daily Citizen* December 15, 1894: p. 11.

[185] *Jackson Daily Citizen* June 21, 1894: p. 5.

[186] *Jackson Daily Citizen* December 15, 1894: p. 11.

[187] *Jackson Daily Citizen* January 31, 1896: p. 6 / *Jackson Daily Citizen* February 25, 1896: p. 6 / *Jackson Daily Citizen* February 29, 1896: p. 3 / *Jackson Daily Citizen* June 12, 1897: p. 7.

[188] *Jackson Daily Citizen* February 28, 1895: p. 7.

[189] *Jackson Daily Citizen* July 17, 1897: p. 7.

[190] Ibid.

[191] *Jackson Daily Citizen* July 5, 1898: p. 6 / *Jackson Daily Citizen* January 4, 1899: p. 3 / *Jackson Daily Citizen* January 30, 1899: p. 3.

[192] *Jackson Daily Citizen* September 18, 1899: p. 7.

[193] Ibid.

[194] Ibid.

[195] Ibid.

[196] *Jackson Citizen Patriot* April 26, 1964: p. 56.

[197] *Jackson Daily Citizen* March 14, 1898: p. 6.

[198] Ibid.

[199] *Jackson Daily Citizen* May 26, 1899: p. 3.

[200] *Jackson Daily Citizen* December 15, 1894: p. 11 / *R. L. Polk & Co.'s 1896 Jackson City Directory*: p. 494 / *R. L. Polk & Co.'s 1897 Jackson City Directory*: p. 417.

[201] *Jackson Daily Citizen* October 26, 1895: p. 7.

[202] *Jackson Citizen Patriot* September 14, 1919: p. 5.

[203] *Jackson Daily Citizen* December 19, 1902: p. 7.

[204] *Jackson Daily Citizen* March 4, 1903: p. 7.

[205] *R. L. Polk & Co.'s 1905 Jackson City Directory*: p. 241 / *Jackson Daily Citizen* January 14, 1904: p. 1.

[206] *Jackson Citizen Patriot* April 26, 1964: p. 56.

[207] Courtesy of Sallie Sparks Kendall: January 6, 1940 Letter from Charles A. Trask to Della Carter / *R. L. Polk & Co.'s 1906 Ypsilanti City Directory*: p. 515 / *R. L. Polk & Co.'s 1907 Ypsilanti City Directory*: p. 555.

[208] *R. L. Polk & Co.'s 1907 Detroit City Directory*: p. 2271 / *R. L. Polk & Co.'s 1908 Detroit City Directory*: p. 2098.

[209] *The Horseless Age* March 27, 1912: p. 600 / *Detroit Free Press* April 28, 1912: p. C6 / *The Automobile* February 12, 1914: p. 432.

[210] *Detroit Free Press* September 26, 1909: p. 8 / *Detroit Free Press* September 29, 1909: p. 6 / *Detroit Free Press* October 3, 1909: p. 8.

[211] *The Horseless Age* March 27, 1912: p. 600 / *The Automobile* March 28, 1912: p. 815 / *The Iron Trade Review* April 18, 1912: p. 864 / *Detroit Free Press* April 28, 1912: p. C6 / *Motor Age* May 2, 1912: p. 47.

[212] *Automobile Topics* April 27, 1912: p. 582 / *Detroit Free Press* April 28, 1912: p. C6.

[213] *The Horseless Age* May 1, 1912: p. 822 / *The Automobile* May 2, 1912: p. 1052.

[214] *The Hub* May 1912: p. 56 / *Automobile Topics* May 11, 1912: p. 707 / *Automobile Topics* June 15, 1912: p. 283.

[215] *Automobile Topics* June 15, 1912: p. 283.

[216] Ibid.

[217] Ibid.

[218] Ibid.

[219] *Automobile Topics* May 11, 1912: p. 707 / *Automobile Trade Journal* June 1, 1912: p. 90 / *Indianapolis 1913 City Directory*: p. 1601 / *Indianapolis 1914 City Directory*: p. 1403 / *Indianapolis 1915 City Directory*: p. 1393.

[220] *The Horseless Age* November 27, 1912: p. 819.

[221] *The Horseless Age* January 22, 1913: p. 212 / *The Horseless Age* January 29, 1913: p. 253 / *The Automobile* February 20, 1913: p. 530.

222 Beverly Rae Kimes and Henry Austin Clark Jr., *Standard Catalog of American Cars, 1805 - 1942* (Iola: Krause Publications, Third Edition 1996), p. 924.

223 *Jackson Citizen Patriot* April 26, 1964: p. 56.

224 Beverly Rae Kimes and Henry Austin Clark Jr., *Standard Catalog of American Cars, 1805 - 1942* (Iola: Krause Publications, Third Edition 1996), pp. 1593, various others.

225 *Automobile Topics* February 7, 1914: p. 1075.

226 *The Automobile* January 15, 1914: p. 175.

227 *Automobile Topics* February 7, 1914: p. 1075 / *Industrial World* February 23, 1914: p. 237 / *The American Cyclecar* March 1914: p. 9 / *Robert D. Cunningham. "The Comet – The* World's Greatest Cycle Car" *The Old Motor* (theoldmotor.com), October 26, 2014 comment, http://theoldmotor.com/?tag=comet-cycle-car. Retrieved May 28, 2015.

228 *Automobile Topics* February 7, 1914: p. 1075 / *The American Cyclecar* March 1914: p. 9 / Robert D. Cunningham. "The Comet – The World's Greatest Cycle Car" *The Old Motor* (theoldmotor.com), October 26, 2014 comment, http://theoldmotor.com/?tag=comet-cycle-car. Retrieved May 28, 2015.

229 *Automobile Topics* February 7, 1914: p. 1075 / *The Automobile* February 12, 1914: p. 432 / *The American Cyclecar* March 1914: p. 9.

230 *Automobile Topics* February 7, 1914: p. 1075 / *The Automobile* February 12, 1914: p. 432.

231 *Automobile Topics* February 7, 1914: p. 1075 / *The Automobile* February 12, 1914: p. 432 / *The American Cyclecar* March 1914: p. 2.

232 *The American Cyclecar* March 1914: pp. 2, 9.

233 Courtesy of Buzzy Carter Maurer: March 28, 1920 Letter from Charles A. Trask to Kenneth G. Carter.

234 *Automobile Topics* February 7, 1914: p. 1075 / *The American Cyclecar* March 1914: p. 2.

235 *The American Cyclecar* March 1914: p. 2 / *Automobile Topics* July 4, 1914: p. 627 / Beverly Rae Kimes and Henry Austin Clark Jr., *Standard Catalog of American Cars, 1805 - 1942* (Iola: Krause Publications, Third Edition 1996), p. 517.

236 *Automobile Topics* July 4, 1914: p. 627 / Beverly Rae Kimes and Henry Austin Clark Jr., *Standard Catalog of American Cars, 1805 - 1942* (Iola: Krause Publications, Third Edition 1996), p. 963.

237 *Automobile Topics* July 4, 1914: p. 627.

238 *Automobile Trade Journal* January 1, 1914: p. 159 / *Motor* February 1914: p. 83.

239 Robert D. Cunningham. "The Comet – The World's Greatest Cycle Car" *The*

240 *Old Motor* (theoldmotor.com), October 26, 2014 comment, http://theoldmotor.com/?tag=comet-cycle-car. Retrieved May 28, 2015 / *Jackson Citizen Patriot* April 26, 1964: p. 56.

240 Courtesy of Buzzy Carter Maurer: March 28, 1920 Letter from Charles A. Trask to Kenneth G. Carter.

241 Robert D. Cunningham. "The Comet – The World's Greatest Cycle Car" *The Old Motor* (theoldmotor.com), October 26, 2014 comment, http://theoldmotor.com/?tag=comet-cycle-car. Retrieved May 28, 2015.

242 Charles A. Trask, "Tractor Friction Transmissions," *Journal of the Society of Automotive Engineers* June 1918: page 440.

243 *Automotive Industries* March 19, 1925: p. 558.

244 *The Journal of the Society of Automotive Engineers* October 1920: p. 404.

245 *Automobile Trade Journal* June 1, 1929: p. 65.

246 *Automobile Trade Journal* August 1, 1917: p. 370 / http://www.paperpulleys.com/pages/home.html.

247 *Jackson Citizen Patriot* April 26, 1964: p. 56.

The Carter Enterprise at the End of the 1890s

248 *Jackson Daily Citizen* July 3, 1896: p. 4.

249 *R. L. Polk & Co.'s 1897 Jackson City Directory*: pp. 118, 422, 465, 492 / *R. L. Polk & Co.'s 1898/1899 Jackson City Directory:* pp. 129, 130, 505, 577 / *Jackson Daily Citizen* April 19, 1899: p. 6 / *Jackson Daily Citizen* May 13, 1899: p. 12 / *Jackson Daily Citizen* February 13, 1900: p. 7 / *R. L.Polk & Co.'s 1900/1901 Jackson City Directory*: pp. 136, 543.

250 *R. L. Polk & Co.'s 1897 Jackson City Directory*: pp. 118, 536, 562 / *R. L. Polk & Co.'s 1898/1899 Jackson City Directory:* pp. 129, 130, 505, 608.

251 *R. L. Polk & Co.'s 1901 Jackson City Directory*: p. 137 / *R. L. Polk & Co.'s 1902 Jackson City Directory*: p. 138.

First Automobile Assembled in Jackson, Michigan

252 *Jackson Daily Citizen* June 26, 1899: p. 7.

253 *The Horseless Age* August 9, 1899: p. 15.

254 *Detroit News* April 6, 1908: p. 2 / *Detroit Journal* April 6, 1908 / *Cleveland Plain Dealer* April 12, 1908: p. 35.

255 Charles Brady King Collection, National Automotive History Collection, Detroit Public Library (outline completed by King titled "Cars Built and Designed by Charles B. King – 1893-1903" and other materials).

256 *Jackson Citizen Patriot* September 14, 1919: p. 5.

257 Joshua Wicks, "Charles B. King" (Detroit Historical.Wordpress.com), July 5, 2013 article, http://detroithistorical.wordpress.com/2013/07/05/charles-b-king/. Retrieved June 28, 2015.

258 Charles Brady King, *Psychic Reminiscences* (Larchmont: Charles B. King, First Edition 1935) / Charles Brady King, *A Golden Anniversary, 1895 – 1945, Personal Side-Lights of America's First Automobile Race* (Larchmont: Charles B. King, November 1, 1945).

259 Charles Brady King, *A Golden Anniversary, 1895 – 1945, Personal Side-Lights of America's First Automobile Race* (Larchmont: Charles B. King, November 1, 1945), pp. 12-14 / *The National Cyclopaedia of American Biography* (New York: James T. White and Company, Current Volume D, 1934) "Charles Brady King."

260 Charles Brady King, *A Golden Anniversary, 1895 – 1945, Personal Side-Lights of America's First Automobile Race* (Larchmont: Charles B. King, November 1, 1945), p. 12.

261 Charles Brady King, *A Golden Anniversary, 1895 – 1945, Personal Side-Lights of America's First Automobile Race* (Larchmont: Charles B. King, November 1, 1945), pp. 8, 14.

262 Charles Brady King, *A Golden Anniversary, 1895 – 1945, Personal Side-Lights of America's First Automobile Race* (Larchmont: Charles B. King, November 1, 1945), p. 14.

263 Charles Brady King, *A Golden Anniversary, 1895 – 1945, Personal Side-Lights of America's First Automobile Race* (Larchmont: Charles B. King, November 1, 1945), pp. 14, 44.

264 Charles Brady King, *A Golden Anniversary, 1895 – 1945, Personal Side-Lights of America's First Automobile Race* (Larchmont: Charles B. King, November 1, 1945), p. 14.

265 Charles Brady King, *A Golden Anniversary, 1895 – 1945, Personal Side-Lights of America's First Automobile Race* (Larchmont: Charles B. King, November 1, 1945), p. 12 / George S. May, *A Most Unique Machine: The Michigan Origins of the American Automobile Industry* (Grand Rapids: William B. Eerdmans Publishing Co., 1975), p. 27.

266 Charles Brady King, *A Golden Anniversary, 1895 – 1945, Personal Side-Lights of America's First Automobile Race* (Larchmont: Charles B. King, November 1, 1945), pp. 19, 27, 31-37.

267 Charles Brady King, *A Golden Anniversary, 1895 – 1945, Personal Side-Lights of America's First Automobile Race* (Larchmont: Charles B. King, November 1, 1945), pp. 19, 27, 33, 39 / *The Horseless Age* January 1896: p. 29.

268 Charles Brady King Collection, National Automotive History Collection, Detroit Public Library (p. 2 of narrative titled "Charles B. King").

269 Charles Brady King, *A Golden Anniversary, 1895 – 1945, Personal Side-Lights of America's First Automobile Race* (Larchmont: Charles B. King, November 1, 1945), pp. 14, 38 / Charles Brady King Collection, National Automotive History Collection, Detroit Public Library (outline completed by King titled "Cars Built and Designed by Charles B. King – 1893-1903" and p. 9 of narrative titled "Charles B. King and Lauer's Shop") / J. F. Duryea. Engine or Motor. U.S . Patent 557,496, filed June 7, 1895, and issued March 31, 1896.

270 George S. May, *A Most Unique Machine: The Michigan Origins of the American Automobile Industry* (Grand Rapids: William B. Eerdmans Publishing Co., 1975), p. 17.

271 Charles Brady King, *A Golden Anniversary, 1895 – 1945, Personal Side-Lights of America's First Automobile Race* (Larchmont: Charles B. King, November 1, 1945), pp. 21, 39.

272 Charles Brady King, *A Golden Anniversary, 1895 – 1945, Personal Side-Lights of America's First Automobile Race* (Larchmont: Charles B. King, November 1, 1945), p. 44 / George S. May, *A Most Unique Machine: The Michigan Origins of the American Automobile Industry* (Grand Rapids: William B. Eerdmans Publishing Co., 1975), p. 89.

273 *Detroit Journal* March 7, 1896 (Note: newspaper citation from *A Golden Anniversary, 1895 – 1945, Personal Side-Lights of America's First Automobile Race).*

274 Charles Brady King, *A Golden Anniversary, 1895 – 1945, Personal Side-Lights of America's First Automobile Race* (Larchmont: Charles B. King, November 1, 1945), p. 44 / *The Horseless Age* November 1895: p. 16.

275 *Detroit Journal* March 7, 1896 / *Detroit Free Press* March 7, 1896 / *Detroit Tribune* March 8, 1896 (Note: newspaper citations from *A Golden Anniversary, 1895 – 1945, Personal Side-Lights of America's First Automobile Race).*

276 Charles Brady King, *A Golden Anniversary, 1895 – 1945, Personal Side-Lights of America's First Automobile Race* (Larchmont: Charles B. King, November 1, 1945), p. 45 / Charles Brady King Collection, National Automotive History Collection, Detroit Public Library ("Selected references from King Letterbooks about Lauer Shop engines" and other materials).

277 *Detroit Journal* March 7, 1896 (Note: newspaper citation from *A Golden Anniversary, 1895 – 1945, Personal Side-Lights of America's First Automobile Race).*

278 Joshua Wicks, "Charles B. King" (Detroit Historical.Wordpress.com), July 5, 2013 article, http://detroithistorical.wordpress.com/2013/07/05/charles-b-king/. Retrieved June 28, 2015.

279 Charles Brady King, *A Golden Anniversary, 1895 – 1945, Personal Side-Lights of America's First Automobile Race* (Larchmont: Charles B. King, November 1, 1945), p. 12.

280 Charles Brady King, *A Golden Anniversary, 1895 – 1945, Personal Side-Lights of America's First Automobile Race* (Larchmont: Charles B. King, November 1, 1945), p. 14 / Charles Brady King Collection, National Automotive History Collection, Detroit Public Library (outline completed by King titled "Cars Built and Designed by Charles B. King – 1893-1903") / Oliver Edward Barthel Collection, National

Automotive History Collection, Detroit Public Library (April 6, 1942 letter from Barthel to William E. Scripps of the *Detroit News*).

281 Charles Brady King and Oliver Edward Barthel Collections, National Automotive History Collection, Detroit Public Library (p. 5 of narrative titled "Charles B. King and Lauer's Shop") / Note: Several different Cartercar sales catalogs include the same promotional account of B. J. Carter's efforts to develop a successful friction-drive transmission for automobiles and indicate that Carter had begun experimentation in 1901.

282 Charles Brady King Collection, National Automotive History Collection, Detroit Public Library ("Narrative of Oliver E. Barthel concerning early automobile activities and associations, prepared by him in the month of December, 1939, in response to the request of M.M. Quaife," pp. 3-4).

283 *Jackson Citizen Patriot* September 14, 1919: p. 5.

284 Charles Brady King Collection, National Automotive History Collection, Detroit Public Library (Transcribed from notes taken during January 17, 1940 interview with Charles B. King).

285 Beverly Rae Kimes and Henry Austin Clark Jr., *Standard Catalog of American Cars, 1805 - 1942* (Iola: Krause Publications, Third Edition 1996), p. 1556 / "Winton Motor Carriage Co.," Cleveland Historical, http://clevelandhistorical.org/items/show/267. Retrieved July 4, 2015 / "Winton Motor Carriage Co.," The Encyclopedia of Cleveland History, http://ech.case.edu/cgi/article.pl?id=WMCC. Retrieved July 4, 2015 / *The Reminiscences of Mr. Oliver E. Barthel*, p. 69 (Interview conducted: July 1952), Collections of The Henry Ford, Accession 65, Benson Ford Research Center, The Henry Ford.

286 Charles Brady King Collection, National Automotive History Collection, Detroit Public Library (outline completed by King titled "Cars Built and Designed by Charles B. King – 1893-1903") / Mark Theobald. "Sievers & Erdman, 1875-1935; Erdman-Guider Company, 1913-1926; Detroit, Michigan; 1919-1926; Saginaw, Michigan" (*Coachbuilt.com*), 2004 narrative, http://www.coachbuilt.com/bui/s/sievers_erdman/sievers_erdman.htm. Retrieved April 14, 2015 / *The Horseless Age* November 1895: p. 12.

287 Mark Theobald. "Sievers & Erdman, 1875-1935; Erdman-Guider Company, 1913-1926; Detroit, Michigan; 1919-1926; Saginaw, Michigan" (Coachbuilt.com), 2004 narrative, http://www.coachbuilt.com/bui/s/sievers_erdman/sievers_erdman.htm. Retrieved April 14, 2015.

288 Charles Brady King Collection, National Automotive History Collection, Detroit Public Library (outline completed by King titled "Cars Built and Designed by Charles B. King – 1893-1903").

289 Ibid.

290 Charles Brady King and Oliver Edward Barthel Collections, National Automotive History Collection, Detroit Public Library (page 11 of narrative titled "Charles B. King and Lauer's Shop") / Charles Brady King, *A Golden Anniversary, 1895 – 1945, Personal Side-Lights of America's First Automobile Race* (Larchmont: Charles B.

King, November 1, 1945), p. 12.

291 Charles Brady King, *A Golden Anniversary, 1895 – 1945, Personal Side-Lights of America's First Automobile Race* (Larchmont: Charles B. King, November 1, 1945), p. 14.

292 Charles Brady King Collection, National Automotive History Collection, Detroit Public Library (list prepared by King titled "First Engines built and tested at Lauer's Shop are numbered as follows").

293 Ibid.

294 Charles Brady King and Oliver Edward Barthel Collections, National Automotive History Collection, Detroit Public Library (list prepared by King titled "First Engines built and tested at Lauer's Shop are numbered as follows" and p. 9 of narrative titled "Charles B. King and Lauer's Shop") / Charles Brady King, *A Golden Anniversary, 1895 – 1945, Personal Side-Lights of America's First Automobile Race* (Larchmont: Charles B. King, November 1, 1945), p. 14.

295 Charles Brady King and Oliver Edward Barthel Collections, National Automotive History Collection, Detroit Public Library (outline completed by King titled "Cars Built and Designed by Charles B. King – 1893-1903," a list prepared by King titled "First Engines built and tested at Lauer's Shop are numbered as follows," p. 9 of narrative titled "Charles B. King and Lauer's Shop," and a sheet written in King's hand with detailed specifications for the two-cylinder engine installed in Carter's vehicle) / *The Horseless Age* September 1896: p. 19 / Charles Brady King, *A Golden Anniversary, 1895 – 1945, Personal Side-Lights of America's First Automobile Race* (Larchmont: Charles B. King, November 1, 1945), p. 14.

296 *Detroit Free Press* August 16, 1896: p. 5.

297 *The Horseless Age* September 1896: p. 19 / *The Motocycle* September 1896: pp. 17, 18.

298 Ibid.

299 Charles Brady King and Oliver Edward Barthel Collections, National Automotive History Collection, Detroit Public Library (p. 11 of narrative titled "Charles B. King and Lauer's Shop" and a sheet written in King's hand with detailed specifications for the two-cylinder engine installed in Carter's vehicle).

300 Beverly Rae Kimes and Henry Austin Clark Jr., *Standard Catalog of American Cars, 1805 - 1942* (Iola: Krause Publications, Third Edition 1996), pp. 39, 687, 900, 1105, 1090, 1319, 1388, 1556.

301 *Jackson Citizen Patriot* September 14, 1919: p. 5.

302 Beverly Rae Kimes and Henry Austin Clark Jr., *Standard Catalog of American Cars, 1805 - 1942* (Iola: Krause Publications, Third Edition 1996), p. 1377.

303 *Jackson Citizen Patriot* September 14, 1919: p. 5.

304 *Jackson Daily Citizen* April 16, 1900: p. 6 / *Jackson Daily Citizen* April 17, 1900: p. 7.

305 *Jackson Daily Citizen* July 7, 1897: p. 6 / *Jackson Daily Citizen* July 10, 1897: p. 6.

306 *The Horseless Age* May 1896: p. 30 / Charles Brady King, *A Golden Anniversary, 1895 – 1945, Personal Side-Lights of America's First Automobile Race* (Larchmont: Charles B. King, November 1, 1945), p. 14 / Charles Brady King Collection, National Automotive History Collection, Detroit Public Library (outline completed by King titled "Cars Built and Designed by Charles B. King – 1893-1903").

307 *The Horseless Age* May 1896: p. 30 / Charles Brady King, *A Golden Anniversary, 1895 – 1945, Personal Side-Lights of America's First Automobile Race* (Larchmont: Charles B. King, November 1, 1945), p. 14 / Charles Brady King Collection, National Automotive History Collection, Detroit Public Library (outline completed by King titled "Cars Built and Designed by Charles B. King – 1893-1903").

308 Charles Brady King, *A Golden Anniversary, 1895 – 1945, Personal Side-Lights of America's First Automobile Race* (Larchmont: Charles B. King, November 1, 1945), p. 14 / Charles Brady King Collection, National Automotive History Collection, Detroit Public Library (p. 2 of narrative titled "Charles B. King").

309 *The Horseless Age* April 1896: p. 32 / *The Horseless Age* May 1896: p. 30.

310 Charles Brady King and Oliver Edward Barthel Collections, National Automotive History Collection, Detroit Public Library (p. 7 of narrative titled "Charles B. King and Lauer's Shop").

311 Charles Brady King and Oliver Edward Barthel Collections, National Automotive History Collection, Detroit Public Library (p. 7 of narrative titled "Charles B. King and Lauer's Shop") / *The Horseless Age* April 1896: p. 32.

312 *Jackson Daily Citizen* July 12, 1897: p. 6 / *Jackson Daily Citizen* July 13, 1897: p. 6.

313 *Jackson Daily Citizen* July 9, 1895: p. 1 / *Jackson Daily Citizen* November 29, 1895: p. 2 / *Jackson Daily Citizen* December 3, 1895: p. 1 / Charles Brady King, *A Golden Anniversary, 1895 – 1945, Personal Side-Lights of America's First Automobile Race* (Larchmont: Charles B. King, November 1, 1945), p. 26.

314 *Cleveland Plain Dealer* December 26, 1897: p. 10.

315 *Jackson Daily Citizen* September 20, 1897: p. 9.

The Erroneous Butcher & Gage Attribution

316 *The Flying A* March 1952: p. 3 / *Jackson Citizen Patriot* March 23, 1952: Part 4, Feature Page / *Horseless Carriage Gazette* March-April 1968: p. 18.

317 Ibid.

Coe Smith Reeves, Another Jackson Automotive Pioneer

318 *Jackson Daily Citizen* May 17, 1901: p. 7.

319 *R. L. Polk & Co.'s 1898/1899 Jackson City Directory*: pp. 384, 505, 554 / *R. L. Polk & Co.'s 1900/1901 Jackson City Directory*: pp. 412, 591 / *Jackson Daily Citizen* August 31, 1901: p. 3.

320 *Jackson Daily Citizen* May 17, 1901: p. 7 / *Jackson Citizen Patriot* March 17, 1946: p. 2 / *The Flying A* March 1952: p. 3 / *Horseless Carriage Gazette* March-April 1968: p. 18.

321 *Jackson Citizen Patriot* March 17, 1946: p. 2.

322 Ibid.

323 Ibid.

324 *The Flying A* March 1952: p. 3.

Early Gasoline-Engine Manufacturing Endeavors and Work with Oliver E. Barthel

325 *The Horseless Age* November 8, 1899: p. 23.

326 *The Motor Vehicle Review* December 12, 1899: p. 12.

327 *The Horseless Age* March 28, 1900: p. 28.

328 Ibid.

329 Charles Brady King Collection, National Automotive History Collection, Detroit Public Library ("Narrative of Oliver E. Barthel concerning early automobile activities and associations, prepared by him in the month of December, 1939, in response to the request of M.M. Quaife," p. 4).

330 *The Reminiscences of Mr. Oliver E. Barthel* (Interview conducted July 1952), p. 12, Collections of The Henry Ford, Accession 65, Benson Ford Research Center, The Henry Ford.

331 George S. May, *A Most Unique Machine: The Michigan Origins of the American Automobile Industry* (Grand Rapids: William B. Eerdmans Publishing Co., 1975), p. 28 / Charles Brady King Collection, National Automotive History Collection, Detroit Public Library ("Narrative of Oliver E. Barthel concerning early automobile activities and associations, prepared by him in the month of December, 1939, in response to the request of M.M. Quaife," p. 2) / *The Reminiscences of Mr. Oliver E. Barthel* (Interview conducted July 1952), Collections of The Henry Ford, Accession 65, Benson Ford Research Center, The Henry Ford / "Oliver Barthel, man of motors," Mac's Motor City Garage, http://www.macsmotorcitygarage.com/2012/06/06/oliver-bethel-man-of-motors/. Retrieved February 15, 2015.

332 John Nichols and Kathy Quirarte, "Dr. Milo Milton Quaife," Famous Chickasawians Surname Q, Iowa Gen Web, Chickasaw County, http://iagenweb.org/chickasaw/biographies/famousq.htm. Retrieved July 7, 2015 / Charles Brady King Collection, National Automotive History Collection, Detroit Public Library ("Narrative of Oliver E. Barthel concerning early automobile activities and associations, prepared by him in the month of December, 1939, in response to the request of M.M. Quaife," p. 2).

333 H. Eugene Weiss, *Chrysler, Ford, Durant and Sloan: Founding Giants of the American Automotive Industry* (Jefferson: McFarland & Company, Inc., August 27, 2003), pp. 7-9 / Joseph P. Cabadas, *River Rouge: Ford's Industrial Colossus* (Minneapolis: Motorbooks International Inc., First Edition, October 15, 2004), p. 17.

334 Entire Paragraph: Charles Brady King Collection, National Automotive History Collection, Detroit Public Library ("Narrative of Oliver E. Barthel concerning early automobile activities and associations, prepared by him in the month of December, 1939, in response to the request of M.M. Quaife," pp. 2-12) / *The Reminiscences of Mr. Oliver E. Barthel* (Interview conducted July 1952), Collections of The Henry Ford, Accession 65, Benson Ford Research Center, The Henry Ford / "Oliver Barthel, man of motors," Mac's Motor City Garage, http://www.macsmotorcitygarage.com/2012/06/06/oliver-bethel-man-of-motors/. Retrieved February 15, 2015.

335 Charles Brady King Collection, National Automotive History Collection, Detroit Public Library ("Narrative of Oliver E. Barthel concerning early automobile activities and associations, prepared by him in the month of December, 1939, in response to the request of M.M. Quaife," pp. 2-12) / *The Reminiscences of Mr. Oliver E. Barthel* (Interview conducted July 1952), Collections of The Henry Ford, Accession 65, Benson Ford Research Center, The Henry Ford.

336 Ibid.

337 *The Reminiscences of Mr. Oliver E. Barthel* (Interview conducted July 1952), p. 12, Collections of The Henry Ford, Accession 65, Benson Ford Research Center, The Henry Ford.

338 *Jackson Daily Citizen* July 24, 1899: p. 7.

339 Ella Sharp Museum Staff, *The History of Business and Industry in Jackson, Michigan* (St. Louis: G. Bradley Publishing, Inc., Second Printing December 1993), pp. 24-37.

340 Ibid.

341 Ella Sharp Museum Staff, *The History of Business and Industry in Jackson, Michigan* (St. Louis: G. Bradley Publishing, Inc., Second Printing December 1993), pp. 24-37 / *Jackson Daily Citizen* August 31, 1899: p. 6.

342 Ibid.

343 *1896 Detroit City Directory*: p. 249 / *R. L. Polk & Co.'s 1901 Detroit City Directory*: p. 260 / Author's Collection (copies from Ronald G. Bean): B. J. Carter's May 29, 1900, June 15, 1900, and June 25, 1900 letters to Oliver E. Barthel.

344 Author's Collection (copies from Ronald G. Bean): B. J. Carter's May 29, 1900, June 15, 1900, and June 25, 1900 letters to Oliver E. Barthel.

345 Ibid.

346 *The Reminiscences of Mr. Oliver E. Barthel* (Interview conducted July 1952), p. 12, Collections of The Henry Ford, Accession 65, Benson Ford Research Center, The Henry Ford.

347 Author's Collection (copies from Ronald G. Bean): B. J. Carter's May 29, 1900, June 15, 1900, and June 25, 1900 letters to Oliver E. Barthel.

Automobile Sales and Service at 204 West Cortland Street and Carter's Eccentric Associate, Professor L. A. Harraden

348 Author's Collection (copies from Ronald G. Bean): B. J. Carter's May 29, 1900, June 15, 1900, and June 25, 1900 letters to Oliver E. Barthel.

349 *Jackson Daily Citizen* May 29, 1900: p. 7 / *Jackson Citizen Patriot* January 5, 1941: p. 4.

350 *Jackson Daily Citizen* February 8, 1900: p. 7 / *Jackson Daily Citizen* May 28, 1900: p. 6 / *R. L. Polk & Co.'s 1900/1901 Jackson City Directory*: p. 598 / *R. L. Polk & Co.'s 1902 Jackson City Directory*: p. 246.

351 Beverly Rae Kimes and Henry Austin Clark Jr., *Standard Catalog of American Cars, 1805 - 1942* (Iola: Krause Publications, Third Edition 1996), pp. 890, 1377.

352 *Jackson Citizen Patriot* January 5, 1941: p. 4.

353 Ibid.

354 *R. L. Polk & Co.'s 1898/1899 Jackson City Directory*: p. 356 / *R. L. Polk & Co.'s 1900/1901 Jackson City Directory*: p. 358 / *Jackson Citizen Patriot* January 5, 1941: p. 4.

355 *Jackson Citizen Patriot* January 5, 1941: p. 4.

356 Tony Long, "Nov. 3, 1900: The Grandmother of All Auto Shows," *Wired* (Wired.com), *The New York Times* November 3, 2010 (article first appeared on Wired.com November 3, 2008), http://www.wired.com/2010/11/1103first-us-car-show-new-york/. Retrieved July 23, 2015 / *Jackson Citizen Patriot* January 5, 1941: p. 4.

357 *Jackson Citizen Patriot* January 5, 1941: p. 4.

358 Ibid.

359 *Jackson Daily Citizen* February 26, 1901: p. 1 / *Jackson Citizen Patriot* January 5, 1941: p. 4.

360 *Jackson Daily Citizen* September 20, 1900: p. 7.

361 Automobile Topics March 2, 1901: p. 739 / "Chicago Auto Show – 1901," Chicago Auto Show 2015, Show History (chicagoautoshow.com), http://www.chicagoautoshow.com/history/1901/. Retrieved July 23, 2015 / "Chicago's Auto Show (3-23-1901)," Chicago History Today (chicagohistorytoday.wordpress.com), March 23, 2015, https://chicagohistorytoday.wordpress.com/2015/03/23/first-chicago-auto-show-3-23-1901/. Retrieved July 23, 2015.

362 *Jackson Daily Citizen* April 19, 1899: p. 6 / *Jackson Daily Citizen* May 13, 1899: p. 12 / *Jackson Daily Citizen* February 13, 1900: p. 7 / *R. L. Polk & Co.'s 1900/1901 Jackson City Directory*: p. 136.

363 *Jackson Citizen Patriot* January 5, 1941: p. 4.

364 *Jackson Daily Citizen* July 25, 1903: p. 8.

365 *Jackson Daily Citizen* April 27, 1901: p. 7.

366 *Jackson Daily Citizen* April 27, 1901: p. 7 / Nick Baldwin and others, The World Guide to Automobile Manufacturers (New York and Oxford, England: Facts On File, Inc., 1987), p. 133.

367 *Jackson Daily Citizen* April 26, 1901: p. 7.

First Automobile Races

368 *Jackson Daily Citizen* June 30, 1900: p. 6.

369 *Jackson Daily Citizen* June 30, 1900: p. 6 / *Jackson Daily Citizen* July 5, 1900: p. 6 / *R. L. Polk & Co.'s 1900/1901 Jackson City Directory*: p. 415 / *R. L. Polk & Co.'s 1902 Jackson City Directory*: p. 425.

370 *Jackson Daily Citizen* July 5, 1900: p. 6.

371 *Jackson Daily Citizen* March 27, 1897: p. 11 / *Jackson Daily Citizen* September 27, 1900: p. 6.

372 *Jackson Semi-Weekly Citizen* October 2, 1900: p. 4.

Carter's Automotive Ambitions Shift from Gasoline-Propelled Machines to Steam Carriages

373 Author's Collection (copies from Ronald G. Bean): B. J. Carter's May 29, 1900, June 15, 1900, and June 25, 1900 letters to Oliver E. Barthel.

The 1900 Carter Steam Carriages

374 *Jackson Daily Citizen* October 12, 1900: p. 7.

375 Beverly Rae Kimes and Henry Austin Clark Jr., *Standard Catalog of American Cars, 1805 - 1942* (Iola: Krause Publications, Third Edition 1996), p. 890.

376 *Jackson Daily Citizen* November 8, 1900: p. 6.

377 *Cycle and Automobile Trade Journal* January 1, 1901: p. 62.

378 *The Motor Age* January 9, 1901: p. 810 / *The Motor Age* February 27, 1901: p. 1147.

379 *Cycle and Automobile Trade Journal* January 1, 1901: p. 62.

380 *The Motor Vehicle Review* November 8, 1900: p. 85 through January 3, 1901: p. 45 / *The Horseless Age* March 28, 1900: p. 28.

381 *Jackson Daily Citizen* June 26, 1901: p. 6.

382 *Jackson Citizen Patriot* January 5, 1941: p. 4.

383 Beverly Rae Kimes and Henry Austin Clark Jr., *Standard Catalog of American Cars, 1805 - 1942* (Iola: Krause Publications, Third Edition 1996), pp. 890, 983, 1377.

384 *Jackson Citizen Patriot* January 5, 1941: p. 4.

385 Ella Sharp Museum Staff, *The History of Business and Industry in Jackson, Michigan* (St. Louis: G. Bradley Publishing, Inc., Second Printing December 1993), p. 58.

386 *Jackson Daily Citizen* October 15, 1900: p. 7 / *R. L. Polk & Co.'s 1898/1899 Jackson City Directory*: p. 296 / *R. L. Polk & Co.'s 1900/1901 Jackson City Directory*: p. 297.

387 *Jackson Daily Citizen* October 15, 1900: p. 7.

388 Ibid.

389 *Jackson Daily Citizen* May 20, 1901: p. 3.

390 Ibid.

391 Ibid.

Carter Urgently Needs a Cash Infusion to Launch Steam-Carriage Manufacturing Operations

392 *Jackson Daily Citizen* October 13, 1900: p. 7.

393 *Jackson Daily Citizen* October 15, 1900: p. 7.

394 *R. L. Polk & Co.'s 1897 Jackson City Directory*: p. 311 / *R. L. Polk & Co.'s 1898/1899 Jackson City Directory*: p. 425.

395 *Jackson Daily Citizen* July 3, 1896: p. 4 / *R. L. Polk & Co.'s 1894/1895 Jackson City Directory*: p. 165 / *R. L. Polk & Co.'s 1896 Jackson City Directory*: p. 201.

396 *1900 United States Federal Census: Jackson Ward 4, Jackson, Michigan*; Roll: 719; Page: 5A; Enumeration District: 0011; FHL microfilm: 1240719 / *R. L. Polk & Co.'s 1900/1901 Jackson City Directory*: pp. 136, 137 / *Jackson Daily Citizen* July 3, 1896: p. 4.

397 *Jackson Daily Citizen* November 12, 1900: p. 7 / *Jackson Daily Citizen* December 10, 1900: p. 7.

398 *R. L. Polk & Co.'s 1900/1901 Jackson City Directory*: pp. 136, 543.

399 *R. L. Polk & Co.'s 1902 Jackson City Directory*: pp. 138, 555.

[400] *The Motor Vehicle Review* November 8, 1900 through January 3, 1901 (first advertisements for Carter Steam Carriages, built in Jackson, Mich.) / *The Motor Vehicle Review* March 14, 1901: p. 21 / *The Horseless Age* December 12, 1900: p. 32 / *Cycle and Automobile Trade Journal* January 1, 1901: p. 62 / *The Motor Age* January 9, 1901: p. 810 & February 27, 1901: p. 1147.

[401] *R. L. Polk & Co.'s 1902 Jackson City Directory*: pp. 138, 611.

Grand Rapids Businessmen and Others Express Interest in Moving Carter's Automobile Company

[402] *Jackson Daily Citizen* October 23, 1900: p. 3.

[403] *Grand Rapids Herald* December 2, 1900: part 1, p. 3

[404] *Grand Rapids Herald* December 2, 1900: part 1, p. 3 / *The Motor Vehicle Review* December 13, 1900: p. 16 / Thomas E. Bonsall, *More Than They Promised: The Studebaker Story* (Palo Alto: Stanford University Press, November 1, 2000), p. 38 / Jan B. Young, *Studebaker and the Railroads, Volume 1* (Raleigh: lulu.com, September 1, 2009), p. 96.

[405] *The Horseless Age* December 12, 1900: p. 32 / *Cycle and Automobile Trade Journal* January 1, 1901: p. 62 / *The Motor Age* January 9, 1901: p. 810.

[406] *The Motor Age* January 9, 1901: p. 810.

The 1901 Carter Steam Carriages with Radically Improved Engine and Lubrication Systems

[407] *Jackson Daily Citizen* August 5, 1901: p. 3.

[408] B. J. Carter. Steam Engine. U.S . Patent 722,206, filed January 18, 1902, and issued March 10, 1903.

[409] *The Motor World* January 1, 1903: p. 420.

[410] Ibid.

[411] Ibid.

[412] *Jackson Daily Citizen* June 26, 1901: p. 6.

[413] *Jackson Daily Citizen* August 5, 1901: p. 3.

[414] *Jackson Daily Citizen* June 26, 1901: p. 6.

[415] *Cycle and Automobile Trade Journal* March 1, 1902: p. 146.

[416] *The Automobile and Motor Review* June 14, 1902: p. 28 through October 18, 1902: p. 39 / *The Horseless Age* June 25, 1902: p. V and July 30, 1902: p. X.

[417] *Jackson Daily Citizen* July 2, 1901: p. 7.

[418] Ibid.

[419] Ibid.

[420] *Jackson Daily Citizen* April 10, 1901: p. 6.

Stymied Attempts to Drive Carter Steam Carriages to the 1901 Pan-American Exposition

[421] *Jackson Daily Citizen* August 5, 1901: p. 3.

[422] University at Buffalo (The State University of New York) Library Staff and Others, "Pan-American Exposition of 1901" University at Buffalo Libraries (library. buffalo.edu), articles and essays 2001, http://library.buffalo.edu/pan-am/. Retrieved May 25, 2015.

[423] Ibid.

[424] Ibid.

[425] *Jackson Daily Citizen* April 8, 1901: p. 3 / University at Buffalo (The State University of New York) Library Staff and Others, "Pan-American Exposition of 1901" University at Buffalo Libraries (library.buffalo.edu), articles and essays 2001, http://library.buffalo.edu/pan-am/. Retrieved May 25, 2015.

[426] *Jackson Daily Citizen* June 29, 1901: p. 6.

[427] *Jackson Daily Citizen* June 26, 1901: p. 6.

[428] *Jackson Daily Citizen* September 17, 1901: p. 3.

[429] *Jackson Daily Citizen* September 17, 1901: p. 3 / *R. L. Polk & Co.'s 1900/1901 Jackson City Directory*: p. 546.

[430] *Jackson Daily Citizen* February 26, 1901: p. 1 / *Jackson Daily Citizen* May 18, 1901: p. 7 / *Jackson Citizen Patriot* January 5, 1941: p. 4.

[431] *Detroit Times* April 6, 1908: p. 1 / *Detroit News* April 6, 1908: p. 2 / *Detroit Journal* April 6, 1908 / *Jackson Citizen* April 7, 1908.

[432] *Detroit Times* April 6, 1908: p. 1 / *Detroit Journal* April 6, 1908.

[433] *Jackson Citizen Patriot* January 5, 1941: p. 4.

[434] *Jackson Daily Citizen* September 17, 1901: p. 3 / *Jackson Citizen Patriot* January 5, 1941: p. 4.

A Second Scare that Carter's Automobile Operations Might Relocate to Grand Rapids

435 *Jackson Daily Citizen* April 26, 1902: p. 3.

436 Ibid.

437 Ibid.

438 Ibid.

439 *The Motor World* May 8, 1902: p. 177.

440 Ibid.

441 *Automobile Topics* May 10, 1902: p. 160.

442 *Jackson Daily Citizen* April 26, 1902: p. 3.

443 Ibid.

444 *The Motor World* May 8, 1902: p. 177.

445 *Grand Rapids Herald* February 15, 1902: p. 3 / *Cycle and Automobile Trade Journal* April 1, 1902: p. 120.

446 *Grand Rapids Herald* March 22, 1902: pp 2, 8 & March 27, 1902: p. 6 / *Cycle and Automobile Trade Journal* April 1, 1902: p. 120.

447 *The Horseless Age* February 11, 1903: p. XVII.

448 Ibid.

449 *The Horseless Age* June 25, 1902: p. V and July 30, 1902: p. X.

450 *The Automobile and Motor Review* June 14, 1902: p. 28 through October 18, 1902: p. 39 / *The Horseless Age* June 25, 1902: p. V and July 30, 1902: p. X.

The Jackson Automobile Company

451 Articles of Association of Jackson Automobile Company executed with the State of Michigan on July 19, 1902 and recorded July 23, 1902 / *The Horseless Age* August 6, 1902: p. 150.

452 Articles of Association of Jackson Automobile Company executed with the State of Michigan on July 19, 1902 and recorded July 23, 1902 / *Jackson Daily Citizen* August 5, 1902: p. 6.

453 Articles of Association of Jackson Automobile Company executed with the State of Michigan on July 19, 1902 and recorded July 23, 1902 / 1902 Annual Report of the Jackson Automobile Company filed with the Michigan Secretary of State on April 17, 1903.

454 Articles of Association of Jackson Automobile Company executed with the State of Michigan on July 19, 1902 and recorded July 23, 1902 / *Jackson Daily Citizen* July 24, 1902: p. 7 / *The Motor Age* August 7, 1902: p. 36.

455 *Jackson Daily Citizen* July 24, 1902: p. 7.

456 Ibid.

457 *R. L. Polk & Co.'s 1903 Jackson City Directory*: p. 594.

458 *R. L. Polk & Co.'s 1900/1901 Jackson City Directory*: p. 54 / *R. L. Polk & Co.'s 1905 Jackson City Directory*: p. 63 / Charles Moore, *History of Michigan, Volume 3* (Chicago: Lewis Publishing Company, 1915), p. 1297.

459 *R. L. Polk & Co.'s 1900/1901 Jackson City Directory*: p. 52 / 1912 Annual Report of the Fuller Buggy Company (fiscal year ending July 31, 1912) filed with the Michigan Secretary of State on March 17, 1913.

460 *Jackson Saturday Evening Star* June 18, 1904: p. 8 / Charles Moore, *History of Michigan, Volume 3* (Chicago: Lewis Publishing Company, 1915), pp. 1300, 1516.

461 *Jackson Daily Citizen* July 24, 1902: p. 7.

462 1902 Annual Report of the Jackson Automobile Company filed with the Michigan Secretary of State on April 17, 1903.

463 B. J. Carter. Steam Engine. U.S . Patent 722,206, filed January 18, 1902, and issued March 10, 1903.

464 1902 Annual Report of the Jackson Automobile Company filed with the Michigan Secretary of State on April 17, 1903 / *R. L. Polk & Co.'s 1903 Jackson City Directory*: p. 155.

465 *Jackson Daily Citizen* July 24, 1902: p. 7.

466 *The Automobile Review and Automobile News* August 15, 1902: p. 199.

467 *Jackson Daily Citizen* October 11, 1900: p. 7 / *Jackson Daily Citizen* August 23, 1902: p. 4.

468 *Jackson Daily Citizen* May 8, 1884: p. 4 / *Jackson Daily Citizen* January 6, 1885: p. 4 / *Jackson Daily Citizen* October 11, 1900: p. 7 / *Jackson Daily Citizen* November 3, 1900: p. 4.

469 *Jackson Daily Citizen* September 25, 1899: p. 6 / *Jackson Daily Citizen* October 11, 1900: p. 7 / *Jackson Daily Citizen* October 12, 1900: p. 7.

470 *Jackson Daily Citizen* December 31, 1900: p. 6.

471 *Jackson Citizen Patriot* September 14, 1919: p. 5.

472 *Jackson Daily Citizen* September 20, 1902: p. 8.

473 *Jackson Daily Citizen* August 23, 1902: p. 4.

474 *Jackson Daily Citizen* July 28, 1902: p. 7.

475 *Jackson Daily Citizen* July 30, 1902: p. 7.

476 *Jackson Daily Citizen* August 12, 1902: p. 7.

477 *Jackson Daily Citizen* August 23, 1902: p. 4.

478 *Jackson Daily Citizen* August 1, 1902: p. 4 / *R. L. Polk & Co.'s 1903 Jackson City Directory*: p. 153.

479 *R. L. Polk & Co.'s 1903 Jackson City Directory*: pp. 146, 208, 212, 405 / *R. L. Polk & Co.'s 1909 Jackson City Directory*: p. 236 / *R. L. Polk & Co.'s 1910 Jackson City Directory*: p. 232 / *R. L. Polk & Co.'s 1912 Jackson City Directory*: p. 226.

480 *Jackson Daily Citizen* September 4, 1902: p. 7 / *Jackson Daily Citizen* September 20, 1902: pp. 7, 8.

481 *Jackson Daily Citizen* September 20, 1902: pp. 7, 8.

482 *Jackson Daily Citizen* September 20, 1902: pp. 7, 8 / *Jackson Daily Citizen* January 10, 1903: p. 3 / *Jackson Daily Citizen* March 7, 1903: p. 5 / *R. L. Polk & Co.'s 1904 Jackson City Directory*: p. 9.

483 *Jackson Daily Citizen* June 9, 1902: p. 8.

484 *Jackson Daily Citizen* August 19, 1903: p. 7.

485 *Jackson Daily Citizen* July 30, 1902: p. 7.

486 *Jackson Daily Citizen* October 16, 1902: p. 3.

487 *Jackson Daily Citizen* December 10, 1902: p. 7.

488 *Jackson Daily Citizen* December 19, 1902: p. 7.

489 *R. L. Polk & Co.'s 1903 Jackson City Directory*: pp. 539, 589 / *R. L. Polk & Co.'s 1904 Jackson City Directory*: p. 549.

490 *Jackson Daily Citizen* March 4, 1903: p. 7.

491 *Jackson Daily Citizen* March 7, 1903: p. 7 / *Jackson Daily Citizen* June 11, 1903: p. 3 / *Jackson Daily Citizen* July 9, 1903: p. 7 / *Jackson Daily Citizen* September 4, 1903: p. 7.

492 *Jackson Daily Citizen* September 4, 1903: p. 7.

493 *Jackson Daily Citizen* January 14, 1904: p. 1 / *R. L. Polk & Co.'s 1905 Jackson City Directory*: p. 242.

494 *Jackson Daily Citizen* March 30, 1904: p. 1.

495 Courtesy of Sallie Sparks Kendall: January 6, 1940 Letter from Charles A. Trask to Della Carter / *R. L. Polk & Co.'s 1906 Ypsilanti City Directory*: p. 515.

496 *R. L. Polk & Co.'s 1905 Jackson City Directory*: pp. 241, 242 / *R. L. Polk & Co.'s 1915 Jackson City Directory*: p. 61.

497 *R. L. Polk & Co.'s 1905 Jackson City Directory*: p. 241.

498 *R. L. Polk & Co.'s 1903 Jackson City Directory*: p. 155 / *R. L. Polk & Co.'s 1904 Jackson City Directory*: pp. 158, 317.

499 *R. L. Polk & Co.'s 1904 Jackson City Directory*: pp. 158, 317.

500 *R. L. Polk & Co.'s 1905 Jackson City Directory*: p. 166.

501 1902 Annual Report of the Jackson Automobile Company filed with the Michigan Secretary of State on April 17, 1903.

In the Midst of Launching the Jackson Automobile Company, Carter Opines on the Bicycle's Future

502 *Jackson Daily Citizen* August 12, 1902: p. 7.

503 *Jackson Daily Citizen* March 19, 1902: p. 6.

504 *Jackson Daily Citizen* August 12, 1902: p. 7.

505 Ibid.

Jaxon Steam Surrey Production is Finally Under Way

506 *The Automobile Review and Automobile News* January 15, 1903: p. 32.

507 *Cycle and Automobile Trade Journal* January 1, 1905: p. 181.

508 *The Automobile Review and Automobile News* December 15, 1902: p. 331.

509 *The Automobile* January 31, 1903: p. 160.

510 *The Automobile* January 31, 1903: p. 159.

511 *The Iron Trade Review* March 5, 1903: p. 68.

512 *Cycle and Automobile Trade Journal* April 1, 1903: p. 77 / Note: *Cycle and Automobile Trade Journal* March 1, 1903: p. 49 incorrectly stated that Jaxon Steam Surrey Model "A" had a wider main seat than Model "B," which was corrected in the April 1, 1903 issue.

513 *The Automobile* February 21, 1903: p. 220.

514 *The Automobile* January 31, 1903: p. 160 / *The Iron Trade Review* March 5, 1903: p. 68.

515 *The Automobile Review and Automobile News* February 1, 1903: p. 55.

516 *The Horseless Age* February 25, 1903: p. 300.

517 Courtesy of Harrah's Automobile Collection Library, summary of Jackson automobile models compiled by Ralph Dunwoodie.

518 *Cycle and Automobile Trade Journal* March 1, 1903: p. 49 / *Cycle and Automobile Trade Journal* April 1, 1903: pp. 77, 113.

519 *Cycle and Automobile Trade Journal* March 1, 1903: p. 49 / *Cycle and Automobile Trade Journal* April 1, 1903: p. 77.

520 *Jackson Daily Citizen* February 3, 1903: p. 7.

521 *The Automobile* February 21, 1903: p. 220.

522 *The Motor World* February 12, 1903: p. 715.

523 *Detroit Free Press* January 4, 1903: p. 7 / *Detroit Free Press* January 11, 1903: p. B2 / *Detroit Free Press* January 18, 1903: p. 5 / *Detroit Free Press* February 8, 1903: p. B11 / *Detroit Free Press* February 14, 1903: p. 12.

524 *Detroit Free Press* January 18, 1903: p. 5 / *Detroit Free Press* February 8, 1903: p. B11 / *Detroit Free Press* February 10, 1903: p. 11.

525 *The Motor World* February 12, 1903: p. 715.

526 *Detroit Free Press* February 11, 1903: p. 11.

527 *Detroit Free Press* February 11, 1903: p. 11 / *Detroit Free Press* February 14, 1903: p. 12.

528 *The Automobile* February 28, 1903: p. 258 / *The Automobile Review and Automobile News* March 1, 1903: pp. 92, 100, 118.

529 1903 Jackson Automobile Company brochure for Jaxon gasoline automobiles / *Detroit Times* April 6, 1908: p. 1 / *Detroit News* April 6, 1908: p. 2 / *Detroit Journal* April 6, 1908 / *Jackson Citizen* April 7, 1908 / *Detroit News* April 7, 1908: p. 7 / *Cleveland Plain Dealer* April 12, 1908: p. 35 / *Automobile Dealer and Repairer* April 1908: p. 37 / *The Horseless Age* April 15, 1908: p. 450 / *Motor Field* May 1908: p. 64.

530 1903 Jackson Automobile Company brochure for Jaxon gasoline automobiles.

531 *The Horseless Age* November 26, 1902: p. 595.

532 *The Automobile* January 31, 1903: p. 159.

533 *The Automobile* February 21, 1903: p. 220.

534 *Motor Age* February 19, 1903: p. 15 / *The Motor World* February 19, 1903: p. 779 / *The Automobile* February 28, 1903: pp. 258, 262 / *Cycle and Automobile Trade Journal*

March 1, 1903: p. 49 / *The Automobile Review and Automobile News* March 1, 1903: pp. 92, 100, 118.

535 *The Motor World* February 12, 1903: p. 715.

536 1903 Jackson Automobile Company brochure for Jaxon gasoline automobiles / *The Automobile Review and Automobile News* March 1, 1903: p. 118.

537 *The Motor World* February 19, 1903: p. 779 / 1903 Jackson Automobile Company brochure for Jaxon gasoline automobiles / *The Automobile Review and Automobile News* March 1, 1903: p. 118 / *Cycle and Automobile Trade Journal* August 1, 1903: p. 84.

538 *The Automobile Review and Automobile News* March 1, 1903: pp. 92, 118 / 1903 Jackson Automobile Company brochure for Jaxon gasoline automobiles.

539 1903 Jackson Automobile Company brochure for Jaxon gasoline automobiles / *Cycle and Automobile Trade Journal* August 1, 1903: p. 84.

540 1903 Jackson Automobile Company brochure for Jaxon gasoline automobiles / *Cycle and Automobile Trade Journal* March 1, 1903: p. 49.

541 *The Motor World* February 19, 1903: p. 779 / 1903 Jackson Automobile Company brochure for Jaxon gasoline automobiles / *Cycle and Automobile Trade Journal* April 1, 1903: p. 94 / *Cycle and Automobile Trade Journal* August 1, 1903: p. 84.

542 1903 Jackson Automobile Company brochure for Jaxon gasoline automobiles / *Cycle and Automobile Trade Journal* March 1, 1903: p. 49 / *The Automobile Review and Automobile News* March 1, 1903: p. 118 / *Cycle and Automobile Trade Journal* August 1, 1903: p. 84 / 1905 Jackson Automobile Company sales catalog.

543 *Cycle and Automobile Trade Journal* March 1, 1903: p. 49 / *Cycle and Automobile Trade Journal* April 1, 1903: p. 94.

544 *Motor Age* February 19, 1903: p. 15 / *The Motor World* February 19, 1903: p. 779 / *The Automobile* February 21, 1903: p. 220 / *Motor Age* February 26, 1903: p. 4 / *The Automobile* February 28, 1903: p. 258 / *Cycle and Automobile Trade Journal* March 1, 1903: p. 49 / *The Automobile Review and Automobile News* March 1, 1903: pp. 92, 100, 118.

545 Ibid.

546 *The Automobile Review and Automobile News* March 1, 1903: pp. 92, 118.

547 *Motor Age* February 19, 1903: p. 15 / *The Motor World* February 19, 1903: p. 779 / *The Automobile* February 21, 1903: p. 220 / *Motor Age* February 26, 1903: p. 4 / *The Automobile* February 28, 1903: p. 258 / *Cycle and Automobile Trade Journal* March 1, 1903: p. 49 / *The Automobile Review and Automobile News* March 1, 1903: pp. 92, 100, 118.

548 Ibid.

549 1903 Jackson Automobile Company brochure for Jaxon gasoline automobiles.

550 *Jackson Daily Citizen* March 4, 1903: p. 7.

551 Ibid.

At Long Last, Jaxon Gasoline Cars are Ready for Sale

552 *Jackson Daily Citizen* March 4, 1903: p. 7 / *Cycle and Automobile Trade Journal* January 1, 1905: pp. 181-195.

553 *Cycle and Automobile Trade Journal* April 1, 1903: p. 94 / *Automobile Topics* May 9, 1903: p. 240.

554 *Automobile Topics* May 9, 1903: p. 240.

555 1903 Jackson Automobile Company brochure for Jaxon gasoline automobiles / 1904 Jackson Automobile Company brochure for the Jaxon Light Touring Car / 1905 Jackson Automobile Company sales catalog.

556 *The Automobile Review and Automobile News* June 15, 1903: p. 219 / *Jackson Daily Citizen* July 1, 1903: p. 3 / 1903 Jackson Automobile Company brochure for Jaxon gasoline automobiles.

557 *Jackson Daily Citizen* July 1, 1903: p. 3.

558 *Cycle and Automobile Trade Journal* August 1, 1903: p. 84.

559 Ibid.

560 *The Automobile Review and Automobile News* August 15, 1903: p. 82.

561 *Cycle and Automobile Trade Journal* August 1, 1903: p. 84 / 1904 Jackson Automobile Company brochure for the Jaxon Light Touring Car.

562 *Cycle and Automobile Trade Journal* April 1, 1904: p. 97.

563 1903 Jackson Automobile Company brochure for Jaxon gasoline automobiles / 1904 Jackson Automobile Company brochure for the Jaxon Light Touring Car / 1905 Jackson Automobile Company sales catalog.

564 1905 Jackson Automobile Company sales catalog.

Jaxon Cars Featured at the 1903 "Automobile Socials"

565 *Jackson Citizen Patriot* September 16, 1928: p. 7 (Note: an interview with Fred T. Lockwood that incorrectly indicates the photograph was taken on July 4, 1905; Lockwood's identification of Mr. and Mrs. Emmett L. Smith creates ambiguity on whether the photograph was taken on June 9, 1903, July 14, 1903, July 15, 1903 or some other June or July 1903 date [E. L. Smith is only listed in the newspapers as providing an auto for the July 14, 1903 automobile social and July 15, 1903 parade; however, consistent with the photograph, 11 autos were featured at the June 9, 1903 automobile social and only 8 at the July 14, 1903 automobile social and at least 13 at the July 15, 1903 parade]) / *Jackson Daily Citizen* June 10, 1903: p. 3 / *Jackson*

Daily Citizen July 15, 1903: p. 3 / *Jackson Daily Citizen* July 16, 1903: p. 6.

566 *Jackson Daily Citizen* June 5, 1903: p. 3 / *Jackson Daily Citizen* June 10, 1903: p. 3.

567 *Jackson Daily Citizen* June 8, 1903: p. 3.

568 *Jackson Daily Citizen* June 8, 1903: p. 3 / *Jackson Daily Citizen* June 10, 1903: p. 3.

569 *Jackson Daily Citizen* June 10, 1903: p. 3 .

570 Ibid.

571 *Jackson Daily Citizen* July 15, 1903: p. 3.

572 *Jackson Citizen Patriot* September 16, 1928: p. 7 (Note: an interview with Fred T. Lockwood that incorrectly indicates the photograph was taken on July 4, 1905; Lockwood's identification of Mr. and Mrs. Emmett L. Smith creates ambiguity on whether the photograph was taken on June 9, 1903, July 14, 1903, July 15, 1903 or some other June or July 1903 date [E. L. Smith is only listed in the newspapers as providing an auto for the July 14, 1903 automobile social and July 15, 1903 parade; however, consistent with the photograph, 11 autos were featured at the June 9, 1903 automobile social and only 8 at the July 14, 1903 automobile social and at least 13 at the July 15, 1903 parade]) / *Jackson Daily Citizen* June 10, 1903: p. 3 / *Jackson Daily Citizen* July 15, 1903: p. 3 / *Jackson Daily Citizen* July 16, 1903: p. 6.

573 *Jackson Daily Citizen* July 15, 1903: p. 3.

City of Jackson's July 16, 1903 Automobile Races

574 *Jackson Daily Citizen* July 16, 1903: p. 6.

575 Ibid.

576 Ibid.

577 *Jackson Daily Citizen* June 23, 1900: p. 10 & June 30, 1900: p. 6 / *Jackson Daily Citizen* May 27, 1902: p. 6.

578 *Jackson Daily Citizen* July 8, 1903: p. 7 / *Jackson Daily Citizen* July 11, 1903: p. 7 / *Jackson Daily Citizen* July 14, 1903: p. 3.

579 Charles Brady King Collection, National Automotive History Collection, Detroit Public Library ("Narrative of Oliver E. Barthel concerning early automobile activities and associations, prepared by him in the month of December, 1939, in response to the request of M.M. Quaife," pp. 2-12) / *The Reminiscences of Mr. Oliver E. Barthel* (Interview conducted July 1952), Collections of The Henry Ford, Accession 65, Benson Ford Research Center, The Henry Ford / *Motor Age* May 7, 1914: p. 11.

580 *Motor Age* May 7, 1914: p. 11.

581 George S. May, *A Most Unique Machine: The Michigan Origins of the American*

Automobile Industry (Grand Rapids: William B. Eerdmans Publ. Co., 1975), p. 19.

582 *Jackson Daily Citizen* July 8, 1903: p. 7.

583 *Jackson Daily Citizen* July 17, 1903: p. 2.

584 Ibid.

585 Ibid.

586 Ibid.

587 *Jackson Daily Citizen* July 17, 1903: p. 8.

588 Ibid.

589 *Jackson Daily Citizen* July 18, 1903: p. 8.

590 *Jackson Daily Citizen* July 17, 1903: p. 8.

591 Ibid.

Close of the Jackson Automobile Company's First Year in Business

592 *Cycle and Automobile Trade Journal* January 1, 1905: pp. 181-195.

593 *Jackson Daily Citizen* March 4, 1903: p. 7.

594 *The Iron Trade Review* March 5, 1903: p. 68.

595 Beverly Rae Kimes and Henry Austin Clark Jr., *Standard Catalog of American Cars, 1805 - 1942* (Iola: Krause Publications, Third Edition 1996), p. 1059.

596 1903 Annual Report of the Jackson Automobile Company filed with the Michigan Secretary of State on March 7, 1904.

597 Ibid.

598 *Motor Age* August 20, 1903: p. 11 / *The Gateway of Vermont Hartford and its Villages* (Lebanon: Bailey & Hatton Press, 1904), pp. 65, 72.

599 *Automobile Topics* May 9, 1903: p. 240.

600 *The Motor World* October 1, 1903: p. 16.

601 Beverly Rae Kimes and Henry Austin Clark Jr., *Standard Catalog of American Cars, 1805 - 1942* (Iola: Krause Publications, Third Edition 1996), p. 458.

602 *The Horseless Age* October 19, 1904: p. XX.

The Jackson Automobile Company's 1904 Model Year

603 *Jackson Daily Citizen* May 11, 1904: p. 7 / *The Horseless Age* May 18, 1904: p. 545 / *R. L. Polk & Co.'s 1905 Jackson City Directory*: p. 89.

604 *Jackson Daily Citizen* June 1, 1904: p. 7 / B. J. Carter. Transmission Gearing. U.S . Patent 761,146, filed September 21, 1903, and issued May 31, 1904.

605 *Cycle and Automobile Trade Journal* January 1, 1905: pp. 181-195.

606 *The Automobile* January 30, 1904: p. 71 / *Motor Age* February 11, 1904: p. 14 / *The Motor World* February 11, 1904: p. 855 / *Automobile Review* February 20, 1904: p. 434 / *Cycle and Automobile Trade Journal* March 1, 1904: p. 94.

607 *Cycle and Automobile Trade Journal* March 1, 1904: p. 94.

608 *Jackson Daily Citizen* February 8, 1904: p. 7.

609 *The Automobile* January 23, 1904: p. 109 / *The Motor World* February 18, 1904: p. 901 / *The Automobile* February 27, 1904: p. 252.

610 *Cycle and Automobile Trade Journal* April 1, 1904: p. 97 / *Cycle and Automobile Trade Journal* May 1, 1904: p. 13.

611 Ibid.

612 *The Horseless Age* May 4, 1904: p. 491.

613 *Cycle and Automobile Trade Journal* April 1, 1904: p. 97.

614 Ibid.

615 *Cycle and Automobile Trade Journal* April 1, 1904: p. 97 / *Cycle and Automobile Trade Journal* May 1, 1904: p. 13.

616 *Cycle and Automobile Trade Journal* April 1, 1904: p. 97.

617 *Cycle and Automobile Trade Journal* September 1, 1904: p. 9 / *The Horseless Age* September 14, 1904: p. XXI / *The Horseless Age* October 5, 1904: p. IX / *Detroit Saturday Night* August 10, 1912: p. 21.

618 *Automobile Review* July 30, 1903: p. 100.

619 Ibid.

620 Ibid.

621 Ibid.

622 *Automobile Review* July 30, 1903: p. 100 / *The Horseless Age* September 14, 1904: p. XXI / *The Horseless Age* October 5, 1904: p. IX.

[623] *Automobile Review* July 30, 1903: p. 100.

[624] *Automobile Review* July 30, 1903: p. 100 / *Cycle and Automobile Trade Journal* September 1, 1904: p. 9.

[625] *Cycle and Automobile Trade Journal* September 1, 1904: p. 9 / *The Horseless Age* September 14, 1904: p. XXI / *The Horseless Age* October 5, 1904: p. IX.

[626] *Jackson Daily Citizen* April 26, 1904: p. 7.

[627] *The Horseless Age* May 4, 1904: p. 491.

[628] *The Horseless Age* May 4, 1904: p. 491 / *Cycle and Automobile Trade Journal* September 1, 1904: p. 9.

[629] *Cycle and Automobile Trade Journal* September 1, 1904: p. 9.

[630] Ibid.

[631] *Cycle and Automobile Trade Journal* April 1, 1904: p. 97.

[632] 1905 Jackson Automobile Company sales catalog.

[633] *Cycle and Automobile Trade Journal* January 1, 1905: pp. 181-195 / *The Automobile* October 12, 1905: p. 417.

[634] *The Horseless Age* October 19, 1904: p. 406 / *The Horseless Age* December 28, 1904: p. 668 / *The Automobile* January 14, 1905: p. 172 / *The Horseless Age* January 18, 1905: p. LX / *The Motor World* December 28, 1905: p. 687 (note: this article which mistakenly substitutes "Milwaukee" for "Minneapolis" midway through).

[635] *The Automobile* October 12, 1905: p. 417.

[636] 1904 Annual Report of the Jackson Automobile Company Filed with the Michigan Secretary of State on March 3, 1905.

[637] 1905 Jackson Automobile Company sales catalog.

[638] 1906 Jackson Automobile Company sales catalog / 1908 Jackson Automobile Company sales catalog.

A New Direction: B. J. Carter Dedicates His Energies to the Friction-Drive Transmission

[639] B. J. Carter. Transmission Gearing. U.S . Patent 761,146, filed September 21, 1903, and issued May 31, 1904 / *Jackson Daily Citizen* May 11, 1904: p. 7.

[640] *Cycle and Automobile Trade Journal* January 1, 1905: pp. 181-195.

[641] Charles Moore, *History of Michigan, Volume 3* (Chicago: Lewis Publishing Company, 1915), pp. 1515-1516.

[642] *Detroit News* April 6, 1908: p. 2 / *Detroit Free Press* April 7, 1908: p. 12.

[643] *Jackson Citizen* April 9, 1908.

[644] Ibid.

[645] Ibid.

Friction-Drive Transmission Experiments

[646] *Cycle and Automobile Trade Journal* February 1, 1910: p. 78.

[647] 1910 Cartercar sales catalog.

[648] *Motor* February 1909: p. 32B.

[649] *Cycle and Automobile Trade Journal* May 1, 1906: p. 130.

[650] Ibid.

[651] Ibid.

[652] Ibid.

[653] 1906 Cartercar sales catalog / *Cycle and Automobile Trade Journal* May 1, 1906: p. 130.

[654] 1909 Cartercar sales catalog no. 10.

The Motorcar Co.'s Automobile Production in Jackson

[655] *R. L. Polk & Co.'s 1905 Jackson City Directory*: p. 64.

[656] *R. L. Polk & Co.'s 1905 Jackson City Directory*: pp. 165, 622.

[657] *R. L. Polk & Co.'s 1905 Jackson City Directory*: pp. 428, 622.

[658] *Jackson Citizen Press* October 21, 1916: p. 10.

[659] *Jackson Daily Citizen* June 25, 1904: p. 3.

[660] *R. L. Polk & Co.'s 1905 Jackson City Directory*: p. 376.

[661] *Detroit Free Press* November 19, 1905: p. B11.

[662] *Jackson Citizen Patriot* April 26, 1964: p. 56.

[663] Courtesy of Sallie Sparks Kendall: January 6, 1940 Letter from Charles A. Trask to Della Carter / *R. L. Polk & Co.'s 1906 Ypsilanti City Directory*: p. 515.

[664] *R. L. Polk & Co.'s 1907 Ypsilanti City Directory*: p. 555.

665 Courtesy of Sallie Sparks Kendall: January 6, 1940 Letter from Charles A. Trask to Della Carter.

666 *R. L. Polk & Co.'s 1907 Detroit City Directory*: p. 2271 / *R. L. Polk & Co.'s 1908 Detroit City Directory*: p. 2098.

667 *Jackson Citizen* April 9, 1908.

668 *The Horseless Age* March 27, 1912: p. 600 / *Detroit Free Press* April 28, 1912: p. C6 / *The Automobile* February 12, 1914: p. 432.

669 *Detroit Free Press* September 26, 1909: p. 8 / *Detroit Free Press* September 29, 1909: p. 6 / *Detroit Free Press* October 3, 1909: p. 8 / *The Horseless Age* March 27, 1912: p. 600 / *The Automobile* March 28, 1912: p. 815.

670 *The Horseless Age* March 27, 1912: p. 600 / *The Automobile* March 28, 1912: p. 815 / *The Iron Trade Review* April 18, 1912: p. 864 / *Detroit Free Press* April 28, 1912: p. C6 / *Motor Age* May 2, 1912: p. 47 / *Automobile Topics* May 11, 1912: p. 707 / *Automobile Trade Journal* June 1, 1912: p. 90 / *Indianapolis 1913 City Directory*: p. 1601 / *Indianapolis 1914 City Directory*: p. 1403 / *Indianapolis 1915 City Directory*: p. 1393.

671 *Cycle and Automobile Trade Journal* March 1, 1905: p. 105.

672 Ibid.

673 Ibid.

674 Ibid.

675 *R. L. Polk & Co.'s 1898/1899 Jackson City Directory*: p. 301 / *R. L. Polk & Co.'s 1900 Jackson City Directory:* p. 330 / *R. L. Polk & Co.'s 1900/1901 Jackson City Directory:* p. 332 / *R. L. Polk & Co.'s 1903 Jackson City Directory:* pp. 376, 512 / *R. L. Polk & Co.'s 1904 Jackson City Directory*: pp. 268, 370, 519 / *R. L. Polk & Co.'s 1905 Jackson City Directory*: pp. 63, 277, 381 / *R. L. Polk & Co.'s 1906 Jackson City Directory:* pp. 254, 359 / *R. L. Polk & Co.'s 1907 Jackson City Directory:* pp. 382, 515 / *R. L. Polk & Co.'s 1908 Jackson City Directory*: pp. 69, 568 / *The Glen V. Mills 1905 Ann Arbor City Directory*: p. 88 / *Jackson Daily Citizen* March 3, 1903: p. 7 / *Michigan Manufacturer and Financial Record* June 22, 1912: p. 3 / *Automobile Topics* July 13, 1912: p. 1.

The Motorcar Company Is Moved to Detroit to Build the Cartercar

676 1906 Cartercar sales catalog.

677 *Detroit Free Press* November 19, 1905: p. B11.

678 Articles of Association of The Motorcar Company (Detroit) executed with the State of Michigan on September 22, 1905 and recorded September 26, 1905 / *Detroit Free Press* December 12, 1905: p. 8.

679 Articles of Association of The Motorcar Company (Detroit) executed with the State of Michigan on September 22, 1905 and recorded September 26, 1905.

680 *The Horseless Age* October 25, 1905: p. 489.

681 *Detroit Free Press* October 15, 1905: p. B11.

682 1906 Cartercar sales catalog.

683 Articles of Association of The Motorcar Company (Detroit) executed with the State of Michigan on September 22, 1905 and recorded September 26, 1905 / 1905 Annual Report of the Motorcar Company (Detroit) filed with the Michigan Secretary of State on March 5, 1906 / *Detroit Free Press* October 15, 1905: p. B11 / *Automobile Topics* October 21, 1905: p. 213 / *The Horseless Age* October 25, 1905: p. 489.

684 1905 Annual Report of the Motorcar Company (Detroit) filed with the Michigan Secretary of State on March 5, 1906.

685 Articles of Association of The Motorcar Company (Detroit) executed with the State of Michigan on September 22, 1905 and recorded September 26, 1905 / 1905 Annual Report of the Motorcar Company (Detroit) filed with the Michigan Secretary of State on March 5, 1906.

686 1905 Annual Report of the Motorcar Company (Detroit) filed with the Michigan Secretary of State on March 5, 1906.

687 *Detroit Free Press* November 19, 1905: p. B11.

688 *R. L. Polk & Co.'s 1906 Detroit City Directory*: p. 659 / *R. L. Polk & Co.'s 1907 Detroit City Directory*: p. 763.

689 1906 Cartercar sales catalog.

690 *Detroit Free Press* October 15, 1905: p. B11 / *Automobile Topics* October 21, 1905: p. 213.

691 *Detroit Free Press* November 19, 1905: p. B11 / *The Horseless Age* November 22, 1905: p. 688 / *Detroit Free Press* October 11, 1908: p. 2 / 1908 Cartercar sales catalog.

692 *R. L. Polk & Co.'s 1898 Detroit City Directory*: p. 1389 / *R. L. Polk & Co.'s 1899 Detroit City Directory*: p. 1416 / *R. L. Polk & Co.'s 1901 Detroit City Directory*: p. 1515.

693 *R. L. Polk & Co.'s 1906 Detroit City Directory*: p. 1573 / *R. L. Polk & Co.'s 1907 Detroit City Directory*: p. 1740 / *R. L. Polk & Co.'s 1908 Detroit City Directory*: p. 1615.

694 *Detroit Free Press* November 19, 1905: p. B11.

695 *The Automobile* November 30, 1905: p. 618 / *Motor Age* December 14, 1905: p. 26.

696 1905 Annual Report of the Motorcar Company (Detroit) filed with the Michigan Secretary of State on March 5, 1906.

The Motorcar Company's Inaugural 1906 Season

[697] *Detroit Free Press* October 15, 1905: p. B11 / *Cycle and Automobile Trade Journal* May 1, 1906: p. 130.

[698] 1906 Cartercar sales catalog.

[699] Bruce W. McCalley, *Model T Ford: The Car That Changed the World* (Iola: Krause Publications, April 1994), multiple references.

[700] 1906 Cartercar sales catalog / *The Automobile* April 12, 1906: p. 44 / *Cycle and Automobile Trade Journal* May 1, 1906: p. 130.

[701] 1906 Cartercar sales catalog.

[702] Ibid.

[703] *Cycle and Automobile Trade Journal* May 1, 1906: p. 130.

[704] 1906 Cartercar sales catalog / *Cycle and Automobile Trade Journal* May 1, 1906: p. 130.

[705] *The Automobile* November 30, 1905: p. 618 / *The Automobile* April 12, 1906: p. 44 / *The Horseless Age* June 13, 1906: p. 912 / 1906 Cartercar sales catalog supplement, Booklet "B".

[706] *Cycle and Automobile Trade Journal* May 1, 1906: p. 130.

[707] Ibid.

[708] Ibid.

[709] Ibid.

[710] *Motor* April 1906: p. 135 / *Cycle and Automobile Trade Journal* April 1, 1906: p. 245 / *The Automobile* April 12, 1906: p. 44.

[711] 1906 Cartercar sales catalog supplement, Booklet "B" / *The Horseless Age* June 13, 1906: pp 912.

[712] *Detroit Free Press* February 11, 1906: pp. 2, 16.

[713] *Detroit Times* February 13, 1906.

[714] *Cycle and Automobile Trade Journal* May 1, 1906: p. 245.

[715] Ibid.

[716] 1906 Cartercar sales catalog supplement, Booklet "B" / *Cycle and Automobile Trade Journal* May 1, 1906: pp. 130, 245 / *The Horseless Age* June 13, 1906: pp 912.

[717] *The Automobile* September 27, 1906: p. 414.

[718] Ibid.

[719] *Detroit Free Press* January 19, 1913: p. C7.

[720] *Cycle and Automobile Trade Journal* June 1, 1909: p. 137 / Nick Baldwin and others, *The World Guide to Automobile Manufacturers* (New York and Oxford, England: Facts On File, Inc., 1987), p. 86 / George S. May, *Encyclopedia of American Business History and Biography: The Automobile Industry, 1896 – 1920* (New York: Bruccoli Clark Layman, Inc., and Facts On File, Inc., 1990), p. 74.

[721] *Cycle and Automobile Trade Journal* February 1, 1907: p. 204.

[722] Ibid.

[723] 1907 Cartercar sales catalog / *The Horseless Age* July 25, 1906: p. 127 / *The Horseless Age* November 28, 1906: p. 776 / *The Automobile* December 27, 1906: p. 937.

[724] 1906 Annual Report of the Motorcar Company (Detroit) filed with the Michigan Secretary of State on February 1, 1907.

1907 Season for the Cartercar

[725] 1907 Cartercar sales catalog.

[726] Ibid.

[727] 1909 Cartercar sales catalog no. 10.

[728] 1907 Cartercar sales catalog / *A Little Talk about "Cartercar" Motors* one-page flyer.

[729] *Detroit Free Press* February 15, 1907: p. 8.

[730] 1907 Cartercar sales catalog.

[731] 1909 Cartercar sales catalog no. 10.

[732] 1907 Cartercar sales catalog.

[733] *The Horseless Age* August 6, 1906: p. 185 / *Cycle and Automobile Trade Journal* October 1, 1906: p. 138 / *The Motor Way* July 26, 1906: p. 20.

[734] *Cycle and Automobile Trade Journal* October 1, 1906: p. 138.

[735] 1907 Cartercar supplementary catalog showing model "E" only.

[736] Ibid.

[737] *Motor* March 1907: p. 174.

[738] *Cycle and Automobile Trade Journal* October 1, 1906: p. 138 / *The Automobile* June 27, 1907: p. 1048.

739 *The Automobile* June 27, 1907: p. 1048.

740 *Detroit Free Press* June 11, 1907: p. 9.

741 Ibid.

742 *The Horseless Age* June 5, 1907: p. 762.

743 *The Horseless Age* June 19, 1907: p. 828.

744 *Cycle and Automobile Trade Journal* October 1, 1906: p. 138.

745 *The Automobile* September 12, 1907: p. 354 / *The Horseless Age* September 25, 1907: p. 382.

746 *Cycle and Automobile Trade Journal* December 1, 1907: p. 174.

747 *The Automobile* September 12, 1907: p. 354 / *The Horseless Age* September 25, 1907: p. 382.

748 *The Horseless Age* September 25, 1907: p. 382.

749 *Cycle and Automobile Trade Journal* June 1, 1909: p. 137 / Nick Baldwin and others, *The World Guide to Automobile Manufacturers* (New York and Oxford, England: Facts On File, Inc., 1987), p. 86 / George S. May, *Encyclopedia of American Business History and Biography: The Automobile Industry, 1896 – 1920* (New York: Bruccoli Clark Layman, Inc., and Facts On File, Inc., 1990), p. 74.

750 *Cycle and Automobile Trade Journal* December 1, 1907: p. 174.

751 *Detroit Free Press* February 15, 1907: p. 8.

752 1907 Annual Report of the Motorcar Company (Detroit) filed with the Michigan Secretary of State on March 30, 1908.

1908 Season for the Cartercar

753 1908 Cartercar sales catalog.

754 *Detroit Free Press* October 6, 1907: p. 22.

755 1908 Cartercar sales catalog.

756 Ibid.

757 *Cycle and Automobile Trade Journal* March 1, 1908: p. 48.

758 1909 Cartercar sales catalog no. 10.

759 *Cycle and Automobile Trade Journal* December 1, 1907: p. 174 / *Cycle and Automobile Trade Journal* June 1, 1909: p. 137 / Nick Baldwin and others, *The World Guide to Automobile Manufacturers* (New York and Oxford, England: Facts On File, Inc., 1987), p. 86 / George S. May, *Encyclopedia of American Business History and Biography: The Automobile Industry, 1896 – 1920* (New York: Bruccoli Clark Layman, Inc., and Facts On File, Inc., 1990), p. 74.

760 *The Horseless Age* August 26, 1908: p. 266.

Byron J. Carter's Untimely Death

761 *Detroit Times* April 6, 1908: p. 1 / *Detroit News* April 6, 1908: p. 2 / *Detroit Journal* April 6, 1908 / *Grand Rapids Press* April 6, 1908: p. 8 / *Saginaw News* April 6, 1908: p. 1 / *Jackson Citizen* April 7, 1908 / *Detroit Free Press* April 7, 1908: p. 12 / *Detroit News* April 7, 1908: p. 7 / *Flint Journal* April 7, 1908: p. 5 / *Marshall (Michigan) Daily Chronicle* April 7, 1908: p. 1 / *Philadelphia Inquirer* April 7, 1908: p. 10 / *Jackson Citizen* April 9, 1908 / *LaPorte (Indiana) Weekly Herald* April 9, 1908: p. 9 / *The Automobile* April 9, 1908: p. 515 / *Cleveland Plain Dealer* April 12, 1908: p. 35 / *Automobile Dealer and Repairer* April 1908: p. 37 / *The Horseless Age* April 15, 1908: p. 450 / *Automobile Topics* April 18, 1908: p. 125 / *Motor Field* May 1908: p. 64 / *Cycle and Automobile Trade Journal* May 1, 1908: p. 47.

762 *Cycle and Automobile Trade Journal* June 1, 1909: p. 137 / R. A. Palmer. Gear Casing. U.S . Patent 954,400, filed November 14, 1908, and issued April 5, 1910.

763 *R. L. Polk & Co.'s 1909 Jackson City Directory*: p. 174 / *R. L. Polk & Co.'s 1910 Jackson City Directory*: p. 169.

764 *Detroit Times* April 6, 1908: p. 1 / *Detroit News* April 6, 1908: p. 2 / *Detroit Journal* April 6, 1908 / *Grand Rapids Press* April 6, 1908: p. 8 / *Saginaw News* April 6, 1908: p. 1 / *Jackson Citizen* April 7, 1908 / *Detroit Free Press* April 7, 1908: p. 12 / *Detroit News* April 7, 1908: p. 7 / *Flint Journal* April 7, 1908: p. 5 / *Marshall (Michigan) Daily Chronicle* April 7, 1908: p. 1 / *Philadelphia Inquirer* April 7, 1908: p. 10 / *Jackson Citizen* April 9, 1908 / *LaPorte (Indiana) Weekly Herald* April 9, 1908: p. 9 / *The Automobile* April 9, 1908: p. 515 / *Cleveland Plain Dealer* April 12, 1908: p. 35 / *Automobile Dealer and Repairer* April 1908: p. 37 / *The Horseless Age* April 15, 1908: p. 450 / *Automobile Topics* April 18, 1908: p. 125 / *Motor Field* May 1908: p. 64 / *Cycle and Automobile Trade Journal* May 1, 1908: p. 47.

765 T. A. Boyd, *Professional Amateur: The Biography of Charles Franklin Kettering* (New York: E. P. Dutton & Co., Inc., 1957), p. 68.

766 Ottilie M. Leland with Minnie Dubbs Millbrook, *Master of Precision: Henry M. Leland* (Detroit: Wayne State University Press, new edition September 1, 1996), p. 129 / T. A. Boyd, *Professional Amateur: The Biography of Charles Franklin Kettering* (New York: E. P. Dutton & Co., Inc., 1957), p. 68.

767 T. A. Boyd, *Professional Amateur: The Biography of Charles Franklin Kettering* (New York: E. P. Dutton & Co., Inc., 1957), p. 68.

768 Arthur Pound, *The Turning Wheel, The Story of General Motors, Through Twenty-Five Years 1908 – 1933* (Garden City: Doubleday, Doran & Company, Inc., 1934/new edition published by Forgotten Books 2012), p. 272.

A Newly Reorganized Cartercar Company at the Close of the 1908 Season

769 *The Horseless Age* August 26, 1908: p. 266.

770 *Detroit Free Press* October 11, 1908: p. 2 & October 12, 1908: p. 4 / *The Automobile* October 15, 1908: p. 551 / *Automobile Topics* October 17, 1908: p. 117 / *Cycle and Automobile Trade Journal* November 1, 1908: p. 96.

771 *Detroit Free Press* October 11, 1908: p. 2 / *The Automobile* October 15, 1908: p. 551 / *Automobile Topics* October 17, 1908: p. 117 / *Cycle and Automobile Trade Journal* November 1, 1908: p. 96 / 1908 Annual Report of the Cartercar Company filed with the Michigan Secretary of State on February 20, 1909 / Beverly Rae Kimes and Henry Austin Clark Jr., *Standard Catalog of American Cars, 1805 - 1942* (Iola: Krause Publications, Third Edition 1996), p. 1217 / "The Pontiac Automobile & The Pontiac Motor Vehicle Co." American Automobiles (american-automobiles.com), undated article, http://www.american-automobiles.com/Pontiac-2.html. Retrieved April 14, 2015.

772 *Detroit Free Press* October 11, 1908: p. 2 / *Cycle and Automobile Trade Journal* November 1, 1908: p. 96 / *Cycle and Automobile Trade Journal* December 1, 1909: p. 148.

773 *New England Automobile Journal* April 24, 1909.

774 *Detroit Free Press* August 28, 1907: p. 9.

775 *Detroit Free Press* October 11, 1908: p. 2 / Arthur Pound, *The Turning Wheel, The Story of General Motors, Through Twenty-Five Years 1908 – 1933* (Garden City: Doubleday, Doran & Company, Inc., 1934/new edition published by Forgotten Books 2012), p. 119.

776 *Detroit Free Press* October 11, 1908: p. 2.

777 *Detroit Free Press* October 12, 1908: p. 4.

778 *The Horseless Age* October 6, 1909: p. 385.

779 *The Automobile* October 15, 1908: p. 551.

780 *Cycle and Automobile Trade Journal* June 1, 1909: p. 137.

781 1909 Cartercar sales catalog no. 10.

782 *The Automobile* July 22, 1909: p. 156.

783 *Detroit Free Press* October 11, 1908: p. 2 / *The Automobile* October 15, 1908: p. 551 / *Automobile Topics* October 17, 1908: p. 117 / *Cycle and Automobile Trade Journal* November 1, 1908: p. 96 / Beverly Rae Kimes and Henry Austin Clark Jr., *Standard Catalog of American Cars, 1805 - 1942* (Iola: Krause Publications, Third Edition 1996), p. 1217 / "The Pontiac Automobile & The Pontiac Motor Vehicle Co." American Automobiles (american-automobiles.com), undated article, http://www.american-automobiles.com/Pontiac-2.html. Retrieved April 14, 2015.

784 *Detroit Free Press* October 12, 1908: p. 4.

785 Arthur Pound, *The Turning Wheel, The Story of General Motors, Through Twenty-Five Years 1908 – 1933* (Garden City: Doubleday, Doran & Company, Inc., 1934/new edition published by Forgotten Books 2012), p. 120.

786 *Detroit Free Press* October 11, 1908: p. 2 / *The Automobile* October 15, 1908: p. 551 / *Cycle and Automobile Trade Journal* November 1, 1908: p. 96.

787 1910 Annual Report of the Cartercar Company filed with the Michigan Secretary of State on April 13, 1911.

788 *Detroit Free Press* October 11, 1908: p. 2 / 1908 Annual Report of the Cartercar Company filed with the Michigan Secretary of State on February 20, 1909 / Ronald G. Bean, *Cartercar and Jaxon, 1900 - 1923: A Story of the 'Jackson' and 'Cartercar' Automobile Companies* (Saginaw: Ronald G. Bean, Publisher, 1975): p. 33 (citing a June 5, 1939 Federal Trade Commission Report on the Motor Vehicle Industry [House Document No. 468]).

789 1908 Annual Report of the Cartercar Company filed with the Michigan Secretary of State on February 20, 1909.

790 Ibid.

General Motors' Acquisition and Cartercar's Ultimate Demise

791 Ronald G. Bean, *Cartercar and Jaxon, 1900 - 1923: A Story of the 'Jackson' and 'Cartercar' Automobile Companies* (Saginaw: Ronald G. Bean, Publisher, 1975): p. 34 (citing a June 5, 1939 Federal Trade Commission Report on the Motor Vehicle Industry [House Document No. 468]) / 1908 Annual Report of the Cartercar Company filed with the Michigan Secretary of State on February 20, 1909.

792 *Detroit Free Press* November 2, 1909: p. 7 / *The Michigan Manufacturer* November 13, 1909: p. 6.

793 Arthur Pound, *The Turning Wheel, The Story of General Motors, Through Twenty-Five Years 1908 – 1933* (Garden City: Doubleday, Doran & Company, Inc., 1934/new edition published by Forgotten Books 2012), p. 119.

794 1908 Annual Report of the Cartercar Company filed with the Michigan Secretary of State on February 20, 1909 / 1909 Annual Report of the Cartercar Company filed with the Michigan Secretary of State on March 26, 1910 / 1910 Annual Report of the Cartercar Company filed with the Michigan Secretary of State on April 13, 1911.

795 1910 Annual Report of the Cartercar Company filed with the Michigan Secretary of State on April 13, 1911.

796 Ibid.

797 Courtesy of Buzzy Carter Maurer: Correspondence among Della Carter, Lacerne A. Patch, General Motors Company, and E. B. Cadwell & Company (General Motors' investment banker and broker) / *R. L. Polk & Co.'s 1910 Jackson City Directory*: p. 494.

[798] 1909 Annual Report of the Cartercar Company filed with the Michigan Secretary of State on March 26, 1910.

[799] Courtesy of Buzzy Carter Maurer: Correspondence among Della Carter, Lacerne A. Patch, General Motors Company, and E. B. Cadwell & Company (General Motors' investment banker and broker).

[800] Ibid.

[801] Ibid.

[802] 1909 Annual Report of the Cartercar Company filed with the Michigan Secretary of State on March 26, 1910.

[803] Ibid.

[804] *Motor Age* November 4, 1909: p. 54 / *The Automobile* November 11, 1909: p. 853 / *The Motor World* November 11, 1909: p. 319 / *Cycle and Automobile Trade Journal* December 1, 1909: p. 120.

[805] Ibid.

[806] *Motor Age* November 4, 1909: p. 54 / *The Automobile* November 11, 1909: p. 853 / *Cycle and Automobile Trade Journal* December 1, 1909: p. 120 / *Motor Age* September 12, 1912: p. 16.

[807] *The Automobile* November 11, 1909: p. 853 / *Cycle and Automobile Trade Journal* December 1, 1909: p. 120.

[808] *The Automobile* November 11, 1909: p. 853.

[809] Ibid.

[810] *Motor Age* April 4, 1912: p. 35.

[811] *Motor Age* September 12, 1912: p. 16.

[812] *The Motor World* November 28, 1912: p. 31.

[813] *Detroit Free Press* May 29, 1914: p. 6.

[814] *The Automobile* December 31, 1914: p. 1243 / *Motor Age* January 4, 1917: p. 86 / Beverly Rae Kimes and Henry Austin Clark Jr., *Standard Catalog of American Cars, 1805 - 1942* (Iola: Krause Publications, Third Edition 1996), p. 835.

[815] *Automobile Trade Journal* February 1, 1915: p. 162.

[816] *Detroit Free Press* January 17, 1915: p. E8 / *Automobile Trade Journal* February 1, 1915: p. 162.

[817] *The Automobile* April 29, 1915: pp. 776, 784 / *Detroit Free Press* May 1, 1915: p. 11.

[818] Ronald G. Bean, *Cartercar and Jaxon, 1900 - 1923: A Story of the 'Jackson' and 'Cartercar' Automobile Companies* (Saginaw: Ronald G. Bean, Publisher, 1975): p. 34 (citing a June 5, 1939 Federal Trade Commission Report on the Motor Vehicle Industry [House Document No. 468]).

[819] *The Automobile* December 9, 1915: p. 1071 / *The Automobile* March 30, 1916: p. 58.

[820] Ronald G. Bean, *Cartercar and Jaxon, 1900 - 1923: A Story of the 'Jackson' and 'Cartercar' Automobile Companies* (Saginaw: Ronald G. Bean, Publisher, 1975): p. 34 (citing a June 5, 1939 Federal Trade Commission Report on the Motor Vehicle Industry [House Document No. 468]).

[821] Arthur Pound, *The Turning Wheel, The Story of General Motors, Through Twenty-Five Years 1908 – 1933* (Garden City: Doubleday, Doran & Company, Inc., 1934/new edition published by Forgotten Books 2012), p. 164 / *Automobile Topics* February 17, 1917: p. 125 / *Automobile Trade Journal* May 1, 1917: p. 244 / *Motor* September 1917: p. 104.

The Jackson Automobile Company Also Runs Out of Steam

[822] 1908 Annual Report of the Jackson Automobile Company (fiscal year ending September 1, 1908) filed with the Michigan Secretary of State on November 25, 1908.

[823] *R. L. Polk & Co.'s 1907 Jackson City Directory*: p. 396 / *R. L. Polk & Co.'s 1908 Jackson City Directory*: p. 431 / *R. L. Polk & Co.'s 1912 Jackson City Directory*: p. 418 / *R. L. Polk & Co.'s 1918 Jackson City Directory*: p. 662.

[824] Warranty Deed from Charles Lewis and Elizabeth A. Lewis, his wife, to George A. Matthews and Esther C. Matthews, his wife; June 16, 1910. Jackson County Register of Deeds, Jackson, Michigan, Liber 200, p. 365, Abstract Entry No. 35 / *Cycle and Automobile Trade Journal* August 1, 1910: p. 97 / *R. L. Polk & Co.'s 1910 Jackson City Directory*: p. 440 / *R. L. Polk & Co.'s 1912 Jackson City Directory*: p. 418 / *R. L. Polk & Co.'s 1913 Jackson City Directory*: p. 426 / *R. L. Polk & Co.'s 1918 Jackson City Directory*: p. 662 / *R. L. Polk & Co.'s 1920 Jackson City Directory*: p. 557 / *R. L. Polk & Co.'s 1922 Jackson City Directory*: p. 867 / *R. L. Polk & Co.'s 1924 Jackson City Directory*: p. 409.

[825] Articles of Association of Jackson Motors Corporation executed with the State of Michigan on April 18, 1919 and recorded August 5, 1919 / 1919 Annual Report of the Jackson Motors Corporation filed with the Michigan Secretary of State on December 2, 1920 / Warranty Deed from Jackson Motor and Manufacturing Company to Jackson Motors Corporation; April 19, 1919. Jackson County Register of Deeds, Jackson, Michigan, Liber 236, p. 394, Abstract Entry No. 41 / Mortgage from Jackson Motors Corporation to International Trust Company; July 19, 1919. Jackson County Register of Deeds, Jackson, Michigan, Liber 196, p. 11, Abstract Entry No. 97.

[826] November 8, 1920 letter from Carl L. V. Exselsen to Jackson Motors Corporation stockholders / *Automotive Industries* February 12, 1920: p. 478.

[827] June 14, 1921 letter from Howard A. Matthews and Carl L. V. Exselsen to Jackson Motors Corporation stockholders / October 24, 1921 letter from Carl L. V. Exselsen to Jackson Motors Corporation stockholders / October 25, 1921 letter from Howard A. Matthews to Jackson Motors Corporation stockholders / *Automotive Industries* September 29, 1921: p. 645 / *Motor World* October 5, 1921: p. 33 / *Automotive Industries* October 6, 1921: p. 693 / *Motor World* October 12, 1921: p. 84 / Warranty Deed from Jackson Motors Corporation to Associated Motor Industries; October 29, 1921. Jackson County Register of Deeds, Jackson, Michigan, Liber 265, p. 515, Abstract Entry No. 42.

[828] *Automotive Industries* September 29, 1921: p. 645 / *Motor World* October 5, 1921: p. 33 / *Automotive Industries* October 6, 1921: p. 693 / *Motor World* October 12, 1921: p. 84 / *Automotive Industries* October 27, 1921: p. 836 / *Motor World* November 2, 1921: p. 35 / *Automotive Industries* March 2, 1922: p. 546 / *Motor Age* June 22, 1922: p. 30 / *Automotive Industries* July 6, 1922: p. 44 / *Motor Age* July 6, 1922: p. 28 / *Automobile Trade Journal* August 1, 1922: p. 72.

[829] *Automotive Industries* November 9, 1922: p. 954 / *Motor World* November 15, 1922: p. 40 / *Automotive Industries* December 14, 1922: p. 1196 / *Automotive Industries* January 4, 1923: p. 42 / *Motor Age* January 4, 1923: p. 18 / *Automotive Industries* January 24, 1924: p. 202 / Quit Claim Deed from Jackson Motors Corporation to Associated Motor Industries (renamed National Motors Corporation on January 5, 1923); January 27, 1923. Jackson County Register of Deeds, Jackson, Michigan, Liber 256, p. 1, Abstract Entry No. 43.

[830] *Automotive Industries* December 14, 1922: p. 1196 / *Automotive Industries* January 4, 1923: p. 42 / *Motor Age* January 4, 1923: p. 18 / *Automotive Industries* January 24, 1924: p. 202 / *Automotive Industries* February 7, 1924: p. 308 / Quit Claim Deed from Jackson Motors Corporation to Associated Motor Industries (renamed National Motors Corporation on January 5, 1923); January 27, 1923. Jackson County Register of Deeds, Jackson, Michigan, Liber 256, p. 1, Abstract Entry No. 43 / In the Matter of National Motors Corporation , an Involuntary Bankrupt; February 26, 1924. Jackson County Register of Deeds, Jackson, Michigan, Liber 262D, p. 282, No. 716 in bankruptcy, Abstract Entry No. 45.

[831] Stuart H. Loewenthal and Richard J. Parker, *Continuously Variable Transmission – Assessment of Applicability to Advanced Electric Vehicles, NASA Report No. TM-82700* (Washington, D.C.: U.S. Department of Energy, 1981), p. 3 & fig. 3 / "Traction-drive Transmission," *Popular Science*, March 1980: p. 84 / Altshuler, Anderson, Jones, Roos, and Womack, *The Future of the Automobile: The Report of MIT's International Automobile Program* (Cambridge: The MIT Press, 1986), p. 86 / Brian S. Andersen, "An Investigation of a Positive Engagement, Continuously Variable Transmission" (Provo: Brigham Young University Scholars Archive, 2007), *All Theses and Dissertations*, Paper 910: p. 5.

Appendix B: Biographies of Charles Lewis and George A. Matthews

[832] Charles Moore, *History of Michigan, Volume 3* (Chicago: Lewis Publishing Company, 1915), pp. 1297-1300 / Note: additional inserted verbiage from *In Memoriam, Charles Lewis, Born April 10, 1853, Died February 24, 1912* (New York: James T. White & Co., 1918) / *R. L. Polk & Co.'s 1893/1894 Jackson City Directory*: pp. 66, 234, 235 / *R. L. Polk & Co.'s 1894/1895 Jackson City Directory*: pp. 39, 62, 228, 442 / *R. L. Polk & Co.'s 1898/1899 Jackson City Directory*: pp. 48, 293, 294 / *The Motor World* February 29, 1912: p. 958 / *The Horseless Age* March 6, 1912: p. 486.

[833] Charles Moore, *History of Michigan, Volume 3* (Chicago: Lewis Publishing Company, 1915), pp. 1514-1517 / Note: additional inserted verbiage from *R. L. Polk & Co.'s 1890 Jackson City Directory*: pp. 38, 156 / *R. L. Polk & Co.'s 1891/1892 Jackson City Directory*: pp. 39, 157, 243 / *R. L. Polk & Co.'s 1893/1894 Jackson City Directory*: pp. 39, 166, 255 / 1912 Annual Report of the Fuller Buggy Company (fiscal year ending July 31, 1912) filed with the Michigan Secretary of State on March 17, 1913 / *Automobile Topics* May 16, 1914: p. 18 / *The Automobile* May 21, 1914: p. 1087 / *Motor Age* May 21, 1914: p. 17.

Index

Numbers in bold italics indicate pages with illustrations.

Dean M. Nelson is an attorney in Minneapolis, Minnesota. He has been an active collector, researcher, and amateur historian of antique cars for over 40 years. Nelson serves as an Executive Council board member and committee chair for the Minnesota Historical Society and belongs to the Society of Automotive Historians, the Horseless Carriage Club of America, The Veteran Motor Car Club of America, and the Antique Automobile Club of America.